Carpentry and Joinery | 2

R. BAYLISS F.B.I.C.C., F.I.M.Wood T.
Formerly Lecturer at Walsall Technical College, Norwich City College
and Art School and Mid-Essex Technical College and School of Art,
Chelmsford.

Carpentry and Joinery | 2

Hutchinson

London Melbourne Sydney Auckland Johannesburg

Hutchinson Education

An imprint of Century Hutchinson Limited
62-65 Chandos Place, London WC2N 4NW

Century Hutchinson Australia Pty Ltd
PO Box 496, 16-22 Church Street, Hawthorn, Melbourne,
Victoria 3122, Australia

Century Hutchinson New Zealand Limited
PO Box 40-086, Glenfield, Auckland 10, New Zealand

Century Hutchinson South Africa (Pty) Limited
PO Box 337, Bergvlei 2012, South Africa

First published 1963
Revised and metricated 1969
Reprinted 1973, 1975, 1976, 1978, 1979, 1980, 1982, 1983, 1984, 1986

Printed and bound in Great Britain by
Anchor Brendon Ltd, Tiptree, Essex

ISBN 0 09 097931 1

Contents

Preface

This book is the second of four volumes planned to cover the theory and practice of the Carpentry and Joinery and Machine Woodworking Courses of the City and Guilds of London Institute and other examining institutions.

The author's approach and presentation are essentially visual, the text serving largely as an explanation and extension of the diagrams. The amount of subject-matter in each volume more than covers the requirements of the C.G.L.I. syllabus, and provides the reader with an introduction to the next stage.

An introduction to the change to metric is given in Chapter 1, and practice lessons directly related to the subject-matter in the book are given at the end of each main chapter.

The work has a strong practical bias, with emphasis on method and is intended mainly to assist the apprentices and craftsmen with limited practical experience.

The author hopes that the books will stimulate individual study, and enable all those engaged in the woodworking branches of the building industry to gain valuable information in addition to that acquired by attendance at educational institutions.

R. BAYLISS

It is the popular view that the change to the metric system of measurement will give the construction industries a unique opportunity to reconsider the dimensions we have commonly used in buildings and for building components.

It is important that we have ranges of components—such as doors and frames, windows, or curtain walling—that are dimensionally co-ordinated.

A building could be designed around a wide range of standardised components, thus limiting the need for non-standard units, or for the site trimming of units.

It is essential that building craftsmen become rapidly accustomed to working in metric sizes—millimetres, centimetres, metres—and visualise their relative size as against the imperial $\frac{1}{16}$ in–$\frac{1}{4}$ in, $\frac{1}{2}$ in–1 inch and the *foot*.

A diagram illustrating the relative difference between *imperial* and *metric* units of measure is given on page 4.

The metric rule is graduated to measure in millimetres, and the yard (or 3 ft rule) to measure in feet and inches.

Notice that 300 mm on the metric rule is approximately equal to 1 ft (305 mm) on the imperial rule; 200 mm is equal to 8 in (203 mm); 100 mm is equal to 4 in (101 mm); 50 mm equal to 2 in (50 mm) and 25 mm equal to 1 in (25 mm).

These five dimensions (300–200–100–50–25 mm) are the recommended first basic sizes for co-ordinating the dimensions of component parts.

From the illustrations on page 4 it will be seen that a square metre contains 10·76 square feet; a cubic metre 35·31 cubic feet; a square yard 9 square feet; and a cubic yard 27 cubic feet.

It is advisable, therefore, to study the diagrams carefully in order to visualise, and memorise, one millimetre, 100 millimetres, 300 millimetres, and the metre as units of square and cubic measure.

Use of planning grid

A planning grid is a series of lines set out in squares, the intervals of which are based upon multiples of a module, or increment of size. The British Standards Institution recommend 300 millimetres as the first preference and 100 millimetres as a second preference. The lines of the planning grid will control the overall dimensions of the structure, also the location, and size, of the components.

The use of a 300 mm planning grid is illustrated on page 5. The door opening is shown at a standard width of 900 mm and the windows correspond with the grid lines.

An enlarged view of one square, of a 300 mm planning grid, is shown on page 6, and details of door and window openings to suit the grid are given at the foot of the page.

It will be seen that if the overall width of the frame is standard, in this case 900 mm, any variation in the thickness of the framing will give varying door sizes. 50 mm framing will give an 850 mm (2 ft 9½ in imperial measure) door width, and 75 mm framing will give an 800 mm (2 ft 7½ in imperial measure) door width.

Metric height of rooms

The building regulations state that the minimum height of rooms shall not be less than 7 ft 6 in, giving a floor to floor height of approximately 8·2 ft.

The room, and floor to floor, heights, in metric and imperial measure, are given on page 7.

The five room heights are shown set out on the 300 mm planning grid.

Metric sizes of timber

Commencing in the year 1970 softwoods will be imported into the country in a new range of sizes in metric measurement. The section sizes are given in millimetres, and the lengths in metres.

These new sizes are slightly under the corresponding imperial sizes. This is due to the fact that 12 in is taken to equal 300 mm (11·8 in).

The chart below illustrates this.

Section sizes

Imperial measure (inches)	1 × 3	2 × 4	3 × 6	4 × 12
Metric measure (mm)	25 × 75	50 × 100	75 × 150	100 × 300

Lengths

Imperial measure (feet)	8	9	10	15	20
Metric measure (metres)	2·40	2·70	3·00	4·50	6·00

CARPENTRY AND JOINERY.

METRICATION
INTRODUCTION

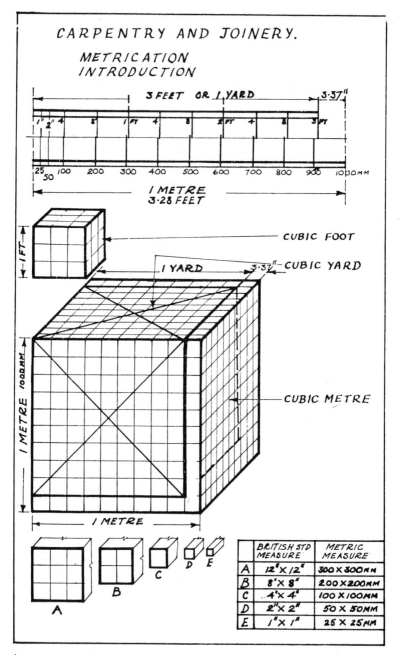

3 FEET OR 1 YARD · 3·37"

1 METRE
3·28 FEET

CUBIC FOOT

1 YARD · 3·37" — CUBIC YARD

CUBIC METRE

1 METRE

	BRITISH STD MEASURE	METRIC MEASURE
A	12" × 12"	300 × 300MM
B	8" × 8"	200 × 200MM
C	4" × 4"	100 × 100MM
D	2" × 2"	50 × 50MM
E	1" × 1"	25 × 25MM

4

CARPENTRY AND JOINERY.
METRICATION
300 MM PLANNING GRID

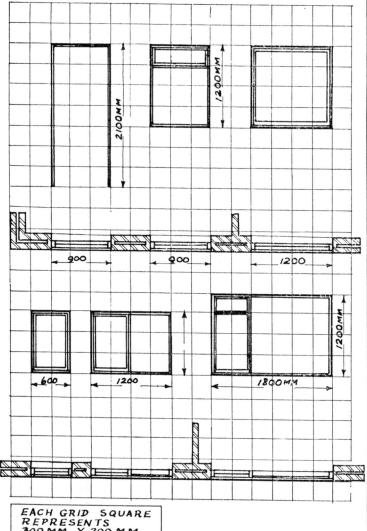

900 900 1200

2100MM 1200MM

600 1200 1800MM 1200MM

EACH GRID SQUARE
REPRESENTS
300 MM X 300 MM

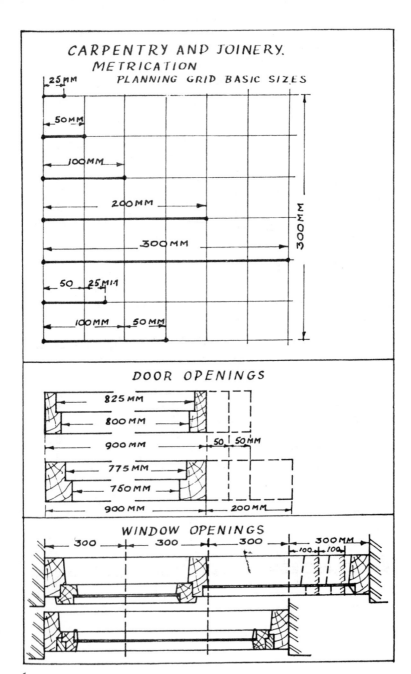

CARPENTRY AND JOINERY.
METRICATION
PLANNING GRID BASIC SIZES

25 MM

50 MM

100 MM

200 MM

300 MM

300 MM

50 25 MM

100 MM   50 MM

DOOR OPENINGS

825 MM

800 MM

900 MM   50 | 50 MM

775 MM

750 MM

900 MM   200 MM

WINDOW OPENINGS

300   300   300   300 MM

100   100

CARPENTRY AND JOINERY.
METRICATION

METRIC STOREY HEIGHTS

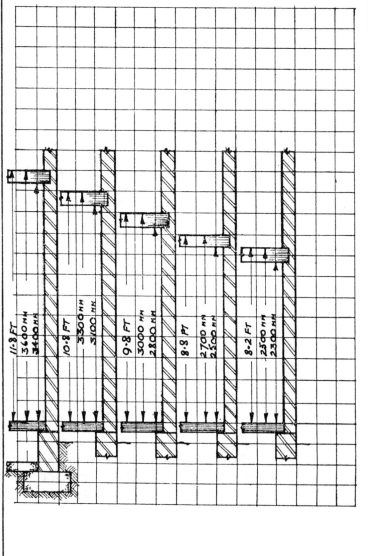

2 | Workshops

It is very difficult to get a perfect layout for the machines and benches in a workshop because of the varying nature of the work they are used for. It is a good plan, however, to arrange the machines in the following groups: first, the cutting-off machines (cross-cut and rip saws), next the planing machines (surface planers, thicknessers, and four siders), then the jointing and finishing machines (mortising, tenoning, and moulding machines, belt, drum, and disc sanders). The joiner's shop should be near the finishing machines so that there is no unnecessary waste of time when work is carried between operations.

Small workshop layout

Two typical layouts for a small workshop employing about eight men are given on page 11. The first example shows the machine shop equipped with one general woodworking machine, one mortise machine, and one band saw. The joiner's shop contains three double benches, with assembly and storage space provided at the end of each bench. The foreman occupies the bench nearest to the office.

In the second example the machine shop contains six machines —a cross-cut saw, a rip saw, a planer and thicknesser, a mortise machine, a spindle moulder, and a band saw. The joiner's shop has two double benches and a single setting-out bench which is placed near the office. The single bench would again probably be occupied by the foreman.

Medium-sized building contractor's shop

The layout given on page 12 is for a medium-sized building contractor's shop employing about thirty-six men and housing sixteen woodworking machines and eight double benches.

The machines are in four groups:

(a)   Sawing machines: cross-cut, circular re-saw, straight line edger, dimension saw, band saw.

(b)   Planers: surface planer, thicknesser, four sider.

(c)   Jointing machines: two mortise machines (chain and square chisel), one tenoning machine (single-ended tenoner), three moulding machines (two spindle moulders), and one router.

(d)   Finishing machines: two belt sanders.

NOTE   The sanding operations are best carried out in a shop apart from, but near to, both the joiner's and the machine shops.

In addition to the machines and the work benches for general work, special benches for wedging up doors and stairs are required, and in the machine shop setting-out benches are also needed.

In a workshop of this size the foreman's office should be large enough to accommodate the setter out, and to provide sufficient storage space for the drawings and details of all work in hand.

The space allotted to each machine depends on the type of work being done. In a general joinery works all rip saws, planing machines, and moulding machines require a distance of 3 to 4 m to the front and rear of each machine. Cross-cut saws and mortise machines require 3 to 4 m on each side. Tenoning machines, dimension saws, and band saws require 3 to 4 m on the working side.

A distance of 1·5 to 2 m between work benches is necessary to enable each man to work in comfort. The assembly space for each workman should be at least 3 m square.

Conveyance of materials

It is an advantage to have a truck or stand conveyor system in all shops. No timber should be stored on the floor; it retains its shape much better when stacked neatly on trucks or on stands which can be picked up by trucks and carried round the shop.

Types of trucks and stands most popular in joinery works are illustrated on page 11 (foot). The stands are usually 1·2 to 1·5 m long, and 600 to 750 mm wide; they should be narrow enough to pass through the smallest door in the factory. The stands must be rigid, straight, and out of twist.

The trucks have a platform framework which should be low enough to pass underneath the stands. This platform can be raised to lift the stand clear of the floor. Only one truck is necessary in a shop, but any number of stands may be used.

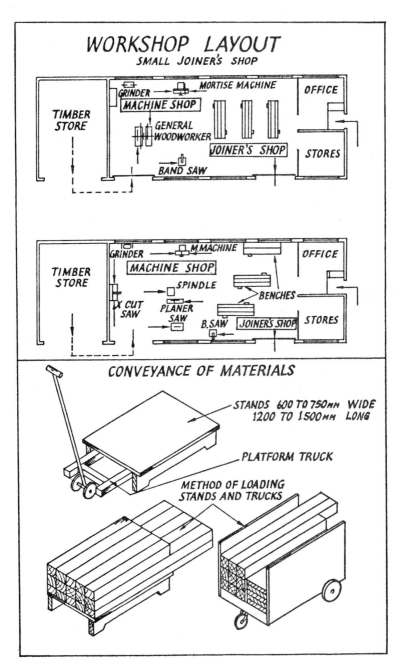

WORKSHOP LAYOUT
SMALL JOINER'S SHOP

GRINDER → MORTISE MACHINE
OFFICE

MACHINE SHOP

TIMBER STORE

GENERAL WOODWORKER

JOINER'S SHOP

STORES

BAND SAW

GRINDER → M.MACHINE
OFFICE

MACHINE SHOP

TIMBER STORE

SPINDLE

X CUT SAW

BENCHES

PLANER
SAW

B.SAW JOINER'S SHOP

STORES

CONVEYANCE OF MATERIALS

STANDS 600 TO 750mm WIDE
1200 TO 1500mm LONG

PLATFORM TRUCK

METHOD OF LOADING
STANDS AND TRUCKS

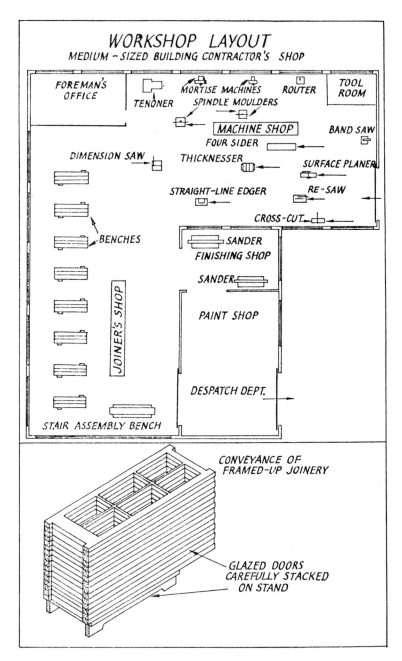

WORKSHOP LAYOUT
MEDIUM – SIZED BUILDING CONTRACTOR'S SHOP

FOREMAN'S OFFICE

TENONER

MORTISE MACHINES

SPINDLE MOULDERS

ROUTER

TOOL ROOM

MACHINE SHOP

BAND SAW

FOUR SIDER

DIMENSION SAW

THICKNESSER

SURFACE PLANER

STRAIGHT-LINE EDGER

RE-SAW

CROSS-CUT

BENCHES

SANDER

FINISHING SHOP

SANDER

JOINER'S SHOP

PAINT SHOP

DESPATCH DEPT.

STAIR ASSEMBLY BENCH

CONVEYANCE OF FRAMED-UP JOINERY

GLAZED DOORS CAREFULLY STACKED ON STAND

3 | Machines and machine operations

A carefully planned machine shop should contain machines able to carry out all the operations of sawing, planing, joint-making, moulding, and finishing.

Feeding of timber

Timber can be fed into the cutting heads of the machines in different ways.

In *hand-operated feeding* the operator can push or guide the timber through the cutting heads, using, of course, the necessary equipment for safety.

Mechanically operated rollers and tracks feed the timber on many sawing, planing, and moulding machines, thus giving the operator a greater degree of safety.

With *tenoning machines* the timber is clamped on to a carriage and is either pushed through the cutting heads by the operator or fed into them by mechanical means.

When *mortising*, the timber is clamped into the machine and the cutting head (chain or chisel) brought down into the timber by the operator.

A small shop would probably have mainly hand-operated machines, with perhaps mechanical feed attachments to the planing machines and spindle moulder.

In the larger shops most of the machines have mechanical feeds or feed attachments. Only machines such as narrow band saws, chisel mortise machines, and routers would be hand operated.

Sawing operations

The five main sawing operations are: resawing timber to smaller sections, splay cutting, removing the waste, cross-cutting to length, and circular cutting. These are all illustrated on pages 21–22.

The main *resawing operations*—ripping and deep cutting—are shown at the top of page 21. In small shops both these operations are usually carried out on a single machine, but in the larger shops it is common practice to use straight line edgers for ripping timber not more than 100 mm thick, and band resaws for deep cutting.

Three methods of *splay cutting* are shown in the next drawing. Tilting fillets, feather-edged boards, fencing rails, and glue blocks are typical products of this operation, in which two members are cut from one rectangular section. In the first method the section is set by tilting the fence; in the second by packing from the fence; and in the third a jig is used, into which the square timber fits at an angle of 45°.

The method of *removing waste* from window sills before the rebating and moulding operation by the spindle or four-cutter is shown on the middle of the page. If one removes waste by sawing instead of by cutter block a substantial saving of timber can be made. The amount of timber to be removed on a large section, such as a sill, may be 1500 or 2500 mm²: so that when one is making many windows much timber may be saved by this method.

When preparing sectional shapes for spindle working two saw cuts are required, but for four-sider working one cut only is necessary, as is shown in the diagram.

The method of *cross-cutting timber to length* is shown in the drawing at the foot of page 21. Here is shown the dimension saw used in the joinery mill. Dimension saws are used for a variety of jobs, including the cutting to size of hardboards, plywoods, and insulating boards. Overhead pull-over saws are used for this purpose in the rough cutting mill.

Three ways of *circular cutting* are illustrated on page 22. The cut may be circular in one plane, circular in two planes, or circular splayed. A face templet is required for marking out the curved shapes as shown. The templet used for the shaping of the member on the spindle moulder is also often used for the marking out here.

In small shops it is usual to *rip large tenons* on the band saw, as illustrated in the drawing at the foot of the page.

Planing operations

As with hand planing, the allowance for machine planing can be taken as 1·5 mm on each surface.

On single-block machines four feed operations are needed to bring timber to a true shape and size, but only one operation is required when a four-sider planing machine is used.

Three types of machines are involved in planing timber to shape and size: a surface planer, which may be hand operated or fitted with a mechanical finger-feed unit; a thicknessing machine, which usually has a mechanical feed unit; and a four-sider planing and moulding machine.

The *surface planer* can be used for two operations, both of which are illustrated at the top of page 23. Planing the face side is called surfacing. Then, with this true face to the fence, the edge is planed. This operation is called edging. The block sizes of surface planer in general use are 225–300–375–450 mm long.

The *thicknessing operation* is shown in the middle of page 23. It is usual to reduce the timber to a thickness first. Bringing the timber to width needs care, particularly when one is handling wide sections. When the sections are thin it is advisable to place two or more boards together.

Four-sider planing machines have at least one block working on each side of the section. The four main cutting heads of a four-sider are each fitted with a pair of planing cutters as standard equipment.

The moulding cutters are added according to the requirements of each job. Many have extra cutting heads, such as splitting saws and solid profile cutter blocks.

In the production of high-class joinery it is usual to plane one side of the stock on a surface planer in order to reach a true working face before one begins operations with the four sider. However, when one is dealing with general joinery this would be done only if the stock were badly warped.

Other uses for planing machines

In well-equipped joinery mills planing machines are primarily used to carry out the operations for which they have been designed. In small shops, however, it is often necessary to adapt them for other work. The surface planer can easily be adapted to rebate and mould framing, and to sink sills.

The drawing in the middle of page 23 shows how the rebating and moulding operation is done and at the foot of the page the three operations necessary to rebate and sink sills are shown.

NOTE   It is advisable to remove the waste by sawing when the sinkings are deep.

Joint-making operations

The main framing joint used in joinery is the mortise and tenon. Three machines are involved in the forming of this joint, and it is necessary to make sure that the setting up of one machine corresponds with the other two.

Mortising operations using a chisel and chain are shown on page 24. The member to be mortised is placed in the machine with the face side to the fence, and held in position with a clamp. The carriage of the machine can be adjusted in the horizontal plane to give varying positions and widths of mortise.

When forming through mortises with a chisel, it is usual to work from both sides of the member in order to obtain a clean-edged mortise. Clean mortises can, however, be formed with a chain in one operation, working from the face side as shown at the foot of page 24.

It is usual to form the mortise first, and to adjust the tenon to fit into it, as no alteration can be made in the thickness of a chain or chisel.

Tenoning and scribing operations are shown on page 25. The two horizontal tenoning heads and the two vertical scribing heads can move upwards, downwards and sideways. This enables the operator to make adjustments without having to reset any of the cutters.

The tenoning heads have a micrometer adjustment which makes

the fitting of the tenon into the mortise a simple matter, but care should be taken to see that when the joint is together the face sides of the meeting members are flush with each other.

First the tenoning heads are set up, then the tenon is cut to fit the mortise accurately; next the scribing heads (with the cutters already attached) are adjusted, and the scribings formed.

NOTE It is essential that the joint should be fitted together and any minor adjustments made before any machining connected with the job is done.

As was said earlier, and shown at the foot of page 22, in small shops large tenons are usually ripped on the band saw.

Moulding operations

Two machines are in general use for the shaping of joinery sections. Four-sider machines are used for long runs of straight work. Vertical-spindle moulders are used for short runs of straight work, curved work, and the numerous small moulding jobs that have to be done.

Square blocks 100 and 150 mm long are used extensively for working both window and door sections. Four pairs of cutters can be set on one block, which means that rebating and moulding operations can be carried out simultaneously.

A square block set up for rebating and moulding is shown on page 26 (top). The middle drawing shows the cutter arrangement for the double moulding of door sections.

Setting and shaping of cutters

Rule-of-thumb methods for shaping and setting scribing and moulding cutters are unnecessary these days, but one must have a knowledge of the geometry of cutter blocks in order to understand the techniques used in a well-organised joinery mill.

The use of a cutter projection scale, when fully understood, can considerably reduce the amount of time taken in grinding and setting cutters, and make rule-of-thumb methods or guesswork unnecessary.

The development of the scale and the application of the projection templet to cutter setting is shown at the bottom of page 26. The geometry of rotary-cutter blocks and the theory of the cutter projection scale is explained in Workshop Geometry pages 277–278.

Other types of cutting heads with their particular uses are illustrated on page 27. The top drawing shows a head with slotted collars set up for single moulding. These collars are obtainable fitted with ball bearings, and are ideal for working curved members. The middle drawing shows a french head set up for panel raising. The drawing at the bottom of the page shows a whitehill head set up for moulding a handrail section.

Working of shaped or curved members

Face templets are necessary for the proper working of curved members. A templet should be accurately made from plywood which must be at least 9 mm thick. The templet is securely fastened to the curved stock, which is then engaged with the ring fence as shown at the top of page 28.

An enlarged sectional view of the cleaning-up operations showing the position of the ring fence, the templet, and the circular cleaning-up block is given in the middle of this page. The drawing at the bottom shows the moulding operation working from the cleaned-up curved surface.

A practical example of machine operations : making a window

The order in which the machine operations are carried out varies according to the type of machines available, the amount of joinery work to be made, and its design and quality. In the large-scale production of standard joinery work it is usual to work the sections, using mainly four-sider planing and moulding machines, before the mortising and tenoning is done. In shops producing high-class work, or when four-sider machines are not available, the mortising and tenoning operation is usually done before the moulding and rebating.

It is of the greatest importance that one should work methodically and follow the correct sequence of machine operations on any specific job. To illustrate this a typical example may be taken in following the stages of making a two-light window with transom 1·65 m high and 1·125 m wide.

The architect's drawings and details on page 29 show 1:20 scale, full-size details, and enlarged details of the joints for the frame and casements. Notice that traditional and modern sections are given for the framing.

From the drawings and specifications the height and width rod is prepared and a cutting list made out. From these particulars the window can be made.

The marking out is the work which chiefly concerns the joiner. He must furnish the machinist with all the information necessary to enable him to carry out the required operations.

The height and width rods are shown at the top of page 30. The marking out of the members in the frame are also shown. They are one pair of jambs, and the head and sill, transom and mullion.

The drawing on page 31 illustrates the marking out of the casements, showing four pairs of stiles, and the pattern rail and bar. A view of the finished bar and rail is also given.

The mortising, tenoning and scribing, rebating and moulding operations are shown on page 32. The assembled joints are illustrated at the bottom of the page.

Practice lessons

1 Working from the information given:
   (a) Draw (full size) the end sectional view of a 125 mm circular cutter block. Show on the drawing the exact position of the cutters in the block, and the cutting, grinding, and clearance angles.
   (b) Draw (full size) the end sectional view of a 90 mm square cutter block. Show the position of the 9 mm thick cutters on the block, and the cutting angle.
   (c) Make plan sectional drawings of—
       (i) A slotted collar cutting head.
       (ii) A french cutting head.
   (d) Make neat diagrams to explain the geometry of a cutter projection scale.
   (e) Show its application to cutter setting.

2 (a) Make neat sketches of the horizontal tenoning heads, and the top and bottom scribing heads, on a single-ended tenoning machine.
   (b) Illustrate how the tenons and scribings are formed.

3 Working from the instructions given:
   (a) Set out a workshop rod for a two-light window with transom, to any convenient size.
   (b) Prepare a cutting list for one window.
   (c) Make a list of the machine operations involved in making the window.
   (d) Work, in conjunction with the woodcutting machinist, to carry out all the machine operations.
   (e) Carry out all the operations involved in assembling and finishing the window.

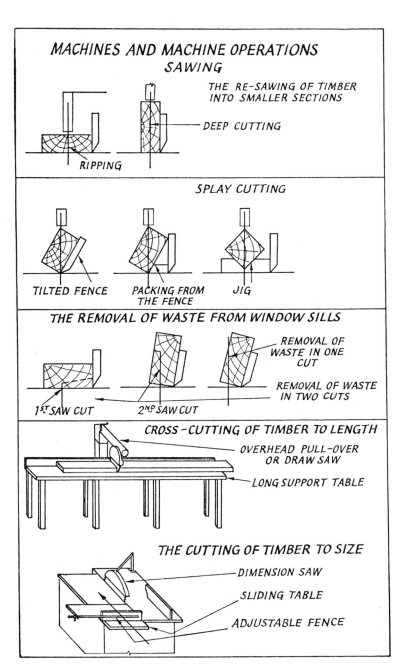

MACHINES AND MACHINE OPERATIONS
SAWING

THE RE-SAWING OF TIMBER
INTO SMALLER SECTIONS

DEEP CUTTING

RIPPING

SPLAY CUTTING

TILTED FENCE   PACKING FROM   JIG
                THE FENCE

THE REMOVAL OF WASTE FROM WINDOW SILLS

REMOVAL OF
WASTE IN ONE
CUT

REMOVAL OF WASTE
IN TWO CUTS

1ST SAW CUT   2ND SAW CUT

CROSS-CUTTING OF TIMBER TO LENGTH

OVERHEAD PULL-OVER
OR DRAW SAW

LONG SUPPORT TABLE

THE CUTTING OF TIMBER TO SIZE

DIMENSION SAW

SLIDING TABLE

ADJUSTABLE FENCE

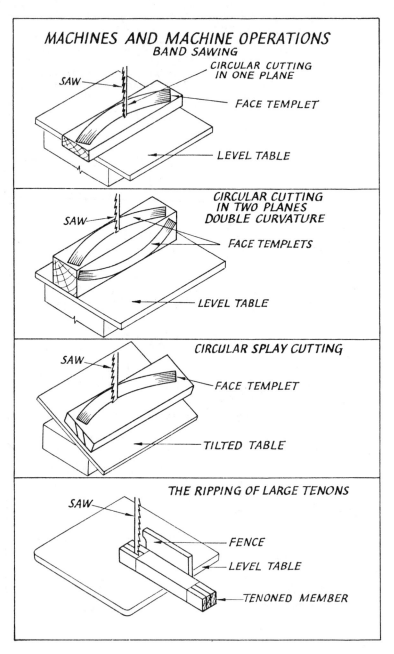

MACHINES AND MACHINE OPERATIONS
BAND SAWING

CIRCULAR CUTTING IN ONE PLANE

SAW

FACE TEMPLET

LEVEL TABLE

CIRCULAR CUTTING IN TWO PLANES DOUBLE CURVATURE

SAW

FACE TEMPLETS

LEVEL TABLE

CIRCULAR SPLAY CUTTING

SAW

FACE TEMPLET

TILTED TABLE

THE RIPPING OF LARGE TENONS

SAW

FENCE

LEVEL TABLE

TENONED MEMBER

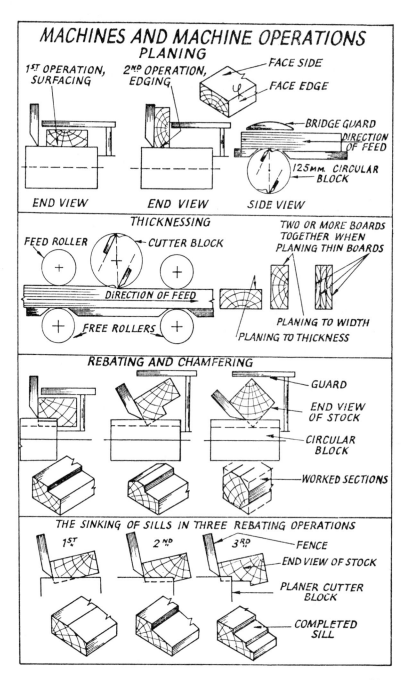

MACHINES AND MACHINE OPERATIONS
PLANING

1ST OPERATION, SURFACING

2ND OPERATION, EDGING

FACE SIDE

FACE EDGE

BRIDGE GUARD

DIRECTION OF FEED

125MM. CIRCULAR BLOCK

END VIEW

END VIEW

SIDE VIEW

THICKNESSING

FEED ROLLER

CUTTER BLOCK

TWO OR MORE BOARDS TOGETHER WHEN PLANING THIN BOARDS

DIRECTION OF FEED

FREE ROLLERS

PLANING TO WIDTH

PLANING TO THICKNESS

REBATING AND CHAMFERING

GUARD

END VIEW OF STOCK

CIRCULAR BLOCK

WORKED SECTIONS

THE SINKING OF SILLS IN THREE REBATING OPERATIONS

1ST

2ND

3RD

FENCE

END VIEW OF STOCK

PLANER CUTTER BLOCK

COMPLETED SILL

23

MACHINES AND MACHINE OPERATIONS
CHISEL MORTISING

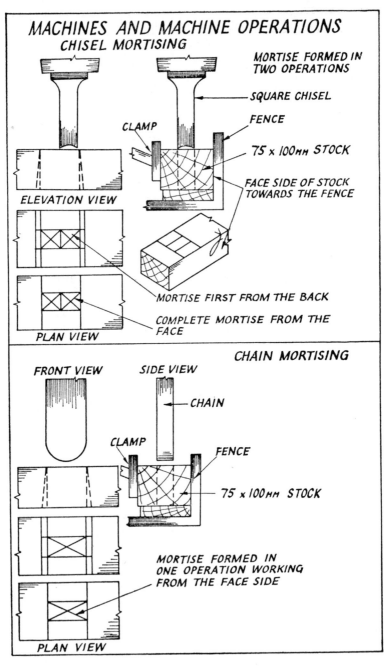

MORTISE FORMED IN TWO OPERATIONS

SQUARE CHISEL

FENCE

75 x 100mm STOCK

FACE SIDE OF STOCK TOWARDS THE FENCE

CLAMP

ELEVATION VIEW

PLAN VIEW

MORTISE FIRST FROM THE BACK

COMPLETE MORTISE FROM THE FACE

CHAIN MORTISING

FRONT VIEW

SIDE VIEW

CHAIN

CLAMP

FENCE

75 x 100mm STOCK

MORTISE FORMED IN ONE OPERATION WORKING FROM THE FACE SIDE

PLAN VIEW

MACHINES AND MACHINE OPERATIONS
TENONING AND SCRIBING

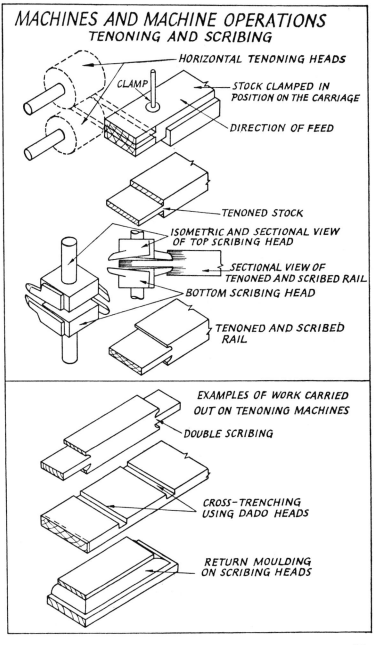

HORIZONTAL TENONING HEADS

CLAMP

STOCK CLAMPED IN POSITION ON THE CARRIAGE

DIRECTION OF FEED

TENONED STOCK

ISOMETRIC AND SECTIONAL VIEW OF TOP SCRIBING HEAD

SECTIONAL VIEW OF TENONED AND SCRIBED RAIL

BOTTOM SCRIBING HEAD

TENONED AND SCRIBED RAIL

EXAMPLES OF WORK CARRIED OUT ON TENONING MACHINES

DOUBLE SCRIBING

CROSS-TRENCHING USING DADO HEADS

RETURN MOULDING ON SCRIBING HEADS

MACHINES AND MACHINE OPERATIONS
MOULDING

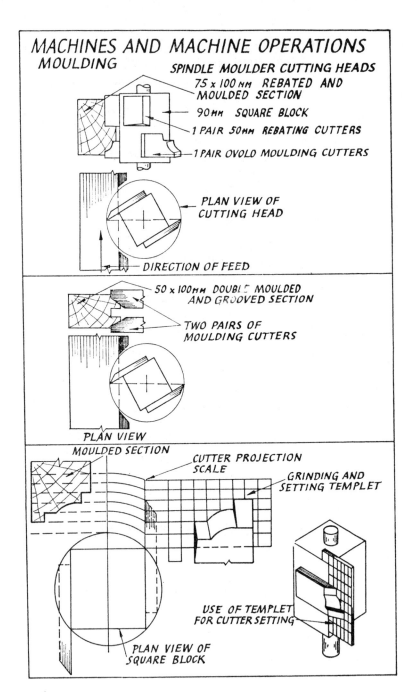

SPINDLE MOULDER CUTTING HEADS

75 x 100 мм REBATED AND MOULDED SECTION

90 мм SQUARE BLOCK

1 PAIR 50мм REBATING CUTTERS

1 PAIR OVOLO MOULDING CUTTERS

PLAN VIEW OF CUTTING HEAD

DIRECTION OF FEED

50 x 100мм DOUBLE MOULDED AND GROOVED SECTION

TWO PAIRS OF MOULDING CUTTERS

PLAN VIEW

MOULDED SECTION

CUTTER PROJECTION SCALE

GRINDING AND SETTING TEMPLET

USE OF TEMPLET FOR CUTTER SETTING

PLAN VIEW OF SQUARE BLOCK

MACHINES AND MACHINE OPERATIONS

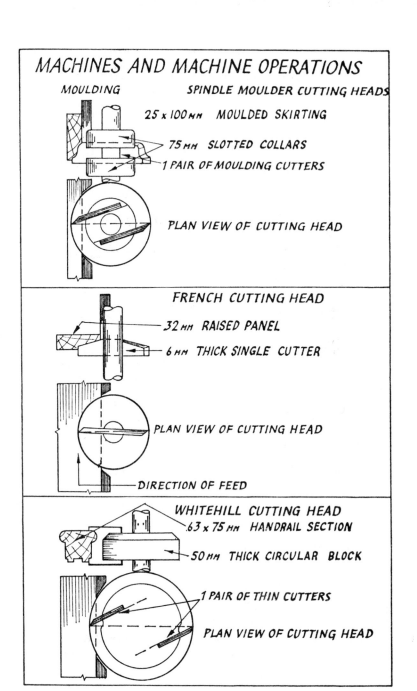

MOULDING

SPINDLE MOULDER CUTTING HEADS

25 x 100 MM MOULDED SKIRTING

75 MM SLOTTED COLLARS

1 PAIR OF MOULDING CUTTERS

PLAN VIEW OF CUTTING HEAD

FRENCH CUTTING HEAD

32 MM RAISED PANEL

6 MM THICK SINGLE CUTTER

PLAN VIEW OF CUTTING HEAD

DIRECTION OF FEED

WHITEHILL CUTTING HEAD

63 x 75 MM HANDRAIL SECTION

50 MM THICK CIRCULAR BLOCK

1 PAIR OF THIN CUTTERS

PLAN VIEW OF CUTTING HEAD

MACHINES AND MACHINE OPERATIONS
CIRCULAR MOULDING

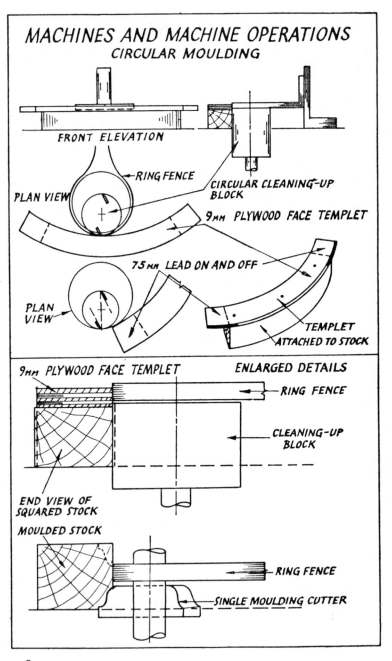

FRONT ELEVATION

PLAN VIEW — RING FENCE

CIRCULAR CLEANING-UP BLOCK

9mm PLYWOOD FACE TEMPLET

75mm LEAD ON AND OFF

PLAN VIEW

TEMPLET ATTACHED TO STOCK

ENLARGED DETAILS

9mm PLYWOOD FACE TEMPLET

RING FENCE

CLEANING-UP BLOCK

END VIEW OF SQUARED STOCK

MOULDED STOCK

RING FENCE

SINGLE MOULDING CUTTER

MACHINE OPERATIONS

OPERATIONS INVOLVED IN THE MANUFACTURE OF WINDOWS
ARCHITECTS' DRAWINGS

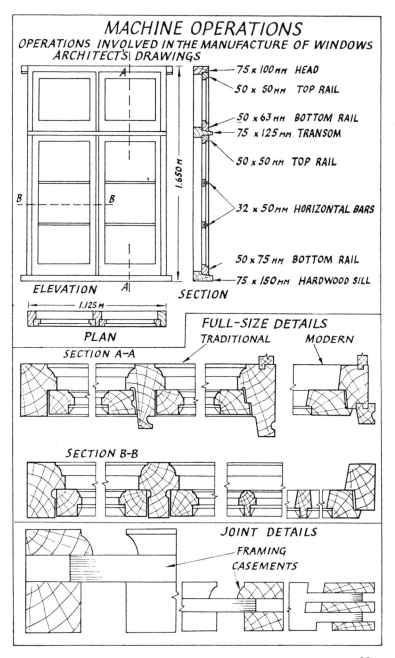

75 × 100 MM HEAD

50 × 50 MM TOP RAIL

50 × 63 MM BOTTOM RAIL

75 × 125 MM. TRANSOM

50 × 50 MM TOP RAIL

32 × 50 MM HORIZONTAL BARS

50 × 75 MM BOTTOM RAIL

75 × 150 MM HARDWOOD SILL

1.650 M

ELEVATION

SECTION

1.125 M

PLAN

FULL-SIZE DETAILS

SECTION A-A

TRADITIONAL   MODERN

SECTION B-B

JOINT DETAILS

FRAMING
CASEMENTS

29

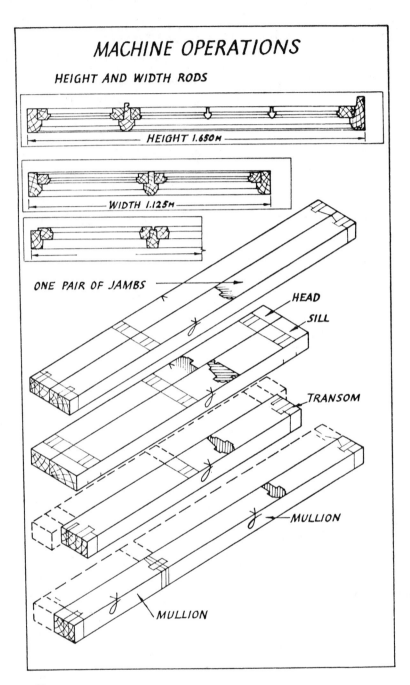

MACHINE OPERATIONS

HEIGHT AND WIDTH RODS

HEIGHT 1.650M

WIDTH 1.125M

ONE PAIR OF JAMBS

HEAD

SILL

TRANSOM

MULLION

MULLION

MACHINE OPERATIONS
METHOD OF MARKING OUT CASEMENTS FOR MACHINE WORKING

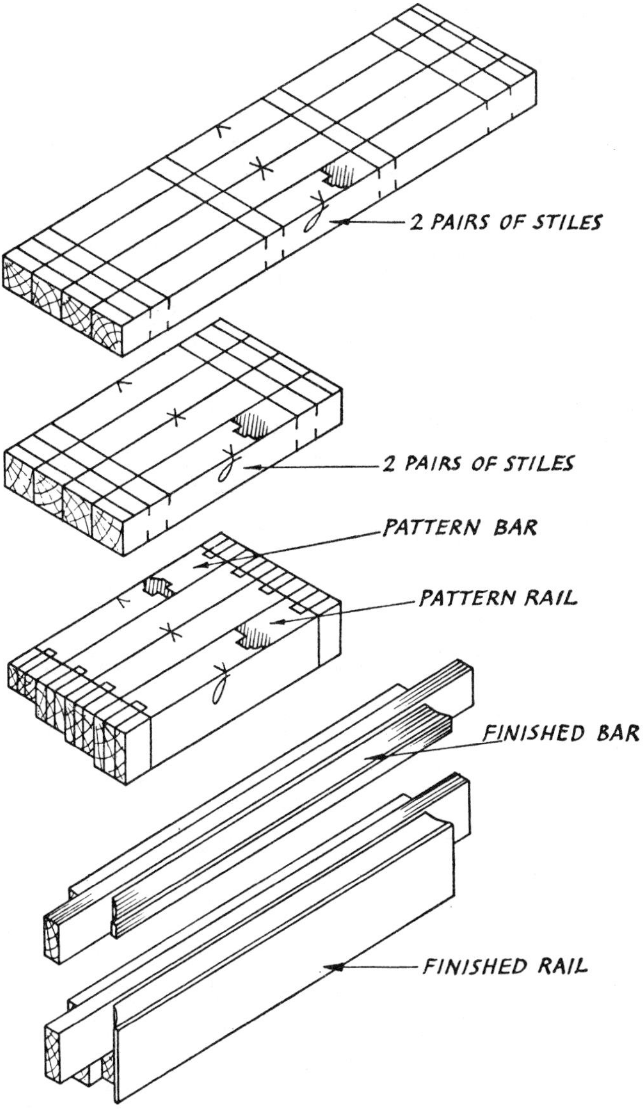

2 PAIRS OF STILES

2 PAIRS OF STILES

PATTERN BAR

PATTERN RAIL

FINISHED BAR

FINISHED RAIL

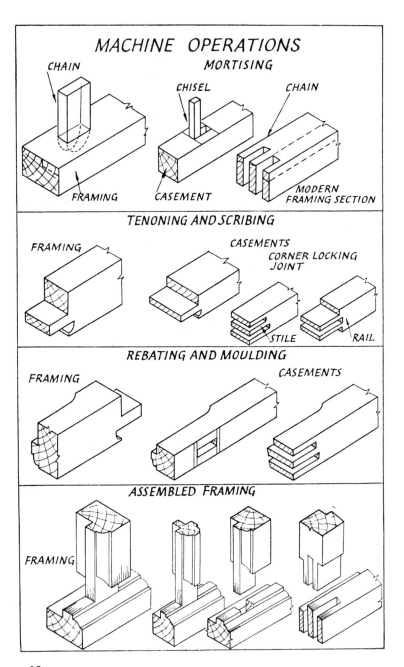

MACHINE OPERATIONS

MORTISING

CHAIN

CHISEL

CHAIN

FRAMING

CASEMENT

MODERN
FRAMING SECTION

TENONING AND SCRIBING

FRAMING

CASEMENTS

CORNER LOCKING
JOINT

STILE

RAIL

REBATING AND MOULDING

FRAMING

CASEMENTS

ASSEMBLED FRAMING

FRAMING

4 | Timber floors

Double floors

Double floors are rarely used in modern building practice. However, the carpenter and joiner should understand these older forms of floor construction, since he may be called upon to deal with them.

The maximum clear span for softwood bridging joists can be considered as 4·8 m, and when the smallest plan dimension of a room exceeds this length it is necessary to construct a double floor. Here relatively large members, called binders, are introduced to give intermediate support to the joists.

The plan and section of a double floor is shown on page 41 (top). The floor is divided into three bays by two 375 × 175 mm solid timber binders. These support 150 × 50 mm bridging joists spaced at 375 mm centres. The binders may be solid timber beams, flitched beams, or rolled-steel joists put in position at 2·4 to 3·6 m centres across the shortest way of the room. They are supported at each end on 225 × 162 × 600 mm stone pads, with an allowance for a free passage of air round the ends of each binder.

Where the ceiling below needs an unbroken surface, ceiling joists are also needed. For the outer bays, these joists may be supported at one end by fillets nailed firmly to the sides of the binders, and at the other end by fillets securely fixed to the wall. The joists for the middle bay are supported on fillets nailed to the binders.

Enlarged details of the floor are given on page 41. The method of supporting the bridging joists and the ceiling joists are shown in the middle of the page. The method of supporting the binder, the free passage of air round the beam, and a section view of the stone pad are also shown here.

The isometric view at the bottom of the page gives details of the jointing of floor and ceiling joists to the binders.

Details of a double floor with steel binders are shown on page 42. At the top are the plan and section of a floor 5·4 m wide and 9 m long, set out in three 3 m bays.

The enlarged details in the middle of the page show a section through the floor with the bridging joists notched up to and over the steel binders, and supported by steel angles. Also shown is a second method where wood bearers are fixed to the steel binder by bolts, to receive the ends of the joists which are notched up to the binder.

The bridging joists are lathed and plastered.

Cradling for the steel binder consists of firrings which are halved at the joints to form frames, fixed to the side of each bridging joist, and arranged around the binder to receive the lath and plaster.

A side view of the steel binder and the cradling are also illustrated (C).

An isometric view of the floor construction, showing the way the bridging joists are notched over the steel binders, is given at the bottom of the page.

Framed floors

When the shortest span of the room exceeds 7·2 m it is necessary to construct a framed floor. This consists of bridging joists, binders, and girders. It is now common practice to use rolled-steel joist sections for both girders and binders, but in older buildings the main supporting units were of solid timber or flitched timber members. The bridging joists are placed the short way of the room; that is, parallel to the main girders. The binders which give support to the bridging joist are themselves supported by the main girders.

The plan and sectional view of a traditional framed floor is given on page 43 (top). This example has 150 × 75 mm bridging joists, 275 × 150 mm binders, and 375 × 200 mm flitched girders.

The enlarged details in the middle of the page show sectional views of the flitched girder and the bridging joists (A–B). Also shown is a sectional view of the binder and the method of supporting the flitched girder (C–D).

The drawing at the bottom of the page indicates the general construction of the floor.

The framed floor illustrated on page 44 (top) has a 375 × 125 mm steel girder, 275 × 150 mm solid wood binders, 150 × 75 mm bridging joists, and 100 × 50 mm ceiling joists.

The enlarged details in the middle of this page show the method of supporting the binders and the fixing of the girder casing.

The general construction for the floor is given in the isometric drawing.

Soundproofing

The transmission of sound from one part of a building to another, particularly in domestic buildings, creates special problems for architects and builders. Sounds may be of two general types: airborne sounds, such as speech or music; or impact sounds, such as those made by walking, hammering, or banging doors.

The practice of eliminating or reducing the transmission of sound in a building structure is known as sound insulation. For timber floors, insulating materials to reduce the transmission of sound between storeys are usually in slab or strip form. They can be applied in three ways: laid over the bridging joists underneath the flooring; as a sound-insulated ceiling, where insulating board is applied to the underside of the floor joists; or as layers of fibre board, which are placed between the joists and supported on fillets.

Three modern examples of soundproof construction are illustrated on page 45. The drawing at the top of the page shows the use of insulating pads, fixed to the top edge of the joists, and panels of board, laid between the joists and supported on fillets nailed to the sides of the joists.

The floor shown in the middle of the page has three layers of insulating boards, with the skirtings bedded on to a felt strip.

Details of an excellent method of soundproofing in which the ceiling is detached from the floor and the floor is insulated from the walls is illustrated at the bottom of the page

Housed framing joints

It is an advantage to use housed joints for the framing together of floor timbers, rather than the traditional tusk tenon joint. By this method the amount of timber to be cut away can be reduced. The three types used are the square, bevelled, and dovetail housed joints. All three types are illustrated on page 46.

Timber connectors

Today, metal framing anchors and hangers are extensively used to connect floor timbers together. Two main types of connectors are produced by a well-known manufacturing company. One is a sheet metal grip which is nailed to the joists, and the other a type of hanger into which the end of the joist is inserted. Details of the grips and hangers are given on page 47. The Trip-L-Grips are made in pairs, and are fixed to the joists as shown at the top of the page. The use of grips to connect floor joists to timber binders is shown in the middle of the page.

The two types of mild steel hangers are illustrated at the foot of page 47. A shows the hanger for building into brickwork, and B the hanger shaped to fit over the top flange of the steel beam or rolled steel joist section.

Wall plates

It is common practice in good-class work to support the floor joists on wall plates. Four examples of wall plates are given on page 48.

The first drawing shows the wall plate, brick size in section, built into the wall with the plate trenched to receive the joist. The second example shows the joist supported on a 75×9 mm mild steel flat bar. The third drawing shows the wall plate supported on the inside 112 mm step back, where a 340 mm wall reduces to a 225 mm wall.

The method of supporting wall plates on corbel brackets is shown at the foot of the page. These brackets are bent to shape from wrought iron or mild steel, 50×6 mm and about 450 mm long, built into the wall at intervals of 750 to 900 mm.

Three further examples of wall plates are given on page 49. The drawing at the top of the page shows the wall plate supported on brick corbelling.

A wall plate bedded on to a damp-proof course and supported

by the inside 112 mm of a 225 mm load-bearing wall is illustrated in the middle of page 49.

The best example, at the bottom of page 49, shows ground-floor joists supported by a wall plate bedded on to a 112 mm sleeper wall.

NOTE   When the ends of the joists are solidly built into the brick-work it is advisable to apply a recognised rot-proofing solution to the joist ends.

Treatment of the hearth

Concrete is used in forming the hearth and this, since it is cast *in situ*, needs to be supported during the casting operation.

The treatment of ground-floor hearths is illustrated on page 50. The first drawing shows a 75 mm stone slab supporting the hearth concrete. The second drawing shows the hearth concrete sup-ported on a hard core infilling.

Where fireplaces occur in upper storeys, local bye-laws require that a timber floor shall have a properly constructed hearth which shall project a minimum of 150 mm beyond the jamb of the fireplace opening and 400 mm into the room. Three examples of the hearth construction for upper floors are given on page 51.

The drawing at the top of page 51 shows the traditional method of supporting the concrete with a brick trimmer arch.

A concrete hearth supported on permanent shuttering (shutter-ing which remains part of the floor structure) is shown in the middle of the page.

In the third example on page 51 a 75 mm stone slab is used.

Floor covering for reinforced concrete

Fire-resistant floors of reinforced concrete usually have wood floor coverings, which may be made up of boards, blocks, or tiles.

The *boards* are fixed to bearers of 50 × 50 mm section. Details of two concrete slab floors given on page 52 show the layout of the bearers. The first drawing shows the bearers laid parallel with the fireplace opening, and the second shows them at right angles to the opening.

Page 53 shows how the bearers may be fixed to the concrete. The top drawing shows splayed bearers embedded in the concrete; the middle drawing shows the bearers fixed to the floor with clips; and the drawing at the foot of the page illustrates the bearers scolloped to form stools at 375 to 450 mm intervals. This method, with air grids fixed into the skirtings as shown, gives a free passage of air under the floor. This system of ventilating floors is common practice on the Continent, but it is essential that the building has a central heating system when this type of ventilation is used.

Block flooring can be made from both softwoods and hardwoods. The timber should be quarter-sawn and carefully kiln-dried. The nominal size of the blocks varies in length from 225 to 300 mm, in width from 50 to 75 mm, and in thickness from 25 to 32 mm. These blocks are usually laid on hot mastic with the dovetail groove in the block providing a good key. Two types of wood blocks are illustrated on page 54. The first drawing shows the traditional wood blocks laid herring-bone pattern and enlarged details of the block. The floor illustrated in the second drawing has 300×75 mm tongued-and-grooved blocks laid in groups of four to form a square.

Plywood may also be used to surface floors. This is a low-cost covering of good appearance, and consists of squares cut from boards of plywood. The stock sizes of the squares are 225, 300, 450, and 900 mm. The thickness is 4–9 mm.

NOTE   A thick surface veneer is essential for the floor to withstand hard wear.

The plywood squares are laid on a sub-floor of 25 mm square-edged boards laid diagonally. They should be well glued and panel-pinned to the sub-floor, with the pins punched in and the holes stopped.

It is an advantage to lay strips of insulating material on the top edge of the joists before the sub-floor is fixed in order to minimise any drumming.

A typical plywood floor is illustrated on page 54 (foot), showing details of sub-floor and floor covering.

The ordinary *parquet flooring* consists of small pieces of highly decorative hardwood (oak and teak are chiefly used), which are hot-glued and panel-pinned to a softwood or plywood sub-floor. The thicknesses in use are 6, 9, and 12 mm; but the 6 mm size is the most popular. In order to obtain a true flat surface, a layer of 4 mm plywood should be introduced between the softwood sub-floor and the parquetry. The floor is illustrated at the top of page 55.

Inlaid parquetry consists of a surface veneer of richly figured and coloured hardwood, 6–9 mm in thickness, which is glued under pressure to a softwood backing. The resulting slabs are then cut into various shapes and sizes, the most popular of which is 300 to 600 mm square. These are then glued and pinned to a softwood or plywood sub-floor.

Laminated floor coverings can be described as a simplified version of parquet flooring. The floor board most popular in Europe consists of a 6 mm hardwood face built up from standard-size pieces which are glued, under pressure, to a softwood base. One design is illustrated on page 55 (middle), and shows the covering, bearers, and an enlarged view of the floor board.

Granulated cork mixed with resin or other bonding agents and pressed into tiles or rolled into sheets is a form of covering extensively used for both public and domestic buildings. It is noiseless, non-slip, and durable if carefully treated. Granulated cork is obtainable in carpet or tile form; the stock sizes of the tiles are 100 to 600 mm square and 6 to 14 mm thick. They may be square-edged or tongued-and-grooved.

The tiles are laid on wood or concrete floors, the surface of which must be free from irregularities. Details of the floor are given at the bottom of page 55, with an enlarged view of the tile and skirting.

Practice lessons

1 Working from the information given:

    (a) Make line diagrams to show the basic difference between a double and framed timber floor.

    (b) Draw the cross-section through the main beam of a double floor with wood binders.

2 *(a)* Make neat sketches showing two methods of insulating a timber floor.

    (b) Give details of an independent ceiling to a timber floor.

3 *(a)* Make sectional and isometric sketches of two types of wood floor coverings on concrete floors.

    (b) Give details of two types of wood block coverings.

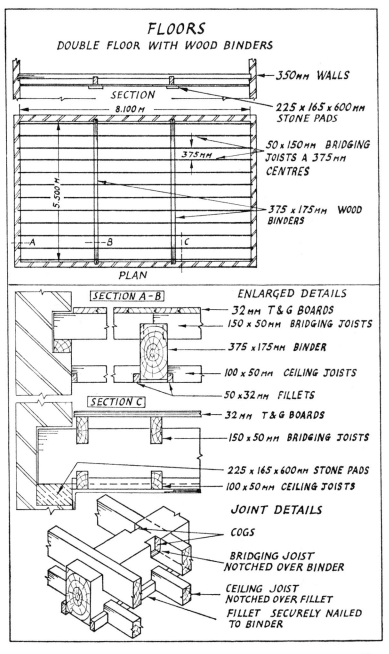

FLOORS
DOUBLE FLOOR WITH WOOD BINDERS

SECTION

350mm WALLS

225 x 165 x 600mm STONE PADS

8.100 M

375mm

5.500 M

50 x 150mm BRIDGING JOISTS A 375mm CENTRES

375 x 175mm WOOD BINDERS

A — B C

PLAN

SECTION A-B

ENLARGED DETAILS

32mm T&G BOARDS
150 x 50mm BRIDGING JOISTS

375 x 175mm BINDER

100 x 50mm CEILING JOISTS

50 x 32mm FILLETS

SECTION C

32mm T&G BOARDS

150 x 50mm BRIDGING JOISTS

225 x 165 x 600mm STONE PADS
100 x 50mm CEILING JOISTS

JOINT DETAILS

COGS

BRIDGING JOIST NOTCHED OVER BINDER

CEILING JOIST NOTCHED OVER FILLET

FILLET SECURELY NAILED TO BINDER

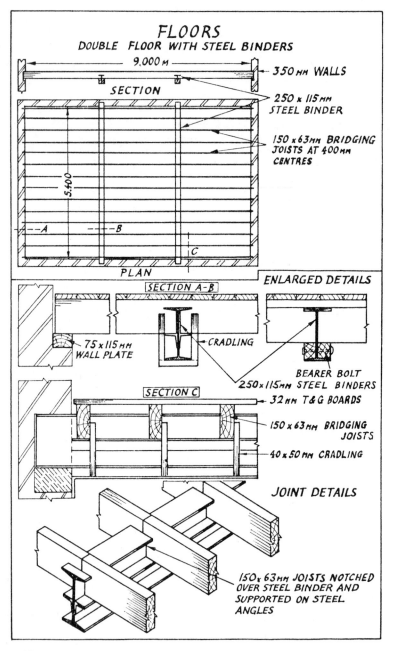

FLOORS
DOUBLE FLOOR WITH STEEL BINDERS

9.000 M

350 MM WALLS

SECTION

250 x 115 MM STEEL BINDER

150 x 63 MM BRIDGING JOISTS AT 400 MM CENTRES

5.400

A   B

C

PLAN

ENLARGED DETAILS

SECTION A-B

CRADLING

75 x 115 MM WALL PLATE

BEARER BOLT

250 x 115 MM STEEL BINDERS

SECTION C

32 MM T&G BOARDS

150 x 63 MM BRIDGING JOISTS

40 x 50 MM CRADLING

JOINT DETAILS

150 x 63 MM JOISTS NOTCHED OVER STEEL BINDER AND SUPPORTED ON STEEL ANGLES

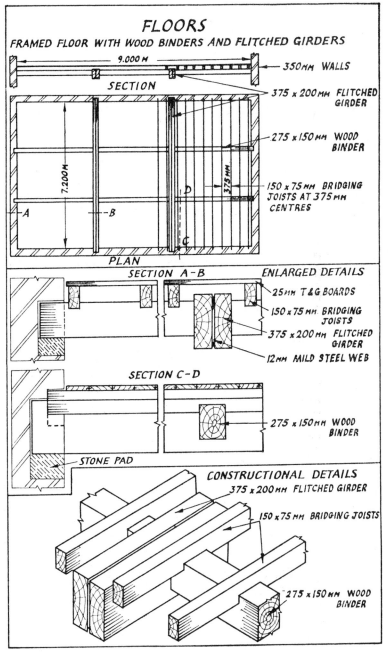

FLOORS
FRAMED FLOOR WITH WOOD BINDERS AND FLITCHED GIRDERS

9.000 M

350MM WALLS

SECTION

375 x 200MM FLITCHED GIRDER

275 x 150MM WOOD BINDER

7.200 M

375 MM

150 x 75 MM BRIDGING JOISTS AT 375 MM CENTRES

A

B

D

C

PLAN

SECTION A-B

ENLARGED DETAILS

25MM T&G BOARDS

150 x 75 MM BRIDGING JOISTS

375 x 200 MM FLITCHED GIRDER

12MM MILD STEEL WEB

SECTION C-D

275 x 150MM WOOD BINDER

STONE PAD

CONSTRUCTIONAL DETAILS

375 x 200MM FLITCHED GIRDER

150 x 75MM BRIDGING JOISTS

275 x 150MM WOOD BINDER

43

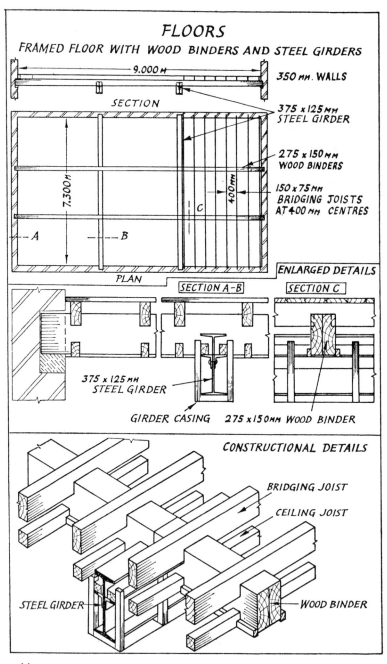

FLOORS

FRAMED FLOOR WITH WOOD BINDERS AND STEEL GIRDERS

9.000 M

350 MM. WALLS

SECTION

375 x 125 MM STEEL GIRDER

275 x 150 MM WOOD BINDERS

150 x 75 MM BRIDGING JOISTS AT 400 MM CENTRES

7.300 M

400 MM

C

A

B

PLAN

ENLARGED DETAILS

SECTION A-B

SECTION C

375 x 125 MM STEEL GIRDER

GIRDER CASING   275 x 150 MM WOOD BINDER

CONSTRUCTIONAL DETAILS

BRIDGING JOIST

CEILING JOIST

STEEL GIRDER

WOOD BINDER

44

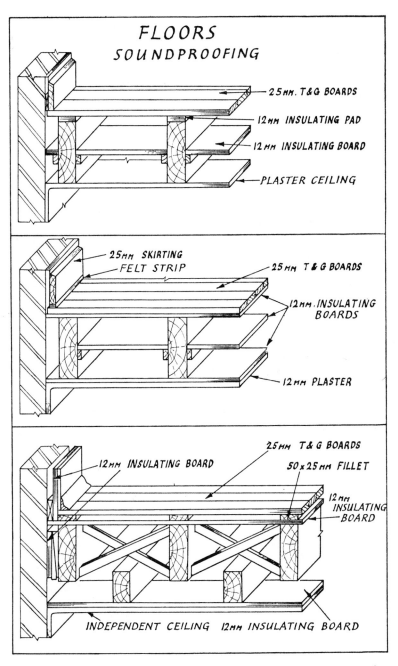

FLOORS
SOUNDPROOFING

25mm. T&G BOARDS

12mm INSULATING PAD

12mm INSULATING BOARD

PLASTER CEILING

25mm SKIRTING
FELT STRIP

25mm T&G BOARDS

12mm INSULATING
BOARDS

12mm PLASTER

12mm INSULATING BOARD

25mm T&G BOARDS

50 x 25mm FILLET

12mm INSULATING BOARD

INDEPENDENT CEILING   12mm INSULATING BOARD

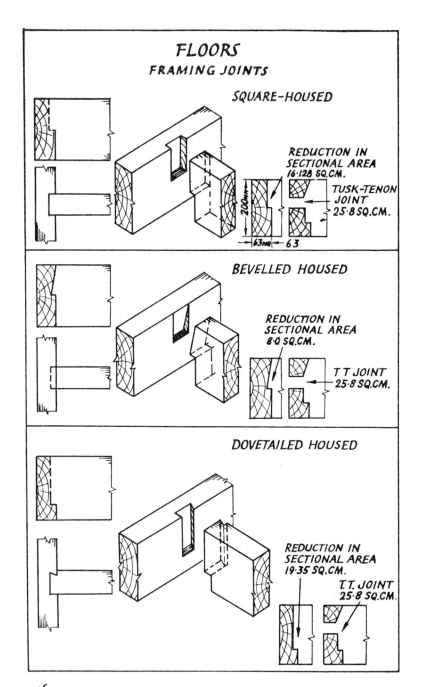

FLOORS
FRAMING JOINTS

SQUARE-HOUSED

REDUCTION IN
SECTIONAL AREA
16·128 SQ.CM.

TUSK-TENON
JOINT
25·8 SQ.CM.

200mm

63mm   63

BEVELLED HOUSED

REDUCTION IN
SECTIONAL AREA
8·0 SQ.CM.

T T JOINT
25·8 SQ.CM.

DOVETAILED HOUSED

REDUCTION IN
SECTIONAL AREA
19·35 SQ.CM.

T.T. JOINT
25·8 SQ.CM.

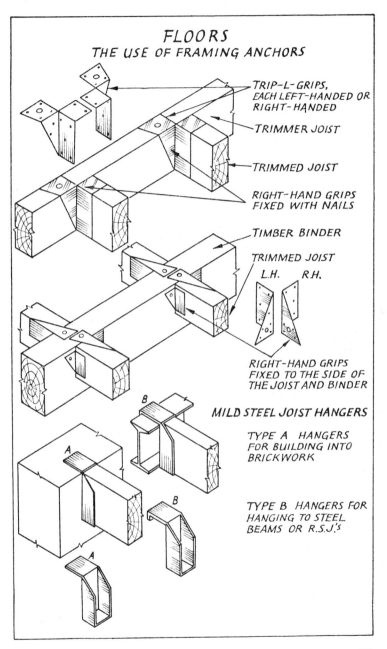

FLOORS
THE USE OF FRAMING ANCHORS

TRIP-L-GRIPS, EACH LEFT-HANDED OR RIGHT-HANDED

TRIMMER JOIST

TRIMMED JOIST

RIGHT-HAND GRIPS FIXED WITH NAILS

TIMBER BINDER

TRIMMED JOIST

L.H.   R.H.

RIGHT-HAND GRIPS FIXED TO THE SIDE OF THE JOIST AND BINDER

MILD STEEL JOIST HANGERS

TYPE A HANGERS FOR BUILDING INTO BRICKWORK

TYPE B HANGERS FOR HANGING TO STEEL BEAMS OR R.S.J.'s

B

A

B

A

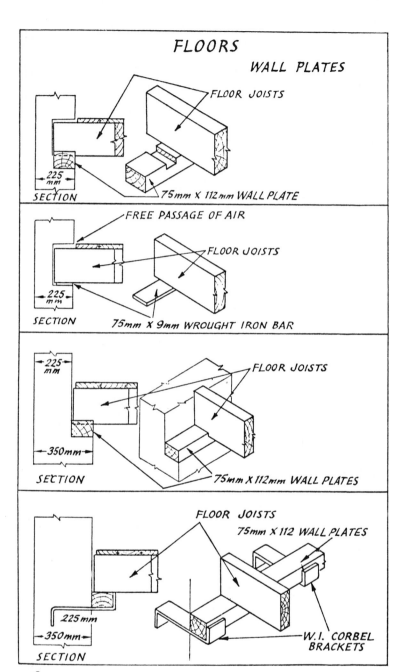

FLOORS

WALL PLATES

FLOOR JOISTS

225 mm

SECTION

75mm X 112mm WALL PLATE

FREE PASSAGE OF AIR

FLOOR JOISTS

225 mm

SECTION

75mm X 9mm WROUGHT IRON BAR

225 mm

FLOOR JOISTS

350mm

SECTION

75mm X 112mm WALL PLATES

FLOOR JOISTS

75mm X 112 WALL PLATES

225 mm

350mm

SECTION

W.I. CORBEL BRACKETS

FLOORS
FLOOR COVERINGS

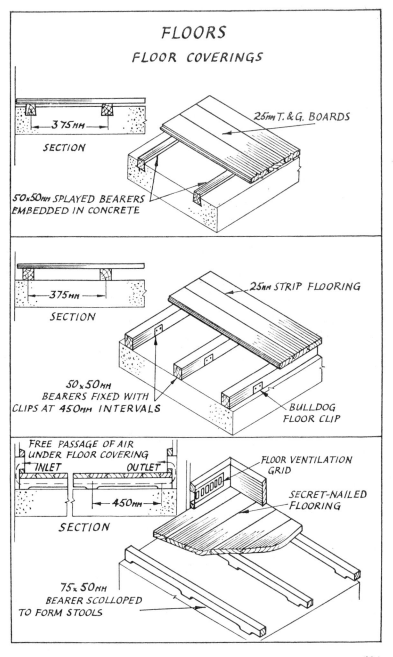

SECTION

375mm

25mm T. & G. BOARDS

50x50mm SPLAYED BEARERS EMBEDDED IN CONCRETE

SECTION

375mm

25mm STRIP FLOORING

50x50mm BEARERS FIXED WITH CLIPS AT 450mm INTERVALS

BULLDOG FLOOR CLIP

FREE PASSAGE OF AIR UNDER FLOOR COVERING

INLET   OUTLET

450mm

SECTION

FLOOR VENTILATION GRID

SECRET-NAILED FLOORING

75x50mm BEARER SCOLLOPED TO FORM STOOLS

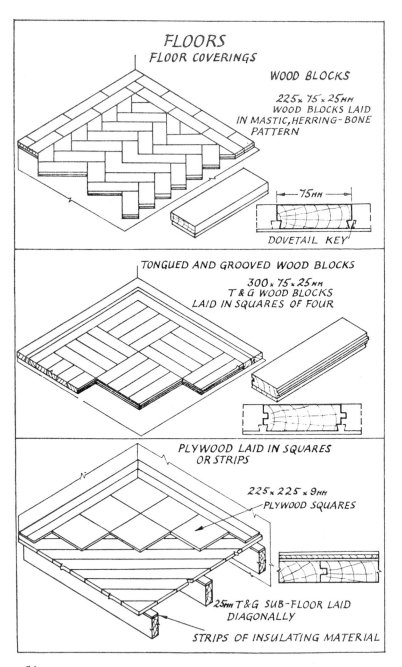

FLOORS
FLOOR COVERINGS

WOOD BLOCKS

225 x 75 x 25mm
WOOD BLOCKS LAID
IN MASTIC, HERRING-BONE
PATTERN

75mm

DOVETAIL KEY

TONGUED AND GROOVED WOOD BLOCKS

300 x 75 x 25mm
T & G WOOD BLOCKS
LAID IN SQUARES OF FOUR

PLYWOOD LAID IN SQUARES OR STRIPS

225 x 225 x 9mm
PLYWOOD SQUARES

25mm T & G SUB-FLOOR LAID
DIAGONALLY

STRIPS OF INSULATING MATERIAL

FLOORS
FLOOR COVERINGS

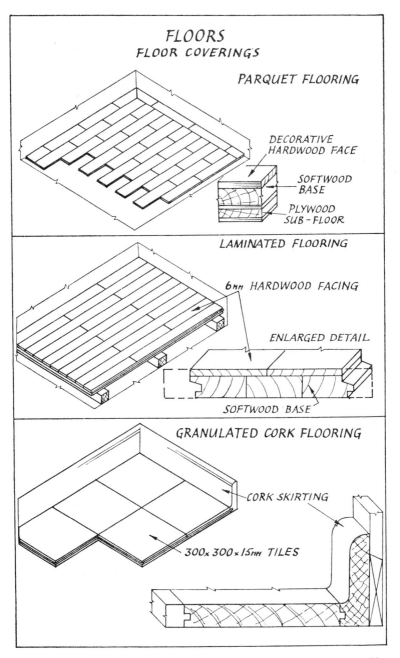

PARQUET FLOORING

DECORATIVE HARDWOOD FACE

SOFTWOOD BASE

PLYWOOD SUB-FLOOR

LAMINATED FLOORING

6mm HARDWOOD FACING

ENLARGED DETAIL

SOFTWOOD BASE

GRANULATED CORK FLOORING

CORK SKIRTING

300 x 300 x 15mm TILES

5 | Roof carpentry

Traditional designs for trussed-roof construction

The traditional methods of truss, or framed, construction are rarely applied to modern buildings, but the principles behind them are sound and should be known.

Both softwoods and hardwoods are used in the construction of the trusses: oak, pitch pine, and Columbian pine for the large spanned roofs, and European redwood for the smaller spans. All the timbers are wrot (planed), and the wrought iron fastenings have a decorative finish.

In the larger permanent buildings of a traditional type each member of a system of framing is jointed, usually with a mortise-and-tenon joint. The joints of the tension members are secured by metal fastenings. Two large-span, framed roofs of this type are illustrated on page 64.

An *open collar-beam roof*, once a common form of construction for small public halls, is shown at the top of the page. Constructional details for a typical decorative roof of this type are given on page 65. The first drawing shows the scale details of the truss, and gives the size and position of each member. The enlarged details show the method of jointing. Notice the form of the joint between the principal rafter and the collar beam, and also the grooving of the curved ribs into the main framing.

A *queen post truss* construction is illustrated on page 64 (middle). Trusses of this type were the main form of construction for large public halls with a roof span of 9 to 13·5 m, where a level ceiling was required.

In factory and storage buildings with large roof spans a cheaper form of construction is used in which the truss members are nailed together.

The *Belfast truss*, shown at the bottom of page 64, is suitable for the roofing of these buildings since it is cheap, and needs less timber than the framed truss. It has a simple, 'sandwich' construction.

Constructional details for this roof are shown on page 66. The truss consists of a string built up from two 25 × 150 mm members, a circular bow of two 25 × 100 mm members, and 25 × 75 mm struts sandwiched in between bow and beam. When the trusses are set at intervals of 3·75 m along the length of the building, the purlins are spaced at 600 to 750 mm apart, and held in position by the struts.

The method of setting out a Belfast truss is given at the top of page 66. The prepared members for the truss are assembled on a heavy trestle platform constructed with baulk timber. The bow curve is set out by means of ordinates (lines at right angles to the spring line) working from the spring line. On this curve the positions of the purlins are marked. The members forming the first layer of the truss are temporarily, but firmly, fixed to the platform. Next the two layers of struts are added, and finally the second bow and string are put on. Enlarged details of the truss and covering are also shown, at the foot of page 66.

Contemporary designs for trussed-roof construction

Modern timber-trussed roofs may be constructed from small-section members fastened together with nails or timber connectors, or they may have a laminated or partly laminated construction. Four contemporary roof-truss designs are illustrated on page 67.

A *built-up* truss made of small-section timber is shown at the top of page 67. Constructional details for this roof are given on page 68. The size of each member and the method of jointing and supporting the truss is shown in the enlarged details at the foot of page 68. Notice that the ties (tension members) and the struts (compression members) are identical in section.

The truss has a sandwich form of construction, and the solid timber members are fastened at the intersections with nails, bolts, or timber connectors. In the early examples of this work rough timbers were used, and all the joints were nailed together. In present-day construction, however, it is usual to use wrot timber and to glue in the packings and stiffeners.

In the roof illustrated the maximum span is 7·5 m, but spans of up to 15 m can be obtained by the introduction of more struts and ties into the truss.

A modern *bow-string truss* is shown in the second drawing on page 67. It is a development of the traditional Belfast truss, and is most suitable for large-span buildings. The curved bow and tie have a glued, laminated construction, but solid timber is used for the struts. The whole structure is fastened together with bolts and connectors.

The *laminated arched rib* illustrated in the third drawing on page 67 has a rectangular section built up of laminates 16 to 25 mm in thickness, glued together under pressure. Because of the size and nature of the work, cold, slow-setting adhesives are necessary; waterproof synthetic resin adhesives are commonly used. The importance of good jointing between the laminates cannot be overstressed. The timber must be planed to size, and the cramping pressure must be adequate and equal at all points.

Arched ribs of small span can be made in one piece, but spans of over 9 m need to be jointed at the crown.

This method of construction was first practised in Switzerland in 1913, and was invented by a German called Otto Helzer.

A *portal frame* type of laminated truss, suitable for civic or school buildings, is shown at the foot of page 67. The cantilever ribs have a varying rectangular section and, like the arched rib, are built up of thin laminates. The complete truss is formed by jointing together the two cantilever ribs at the crown.

Another modern kind of roof is shown on page 69. This is the *trussed rafter* construction, and by its use the ridge, purlins, and binders or ceiling beams are eliminated. Each truss is made up of two rafters, a main tie, two struts, and two ties.

A plan and elevation view of a roof of 7·2 m span and 40° pitch is shown on page 69 (top). The enlarged details show how framing anchors are used to secure the main tie to the wall plate, and how saw-tooth, bulldog connectors fasten the struts and ties to the main tie.

Timber fasteners for roofs

The joints of a roof truss, or framed structure, may be fastened with nails, screws, nuts and bolts, or with bolts and connectors. The number, position, and type of fastenings to be used in a structural joint is usually decided by the architect or engineer, since it involves a knowledge of mechanics and the theory of structure.

When two or more structural members are jointed together and subjected to a tensile stress the fasteners (nails, screws, bolts, and connectors) tend to shear off at the joint line between each member. When two members are joined together the fastenings tend to shear off at one section, and are said to be in *single shear*. When three members are jointed together the fastenings tend to shear at two sections, and are said to be in *double shear*. The strength of a fastening in a double shear is approximately twice that of a similar fastening in single shear.

Two *nailed joints* which are subject to a tensile stress are shown on page 70 (top). Note that in the first illustration the members tend to pull apart from each other, and to prevent this it is necessary to clinch the nails in order to anchor them more firmly. In the second drawing, however, there are three members, so that the nails are in double shear. There is therefore less tendency for the members to pull away from one another.

NOTE   The nails and screws should be evenly distributed over the whole area.

Two examples of *screwed joints* are shown at the foot of page 70.

The strength of joints constructed with ordinary *nuts and bolts* is governed by the amount of timber behind each bolt. Details of two joints showing bolts in double and single shear are given on page 71. The enlarged details show the amount of timber behind each bolt.

When timber connectors are used the shear stress is distributed over a wide area of the section, and the function of the nut and bolt is simply to couple the connectors and members together.

Three types of timber connectors are obtainable for jointing structural members together:

bulldog connectors
'Teco' shear plates
'Teco' split ring connectors.

Bulldog connectors are discs with saw-tooth projections made single or double sided. The discs are inserted between the two members to be jointed together, and are coupled together with a nut and bolt.

Details of bulldog timber connectors are given on page 72, which shows the double-sided connector for wood-to-wood joints, the single-sided connector for wood-to-metal joints, and a sectional view of each joint.

Details of a joint made between a strut and a tie by means of a connector are given on page 73 (top). An enlarged view of a saw-tooth connector, and drawings of the main joints of (A) and (B) of the built-up truss illustrated on page 68, are also given.

Teco shear plates consist of one or two circular flanged discs coupled together with nuts and bolts. Two plates placed back to back are necessary for wood-to-wood joints, but for wood-to-metal joints one plate only is required. Two joints fitted with shear-plate connectors are shown on page 74. A sectional view of these joints gives details of the washers, bolts, and shear plates.

Teco double-bevelled split-ring connectors consist of a single split ring, and a nut and bolt. The split rings are recessed half and half into each timber and the joint is pulled up tight with a nut and bolt. This type of connector is suitable only for wood-to-wood joints. Such a joint fitted with a split-ring connector is shown on page 75 (top).

Many of the operations involved in the insertion of shear-plate and split-ring connectors are now done by machine, but this work can be successfully done by hand with a borer attachment fitted to a drill. Details of a borer attachment and the insertion of the rings are given at the foot of page 75.

If framing anchors are used for the fixing of roof timbers, all traditional forms of jointing can be eliminated.

Trip-L-grips used for fixing rafters to wall plates, ceiling joists to ceiling beams, and purlins to trusses are illustrated on page 76.

This type of framing anchor can also be used to advantage on stud framing and timber-framed buildings, as is illustrated on page 77.

Lead gutters

It is necessary that water should be carried away from several points on the roof, and for this gutters must be installed. They are needed behind chimney stacks, in the angle between roofs (valleys), and behind parapet walls. Examples of the three types of gutters are given on page 78 (top).

The preparation necessary for the plumber's work is done by the carpenter. This includes the preparation and fixing of the gutter bearers and the cutting to shape and fixing of the gutter boards, on which the sheet lead is laid and dressed into position.

Gutters behind chimney stacks

Roofing timber rafters which are interrupted by the chimney stack must be supported, and therefore require trimming round the stack. This is illustrated on page 78. Main trimming rafters run from the ridge to the wall plate on either side of the stack. Cross-trimmers are inserted behind the stack at a high level, and in front of it at a low level.

Enlarged details of the gutter formed over the trimming are given in the middle of page 78. Notice that the cross-trimmers are placed 25 mm away from the brick stack; that the 75 × 150 mm tapered block makes the 150 mm wide gutter level; and that there is a tilting fillet over which the lead sheet is dressed and extended up the roof to give a gutter depth of 150 mm. This depth is necessary to prevent water from flushing over the gutter edges, and thus finding its way into the roofwork below.

Valley gutters

Details of an open and a secret valley gutter, which run in the angle between roofs, are given on page 78 (foot). The gutter boards, which are 25 mm thick, must provide a clean, flat surface for the lead which the plumber will use to form the gutter. All exposed corners should be slightly rounded so that there are no sharp angles on which the lead sheet might crack during or after fixing.

Parapet gutters

There are two types of parapet gutters—tapered and parallel.

A typical two-way, twice-stepped *tapered gutter* is illustrated on page 79, and it can be seen to narrow considerably towards the outlet—hence its name. The gutter is formed of 25 mm boards laid with a fall of not less than 25 mm in 3 m. It is supported on 50 × 40 mm bearers fastened to the side of each rafter.

The gutter has a roll at its highest point, then a fall to a 50 mm drip, and a further fall to a cesspool at its lowest level. Rolls and drips are necessary, since the lead strips cannot be butt-jointed together. Sheet lead 2·1 or 2·4 m in width and weighing 24 kg per square metre is most suitable for gutters, and since the roll and drip are placed at the join, their position will be determined by the length of the strips.

Enlarged details of the rolls and drips are given on page 79 (middle and foot). Notice the shape of the roll and the size of the capillary groove in the 50 mm drip.

NOTE   All parapet gutters must be over 275 mm wide at their narrowest point.

The advantage of using the *parallel gutter* is that it eliminates difficulties at the eaves when slating or tiling. A typical parallel gutter is illustrated on page 80. The gutter falls both ways from the roll situated at the highest point, and discharges into a cesspool at the lowest level. The pole plate is the main member of the gutter. It supports the gutter timbers, and also acts as a wall plate over which the common rafters are bird's-mouthed.

Details of the cesspool are given on page 80 (foot). The box is of 50 mm boards tongued or dovetailed together, and prepared to receive the outlet pipe and lead lining as shown in the vertical section.

Practice lessons

1 Working from the information given:

    (a) Make neat diagrams of a built-up truss. Span 6·6 m. Pitch 30°.

    (b) Give isometric details of the sandwich form of construction.

2 *(a)* Make a sectional and a plan view of trussed rafter construction.

    (b) Draw enlarged details of the joints and connectors used.

3 *(a)* Make neat sketches of the various timber fasteners that are used in roof construction.

    (b) Give examples of fixing with nails, screws, and bolts.

    (c) Explain the terms *single shear* and *double shear*.

4 *(a)* Draw, to any convenient scale, a section through a tapered gutter. Show all construction clearly.

    (b) Draw sectional views of—
      (i) A 50 mm roll
      (ii) A 50 mm drip.

ROOFS

TRUSSED ROOFS

TRADITIONAL DESIGNS

COLLAR-BEAM TRUSS

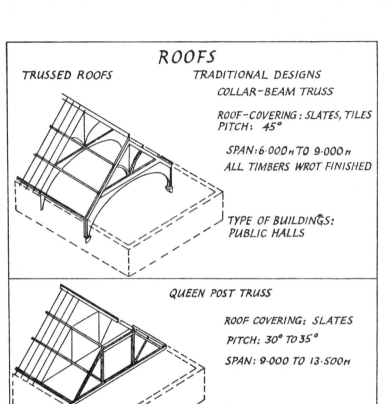

ROOF-COVERING : SLATES, TILES
PITCH: 45°

SPAN: 6.000ᴍ TO 9.000ᴍ
ALL TIMBERS WROT FINISHED

TYPE OF BUILDINGS:
PUBLIC HALLS

QUEEN POST TRUSS

ROOF COVERING: SLATES

PITCH: 30° TO 35°

SPAN: 9.000 TO 13.500ᴍ

TYPE OF BUILDINGS:

FACTORY
PUBLIC BUILDING

BELFAST TRUSS

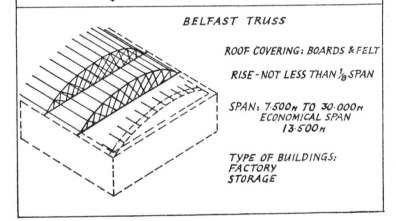

ROOF COVERING: BOARDS & FELT

RISE - NOT LESS THAN ⅛ SPAN

SPAN: 7.500ᴍ TO 30.000ᴍ
ECONOMICAL SPAN
13.500ᴍ

TYPE OF BUILDINGS:
FACTORY
STORAGE

ROOFS

COLLAR - BEAM TRUSS

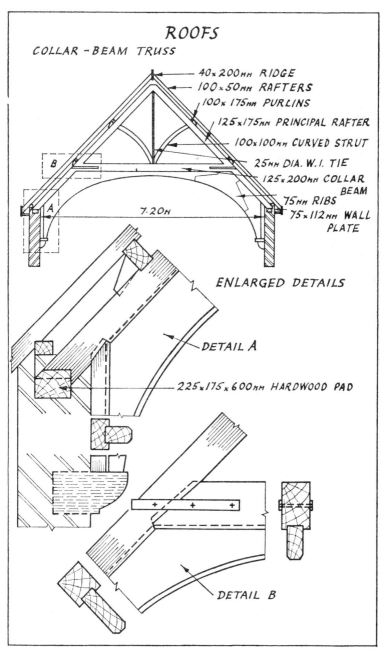

40 × 200 mm RIDGE
100 × 50 mm RAFTERS
100 × 175 mm PURLINS
125 × 175 mm PRINCIPAL RAFTER
100 × 100 mm CURVED STRUT
25 mm DIA. W.I. TIE
125 × 200 mm COLLAR BEAM
75 mm RIBS
75 × 112 mm WALL PLATE

7·20 M

B

A

ENLARGED DETAILS

DETAIL A

225 × 175 × 600 mm HARDWOOD PAD

DETAIL B

ROOFS

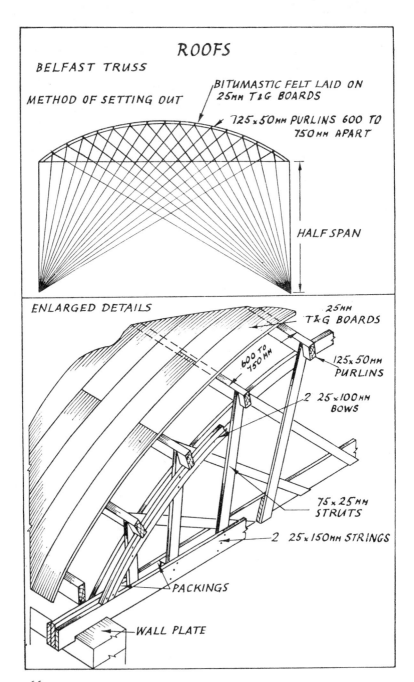

BELFAST TRUSS

METHOD OF SETTING OUT

BITUMASTIC FELT LAID ON
25MM T&G BOARDS

125×50MM PURLINS 600 TO
750MM APART

HALF SPAN

ENLARGED DETAILS

25MM
T&G BOARDS

600 TO
750 MM

125×50MM
PURLINS

2 25×100MM
BOWS

75×25MM
STRUTS

2 25×150MM STRINGS

PACKINGS

WALL PLATE

ROOFS

TRUSSED ROOFS

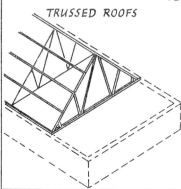

CONTEMPORARY DESIGNS

BUILT-UP TRUSS

ROOF COVERING - ASBESTOS OR
                  METAL SHEETS

PITCH - 30° TO 40°

SPAN - 6·000M TO 7·500M

TIMBERS USUALLY WROT FINISHED

TYPE OF BUILDINGS:
INDUSTRIAL BUILDINGS
STORAGE

LAMINATED BOW STRING TRUSS

ROOF COVERING - INSULATING BOARDS,
               FELT, METAL SHEETS

RISE - NOT LESS THAN $\frac{1}{8}$ SPAN

SPAN - 15·000M TO 30·000 M.

TIMBER WROT FINISHED

TYPE OF BUILDINGS:
           FACTORY, STORAGE

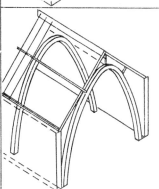

LAMINATED ARCH RIB

SPAN - 6·000M TO 18·000M

ARCHED RIB BUILT UP IN THIN
LAMINATIONS GLUED TOGETHER
UNDER PRESSURE

TYPE OF BUILDINGS:
      PUBLIC HALLS
      SCHOOLS

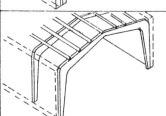

LAMINATED CANTILEVER RIB

SPAN - 6·000M TO 15·000M

TYPE OF BUILDINGS:
      CIVIC BUILDINGS
      SCHOOLS

ROOFS

BUILT-UP TRUSS

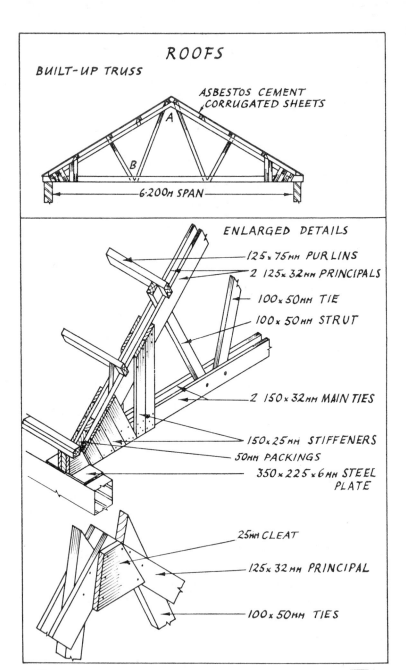

ASBESTOS CEMENT
CORRUGATED SHEETS

A

B

6·200M SPAN

ENLARGED DETAILS

125 x 75MM PURLINS

2 125 x 32MM PRINCIPALS

100 x 50MM TIE

100 x 50MM STRUT

2 150 x 32MM MAIN TIES

150 x 25MM STIFFENERS

50MM PACKINGS

350 x 225 x 6MM STEEL
PLATE

25MM CLEAT

125 x 32 MM PRINCIPAL

100 x 50MM TIES

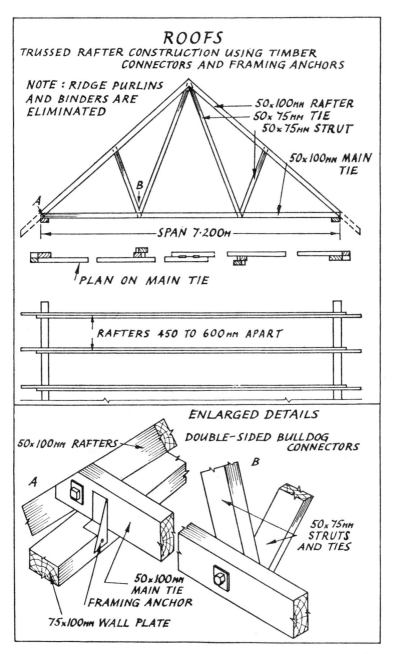

ROOFS
TRUSSED RAFTER CONSTRUCTION USING TIMBER CONNECTORS AND FRAMING ANCHORS

NOTE : RIDGE PURLINS AND BINDERS ARE ELIMINATED

50×100mm RAFTER
50×75mm TIE
50×75mm STRUT

50×100mm MAIN TIE

A

B

SPAN 7·200M

PLAN ON MAIN TIE

RAFTERS 450 TO 600mm APART

ENLARGED DETAILS

DOUBLE-SIDED BULLDOG CONNECTORS

50×100mm RAFTERS

A

B

50×75mm STRUTS AND TIES

50×100mm MAIN TIE
FRAMING ANCHOR

75×100mm WALL PLATE

ROOFS

BUILT-UP TRUSSES

NAILED JOINTS

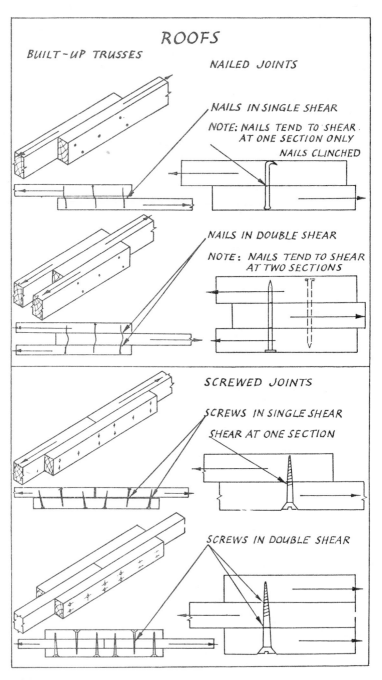

NAILS IN SINGLE SHEAR

NOTE: NAILS TEND TO SHEAR AT ONE SECTION ONLY

NAILS CLINCHED

NAILS IN DOUBLE SHEAR

NOTE: NAILS TEND TO SHEAR AT TWO SECTIONS

SCREWED JOINTS

SCREWS IN SINGLE SHEAR

SHEAR AT ONE SECTION

SCREWS IN DOUBLE SHEAR

ROOFS

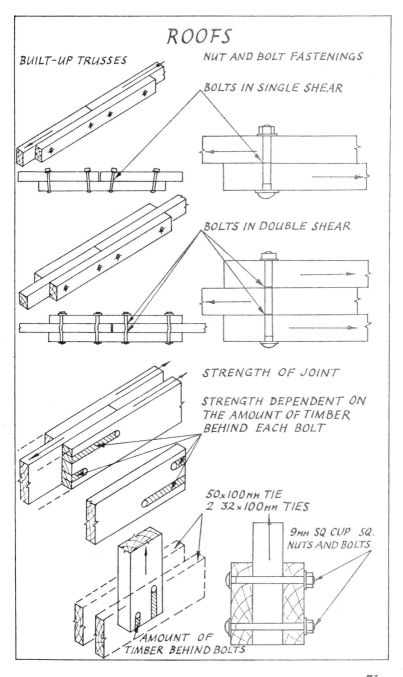

BUILT-UP TRUSSES

NUT AND BOLT FASTENINGS

BOLTS IN SINGLE SHEAR

BOLTS IN DOUBLE SHEAR

STRENGTH OF JOINT

STRENGTH DEPENDENT ON
THE AMOUNT OF TIMBER
BEHIND EACH BOLT

50×100 MM TIE
2 32×100 MM TIES

9 MM SQ CUP SQ.
NUTS AND BOLTS

AMOUNT OF
TIMBER BEHIND BOLTS

ROOFS
BUILT-UP TRUSSES
BULLDOG TIMBER CONNECTORS

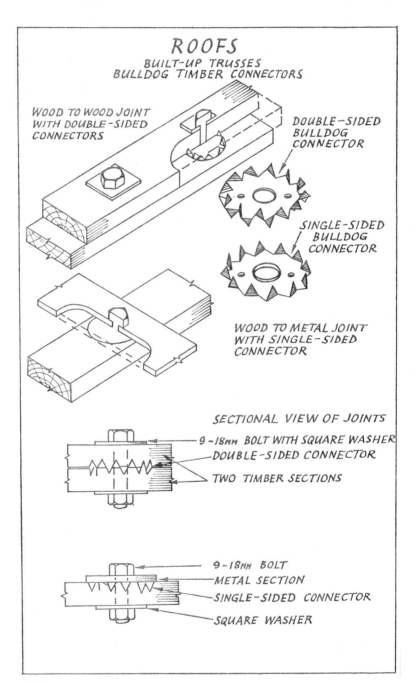

WOOD TO WOOD JOINT
WITH DOUBLE-SIDED
CONNECTORS

DOUBLE-SIDED
BULLDOG
CONNECTOR

SINGLE-SIDED
BULLDOG
CONNECTOR

WOOD TO METAL JOINT
WITH SINGLE-SIDED
CONNECTOR

SECTIONAL VIEW OF JOINTS

9-18MM BOLT WITH SQUARE WASHER
DOUBLE-SIDED CONNECTOR

TWO TIMBER SECTIONS

9-18MM BOLT
METAL SECTION
SINGLE-SIDED CONNECTOR
SQUARE WASHER

ROOFS

THE USE OF FRAMING ANCHORS

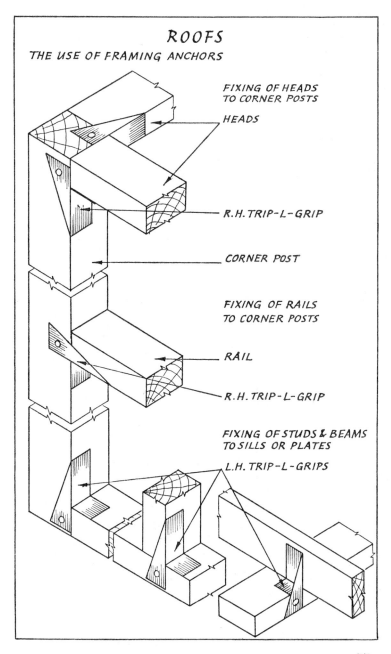

FIXING OF HEADS
TO CORNER POSTS

HEADS

R.H. TRIP-L-GRIP

CORNER POST

FIXING OF RAILS
TO CORNER POSTS

RAIL

R.H. TRIP-L-GRIP

FIXING OF STUDS & BEAMS
TO SILLS OR PLATES

L.H. TRIP-L-GRIPS

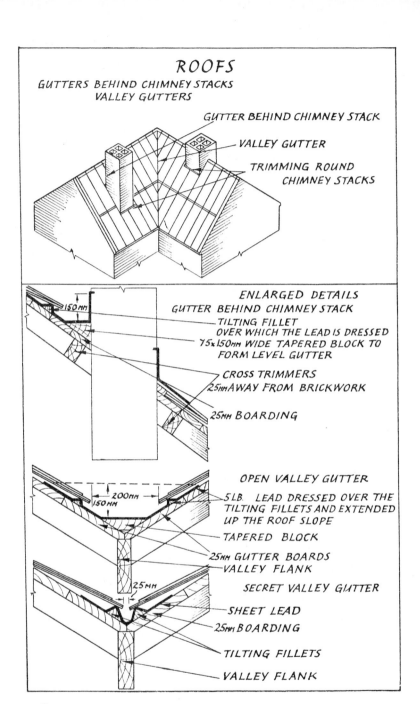

ROOFS

GUTTERS BEHIND CHIMNEY STACKS
VALLEY GUTTERS

GUTTER BEHIND CHIMNEY STACK

VALLEY GUTTER

TRIMMING ROUND
CHIMNEY STACKS

ENLARGED DETAILS
GUTTER BEHIND CHIMNEY STACK

150MM

TILTING FILLET
OVER WHICH THE LEAD IS DRESSED
75 x 150MM WIDE TAPERED BLOCK TO
FORM LEVEL GUTTER

CROSS TRIMMERS
25MM AWAY FROM BRICKWORK

25MM BOARDING

OPEN VALLEY GUTTER

200MM
150MM

5 LB. LEAD DRESSED OVER THE
TILTING FILLETS AND EXTENDED
UP THE ROOF SLOPE

TAPERED BLOCK

25MM GUTTER BOARDS
VALLEY FLANK

25MM

SECRET VALLEY GUTTER

SHEET LEAD

25MM BOARDING

TILTING FILLETS

VALLEY FLANK

78

ROOFS
TAPERED GUTTER

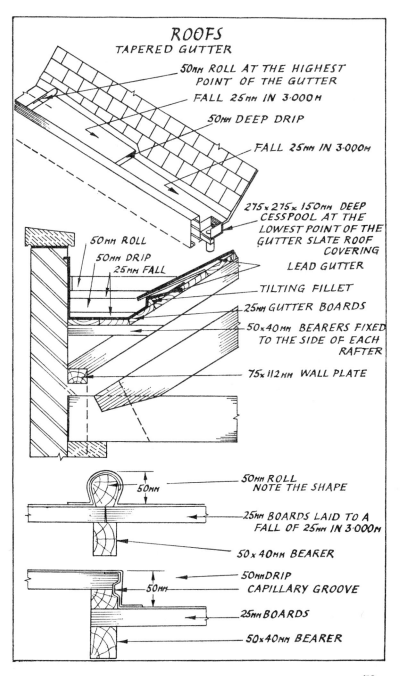

50mm ROLL AT THE HIGHEST POINT OF THE GUTTER

FALL 25mm IN 3·000m

50mm DEEP DRIP

FALL 25mm IN 3·000m

275 x 275 x 150mm DEEP CESSPOOL AT THE LOWEST POINT OF THE GUTTER SLATE ROOF COVERING

LEAD GUTTER

50mm ROLL

50mm DRIP

25mm FALL

TILTING FILLET

25mm GUTTER BOARDS

50 x 40mm BEARERS FIXED TO THE SIDE OF EACH RAFTER

75 x 112mm WALL PLATE

50mm ROLL
NOTE THE SHAPE

50mm

25mm BOARDS LAID TO A FALL OF 25mm IN 3·000m

50 x 40mm BEARER

50mm DRIP
CAPILLARY GROOVE

50mm

25mm BOARDS

50 x 40mm BEARER

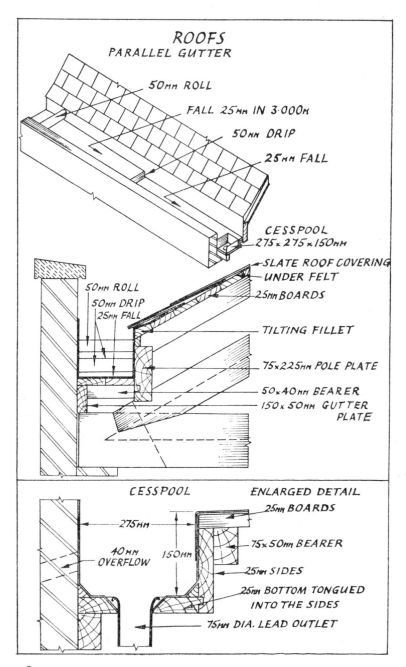

ROOFS
PARALLEL GUTTER

50mm ROLL

FALL 25mm IN 3·000m

50mm DRIP

25mm FALL

CESSPOOL
275 × 275 × 150mm

SLATE ROOF COVERING
UNDER FELT
25mm BOARDS

50mm ROLL
50mm DRIP
25mm FALL

TILTING FILLET

75 × 225mm POLE PLATE

50 × 40mm BEARER

150 × 50mm GUTTER
PLATE

CESSPOOL   ENLARGED DETAIL

25mm BOARDS

275mm

40mm
OVERFLOW

150mm

75 × 50mm BEARER

25mm SIDES

25mm BOTTOM TONGUED
INTO THE SIDES

75mm DIA. LEAD OUTLET

There are four types of windows commonly used for roof lighting. Dormer roof lights and skylights are the usual types used for pitched roofs, lantern lights for flat roofs, and patent glazing systems for glazed-roof areas of factory buildings. These are illustrated on page 84.

Types of roof light

Dormer roof lights are usually of the casement type, and open either outwards or inwards. The cheeks of the dormer are boarded, and may be covered with slates, tiles, lead, copper, or aluminium. The roof can be flat and covered with lead, copper, or asphalt; or alternatively it may be pitched and covered with slates or tiles.

A typical dormer roof light is illustrated on page 85. A plan, elevation, and section view are given at the top of the page, showing the roof trimming and the method of forming the dormer cheeks and the flat roof. Details of the window, showing vertical and horizontal sections of the frame with casements and finishings, are illustrated on page 85 (foot).

Skylights have the opening light fitted over the frame or curb, and not fitted into rebates as is done with ordinary casement windows. This is in order to make the skylight watertight. The curb projects above the roof by at least 150 mm. It has a lead gutter at the back, and lead flashings to the front and sides. The opening light and curb, trimming and gutter, are shown on page 86. Details of construction are illustrated on page 87. The first drawing shows the method of jointing the opening light. Notice the condensation exits, and the jointing of the bar to the bottom rail.

The tongued-and-grooved curb, and an alternative method of construction for the curb, are also shown.

Roof glazing

Putty glazing, wood-bar glazing, and lead-bar or patent glazing are the main methods used for setting glass into large areas of roof. The glazing bars used are of the following standard sections: 40 × 75 mm; 50 × 75 mm; 50 × 100 mm; 50 × 125 mm.

width of bar	maximum length
75 mm	1·8 m
100 mm	2·4 m
125 mm	3 m

Putty glazing, shown on page 88 (top), is used extensively on horticultural buildings. The rebates to receive the glass are 22 × 12 mm. It is important to bed the glass on to the putty (see page 88—top). The bars are spaced 300 to a maximum of 600 mm apart.

Wood glazing consists of a 50 mm wide glazing bar and a cap. The bar is rebated to receive the glass, and has a groove on each side to carry away any condensation. The cap has two asbestos cords inserted into it in order to form a weatherproof joint between it and the glass. It is advisable to use a durable timber for the caps, and teak is especially suitable. Details of the bar and cap are given on page 88 (middle).

Patent glazing has become highly developed, and patent glazing bars made in wood, metal, or reinforced concrete are available.

Details of a typical lead-covered wood glazing bar are given on page 88 (foot). The bar is rebated for the glass and shaped to form condensation grooves. The bar and cap are closely covered with sheet lead. The cap fits over the bar on to the glass, and is fixed by screws inserted through the face into the bar.

Practice lessons

1   Working from the information given:

  (a) Draw 1:20 scale details of a dormer window. Show clearly a plan, elevation, and section view.
  (b) Prepare 1:4 scale section details.

2   Draw (full size) the sectional view of three types, and sizes, of glazing bar.

  (a) Putty glazed 1·8 m long.
  (b) Wood bar and cap 2·4 m long.
  (c) Lead-covered bar 3 m long.

3   Working from the details given on page 86:

  (a) Set out a workshop rod for the skylight and curb.
  (b) From the prepared material supplied, carry out all the operations involved in making the light, and curb, up to the assembly stage.
  (c) Wedge up and clean off the skylight, and assemble the curb.
  (d) Fit and hang the skylight to the curb.

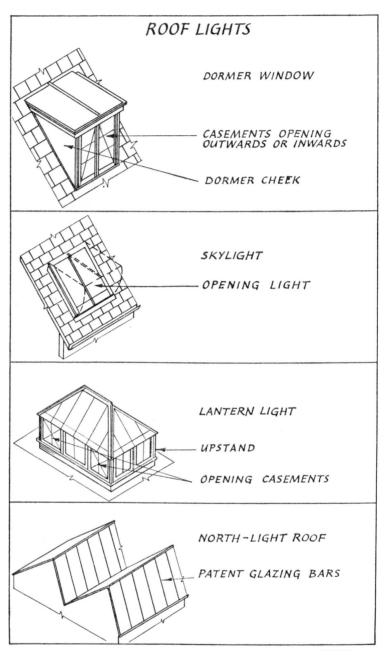

ROOF LIGHTS

DORMER WINDOW

CASEMENTS OPENING
OUTWARDS OR INWARDS

DORMER CHEEK

SKYLIGHT

OPENING LIGHT

LANTERN LIGHT

UPSTAND

OPENING CASEMENTS

NORTH-LIGHT ROOF

PATENT GLAZING BARS

ROOF LIGHTS

DORMER WINDOW

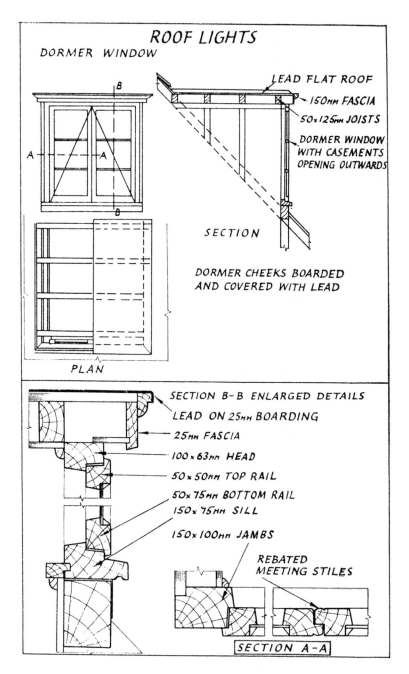

B

A —— A

B

PLAN

LEAD FLAT ROOF

150mm FASCIA

50 x 125mm JOISTS

DORMER WINDOW
WITH CASEMENTS
OPENING OUTWARDS

SECTION

DORMER CHEEKS BOARDED
AND COVERED WITH LEAD

SECTION B-B ENLARGED DETAILS

LEAD ON 25mm BOARDING

25mm FASCIA

100 x 63mm HEAD

50 x 50mm TOP RAIL

50 x 75mm BOTTOM RAIL

150 x 75mm SILL

150 x 100mm JAMBS

REBATED
MEETING STILES

SECTION A-A

ROOF LIGHTS

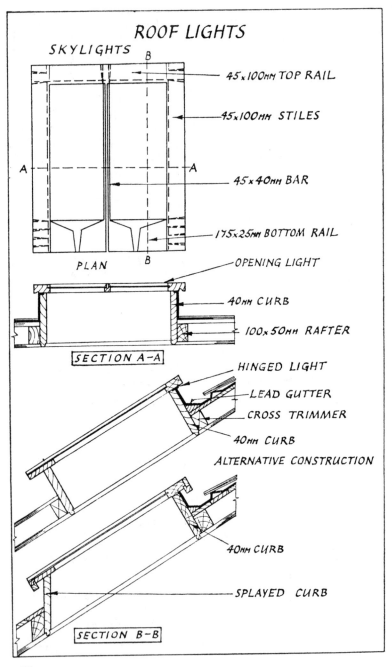

SKYLIGHTS

B

45 x 100mm TOP RAIL

45 x 100mm STILES

A — A

45 x 40mm BAR

175 x 25mm BOTTOM RAIL

PLAN   B

OPENING LIGHT

40mm CURB

100 x 50mm RAFTER

SECTION A-A

HINGED LIGHT

LEAD GUTTER

CROSS TRIMMER

40mm CURB

ALTERNATIVE CONSTRUCTION

40mm CURB

SPLAYED CURB

SECTION B-B

ROOF LIGHTS

SKYLIGHTS CONSTRUCTIONAL DETAILS

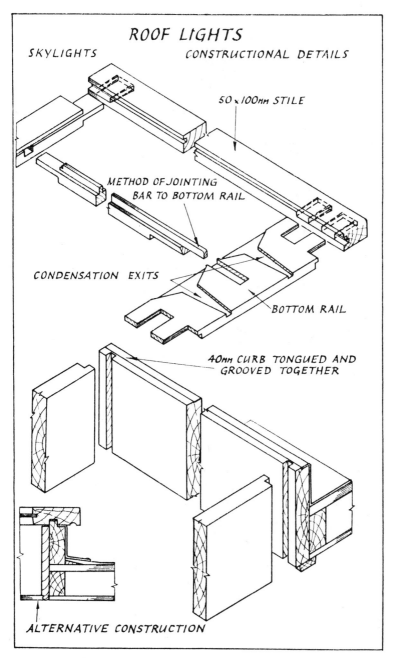

50 x 100mm STILE

METHOD OF JOINTING
BAR TO BOTTOM RAIL

CONDENSATION EXITS

BOTTOM RAIL

40mm CURB TONGUED AND
GROOVED TOGETHER

ALTERNATIVE CONSTRUCTION

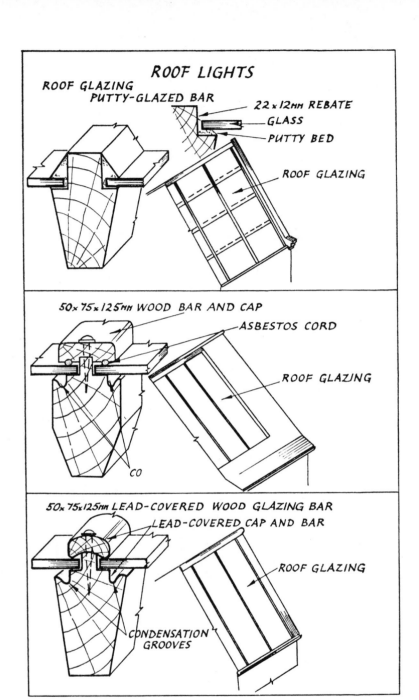

ROOF LIGHTS

ROOF GLAZING
PUTTY-GLAZED BAR

22 x 12mm REBATE
GLASS
PUTTY BED

ROOF GLAZING

50 x 75 x 125mm WOOD BAR AND CAP

ASBESTOS CORD

ROOF GLAZING

CO

50 x 75 x 125mm LEAD-COVERED WOOD GLAZING BAR
LEAD-COVERED CAP AND BAR

ROOF GLAZING

CONDENSATION
GROOVES

Frames with shaped heads

Door frames with shaped heads are classified according to the shape of the head. The most common shapes are segmental-headed, semicircular-headed, and semicircular-headed with transom.

A *segmental-headed door frame* seen in plan and elevation is illustrated on page 93 (top). The head may be cut out in the solid or built up of two or more laminates, as is shown. An enlarged detail of the joint is also given.

Semicircular-headed frames may be made in three ways: using handrail bolts and cross-tongues; using hammer-headed keys; or using tenons and tongues—a method most suitable for mechanised production. These are shown on page 93 (middle).

The *semicircular-headed frame and transom* is illustrated at the foot of the page. The transom must be placed at least 25 mm below the spring line. The enlarged details show a 75 × 100 mm built-up head, and a 75 × 140 mm projecting transom.

The joint between the transom and the jamb is close to the joint in the spring line so that it is necessary, in order to avoid short grain, to have twin tenons in one of the joints. The illustration shows the transom twin-tenoned into the jamb with a single tenon into the semicircular head.

Vestibule frames for double swing doors

Double swing doors are used extensively in public halls, hospitals, shops, offices, and in the more modern domestic buildings. Frames are made to suit a single door or doors hung in pairs. The doors themselves are usually hung on pivoted floor springs, or helical spring hinges. The method of fitting these hinges is described and illustrated in the chapter on ironmongery. The jambs of the door frames are hollowed to receive the rounded edges of the hanging stiles.

The two types of frames are illustrated on page 94. The first drawing shows the plan and elevation of a frame for a *single door* which is hung to swing both ways.

The enlarged details show the method of finding the amount of hollow in the jamb. The centre of the pivot is the centre for the round on the door. The centre for the hollow in the jamb is taken from a point 3 mm away from the pivot centre. This gives the clearance in the centre of the hollow which is necessary for the door to swing freely. The frame is twin-tenoned or dovetailed together.

A frame of modern design, into which a *pair of swing doors* are fitted, is shown on page 94 (foot). The plan and elevation show a 75 × 150 mm frame built into a flush-panelled, timber-partitioned wall. The enlarged details give the section views of the frame.

This frame needs to be mortised and tenoned together and mitred on the face because there are no architraves to form a finish to the opening.

Front entrance frames

Entrance doors to public buildings are usually made to fold back and form panelling when they are open.

The plan, elevation, and section of a typical public-entrance door frame are shown at the top of page 95. Notice how the doors fold back into the recess to form panelling.

The enlarged details at the foot of page 95 show the special joints between door and jamb. In the first detail the door is hung on pivots and in the second on butt hinges. The vertical sections B–B and C–C show a 75 × 100 mm solid head, a fanlight glazed with beads, and a built-up transom with a softwood core.

It is usual to mortise and tenon, wedge and pin these frames together. Only the core of the transom is framed into the jamb; the facings are added afterwards.

Methods of fixing door frames

The usual practice is to build in the door frames as the building work proceeds. The jambs are dowelled into the floor or threshold, and the horns on the head of the frame are built into the wall. Intermediate fixing may also be required. In softwood frames the jambs can be fixed in the centre by being nailed to wood pads. In hardwood frames, 3 × 25 or 40 mm galvanised steel or bronze ties can be fixed to the back of the jambs for building into the wall, and in softwood frames spike nails are often used for the same purpose.

The illustrations on page 96 (top) give details of a built-in door frame, showing the dowels, the horns on the head of the frame, and the use of spike nails for building into the wall. A special steel tie is illustrated in the middle of the page.

A method of fixing from the face with screws is also shown on the middle of page 96. Screws 75–100 mm long are used for this purpose. Notice that the screws are sunk below the surface of the jamb, and the holes plugged with wood pellets.

It is usual, however, in all good-class work, to avoid fixing from the face with nails or screws. Various methods of secret fixing have been developed, and one such method is illustrated at the foot of page 96. Notice that the frame is fixed into the floor with dowels, and by the two wood grounds which are placed into the rebates formed in the jambs.

Practice lessons

1 Working from the information given:

    (a) Make neat diagrams to show methods of constructing a segmental headed door frame.

    (b) Show two methods of butt jointing curved members that are in present-day use.

2 *(a)* Draw (1:20) the plan and elevation view of a double swing single door and frame.

    (b) Draw full size details of the door jambs.

    (c) Show, on the drawing, the method of marking out the hollow in the frame.

3 *(a)* Make neat diagrams to show the various methods of building in, and fixing, door frames.

    (b) State briefly the advantages of fixing frames by the use of grounds.

DOOR FRAMES

SEGMENTAL-HEADED FRAME

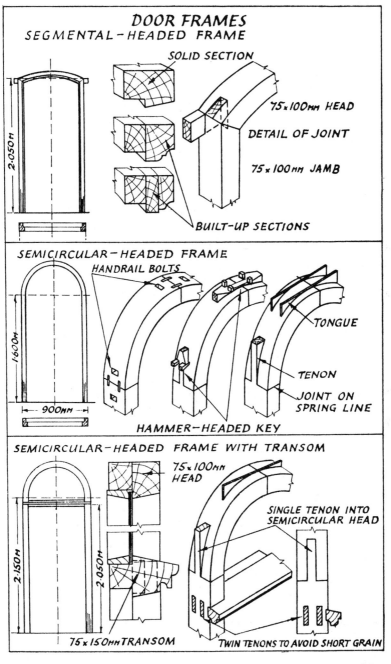

2.050M

SOLID SECTION

75 × 100mm HEAD

DETAIL OF JOINT

75 × 100mm JAMB

BUILT-UP SECTIONS

SEMICIRCULAR-HEADED FRAME

HANDRAIL BOLTS

1.600M

900mm

TONGUE

TENON

JOINT ON SPRING LINE

HAMMER-HEADED KEY

SEMICIRCULAR-HEADED FRAME WITH TRANSOM

2.150M

2.050M

75 × 100mm HEAD

SINGLE TENON INTO SEMICIRCULAR HEAD

75 × 150mm TRANSOM

TWIN TENONS TO AVOID SHORT GRAIN

DOOR FRAMES

VESTIBULE FRAMES
FRAME FOR DOUBLE SWING DOOR

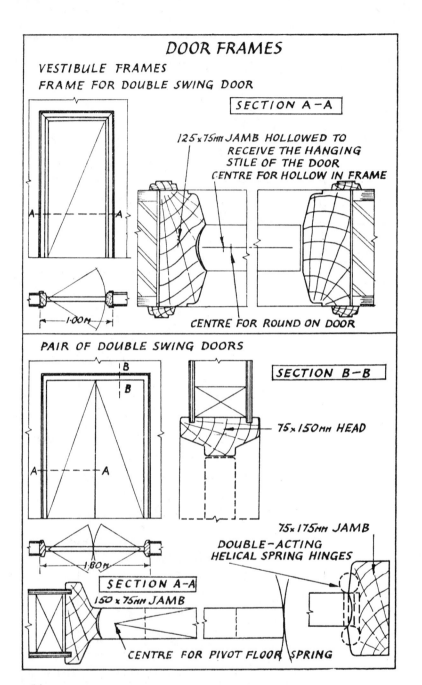

SECTION A–A

125 x 75mm JAMB HOLLOWED TO
RECEIVE THE HANGING
STILE OF THE DOOR
CENTRE FOR HOLLOW IN FRAME

1·00M

CENTRE FOR ROUND ON DOOR

PAIR OF DOUBLE SWING DOORS

SECTION B–B

75 x 150mm HEAD

75 x 175mm JAMB

DOUBLE-ACTING
HELICAL SPRING HINGES

1·80M

SECTION A–A
150 x 75mm JAMB

CENTRE FOR PIVOT FLOOR SPRING

94

DOOR FRAMES

FRONT ENTRANCE FRAMES

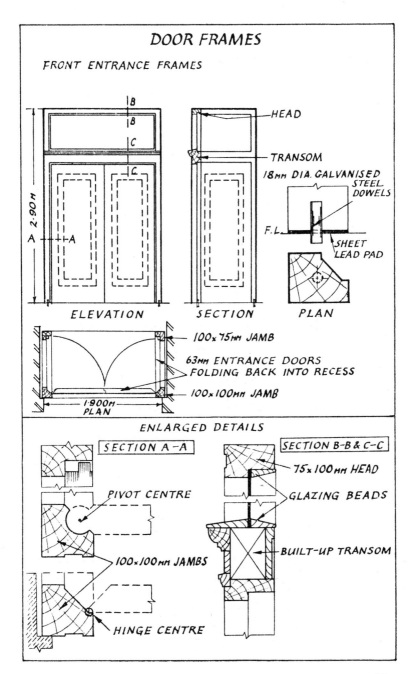

ELEVATION

SECTION

PLAN

HEAD

TRANSOM

18mm DIA. GALVANISED STEEL DOWELS

F.L.

SHEET LEAD PAD

2.90m

A — A

B
B
C
C

100×75mm JAMB

63mm ENTRANCE DOORS FOLDING BACK INTO RECESS

100×100mm JAMB

1·900m
PLAN

ENLARGED DETAILS

SECTION A–A

PIVOT CENTRE

100×100mm JAMBS

HINGE CENTRE

SECTION B–B & C–C

75×100mm HEAD

GLAZING BEADS

BUILT-UP TRANSOM

DOOR FRAMES

METHODS OF FIXING DOOR FRAMES

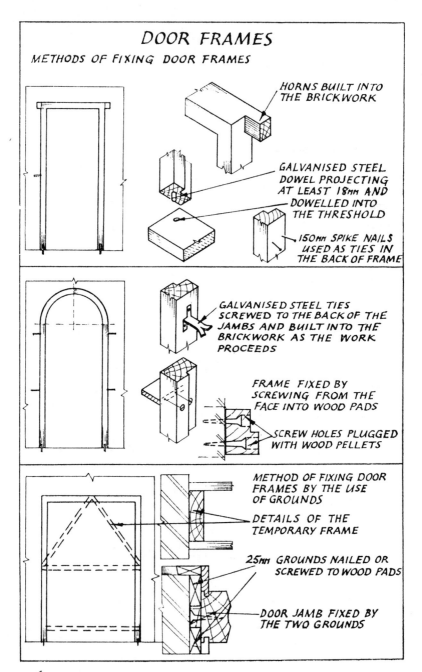

HORNS BUILT INTO THE BRICKWORK

GALVANISED STEEL DOWEL PROJECTING AT LEAST 18mm AND DOWELLED INTO THE THRESHOLD

150mm SPIKE NAILS USED AS TIES IN THE BACK OF FRAME

GALVANISED STEEL TIES SCREWED TO THE BACK OF THE JAMBS AND BUILT INTO THE BRICKWORK AS THE WORK PROCEEDS

FRAME FIXED BY SCREWING FROM THE FACE INTO WOOD PADS

SCREW HOLES PLUGGED WITH WOOD PELLETS

METHOD OF FIXING DOOR FRAMES BY THE USE OF GROUNDS

DETAILS OF THE TEMPORARY FRAME

25mm GROUNDS NAILED OR SCREWED TO WOOD PADS

DOOR JAMB FIXED BY THE TWO GROUNDS

8 | Doors

Entrance doors to public buildings may be hung singly or in pairs. For both traditional and modern designs the framed-and-panelled construction is often used, with the panels made from timber or glass.

Panelled entrance doors

Doors of traditional design commonly have raised panels, with bolection mouldings either in the solid or planted on. For contemporary designs, manufactured boards (plywoods and fibre-boards) are used. Three typical panelled entrance doors are illustrated on page 102.

A *five-panel door*, with single raised panels and bolection mouldings, is shown in the first drawing. The enlarged details show two methods of construction. The first method shows the raised panel grooved into the bolection moulding, which is tongued into the framing. The second example shows the raised panel grooved into the framing, with the bolection moulding planted on and screwed from the back.

The bolection moulding is usually slot mortised and tenoned together, and mitred on the face. This is shown on page 103 (top). Before the introduction of synthetic resin adhesives it was usual to dovetail the moulding together.

When the bolection mouldings are made in the solid the frame must be assembled dry, and both surfaces of the framing must be cleaned off. The bolection moulding is formed round the panel, and the whole is then inserted into the framing as a complete unit.

The *double-margin door* shown on page 102 (middle) is a single door made up from two doors which are made separately and wedged together at the meeting stiles. The finished door therefore resembles a pair of doors. Enlarged details are given showing the folding wedges and cover beads.

The procedure in the assembly of a double-margin door is different from that for an ordinary door (see page 103—middle). The meeting stiles must be first be glued and wedged to the rails, and then they are glued and wedged together. The panels are inserted and the hanging stiles glued and wedged. Finally, vertical-joint beads are fixed and the door is cleaned up on both surfaces. To give the door stability it is necessary to insert a metal bar into its top and bottom edges. Details of the bar and the way it is inserted are given on page 103 (middle).

A pair of entrance doors having one *single-framed panel* in each door are shown on page 103 (foot). The doors consist of an outer frame into which the framed panel is tongued and grooved. The enlarged details show alternative methods of construction. The first example shows a plywood panel and double-moulded framing, and the second, a solid flush panel with single-moulded framing.

The method of jointing framed panelled doors is shown on page 102 (foot). The panel is framed with a 40 mm thick framing, which is mortised and tenoned together and grooved into the outer frame.

Glazed entrance doors

Three typical glazed entrance doors are illustrated on page 104.

A *single door of modern design* is shown at the top of the page, with enlarged details showing single and double glazing. The vertical sections B–B shows the special construction required to prevent the entry of driving rain.

A *contemporary pair of doors* is also shown on page 104 (middle). The enlarged details show a section of the hanging stiles, the meeting stiles, and the weather-proof construction at the threshold.

A *traditional pair of doors*, particularly suitable for shop or office buildings, is illustrated at the foot of page 104. Alternative methods of construction are given in the enlarged details.

The method of jointing the vertical and horizontal bars for glazed entrance doors is shown at the foot of page 105. The horizontal bars are mortised, and the vertical bars tenoned into them.

Wood beads are used, with the glass bedded in with mastic or wash leather.

The heat loss through the glazed area of a door can be reduced considerably by the use of double glazing. A satisfactory way of doing this is shown at the top of page 105. The drawing shows the door glazed with beads from the outside. On the inside, a glazed light is introduced to form the second sheet of glass. It is side-hung to give access for cleaning.

Garage doors

Garage doors are of three main types—doors in pairs hung to open outwards; sliding doors usually made in four leaves; and vertical rising doors. Details of the three types are given on page 106.

A *pair of garage doors* 2·3 m wide, 2·05 m high, and 50 mm thick is shown at the top of the page. The doors are framed together. The upper portion is glazed, and the lower portion sheeted in with match-boarding. It is necessary to brace the garage doors, and the braces should be cut into the rails and clear of the stiles as shown. The enlarged details show sections of the top rails, stiles, bars, and meeting stiles.

Sliding doors are usually made in four leaves and hung on an overhead track. Such a set of doors is shown in the middle of the page. The upper panels are glazed and the lower panels are bead and butt. In the enlarged details section A–A shows the stiles and panels and the method of rebating each leaf together. The section B–B gives details of the track and the method of hanging the doors.

A *vertical rising* garage door made in one leaf is illustrated at the foot of the page. Doors of this type need to have a sound construction and to be braced as shown. The section A–A shows a 63×100 mm stile and 12 mm plywood panel. Section B–B shows a 63×100 mm stile with hardwood glazing bead. The doors may be hung on a track to slide into the roof space or they may have a counter-balanced lifting assembly at each side.

Folding screens

Folding screens are used mainly in schools, places of entertainment, and hotels. They consist of panels or leaves made the full height of the screen and 600 to 900 mm wide. The leaves are hinged together, and hung on to a special track to fold back concertina-wise into a recess.

Screens of traditional design are framed and panelled or glazed, but most contemporary work has a laminated construction.

A typical folding screen is illustrated on page 107. The top drawing gives the plan and elevation, and shows the screen folding back half to the right and half to the left. The enlarged details show a vertical section B–B through the track and casing, the guides, and the floor channel. Section A–A shows the plan of the wall jamb with the half-door hinged to fold back to the wall. Three alternative ways are shown of forming the joint between each leaf.

Fitting and hanging of doors

Details of a door which is to be hung on 100 mm butt hinges are given on page 108. The sequence of operations is as follows:

1 The door is first fitted into the door opening allowing 1 mm, or a penny thickness, play to the jambs and head, and also the necessary allowance for the floor coverings (carpets, etc.).

2 The hinges are fitted and fixed to the door. Note, at the foot of the page, that the bottom hinge has more projection to give a tilt, or cock, to the door.

3 The door is now set up in the opening and the position of the hinges marked on the frame.

4 The door is removed from the opening and the marking out and recessing for the hinges completed.

5 The door is hung by first the top hinge being fixed with one screw only and then the bottom hinge being fixed in the same way. Only after one has made sure that the door is fitted correctly are the remaining screws inserted.

Practice lessons

1 Working from the information given:

    (a) Draw to a 1:20 scale the elevation view of one of the three doors illustrated on page 102.

    (b) Draw full-size details of—
        (i) A single raised panel and bolection moulding
        (ii) A framed panel.

2 *(a)* Draw the plan and elevation view of a pair of garage doors and frame, as illustrated on page 106. Scale 1:20.

    (b) Draw 1:5 scale details of the framing members.

3 *(a)* Set out a workshop rod for the fully glazed door illustrated on page 104.

    (b) Prepare a cutting list for one door.

    (c) From the prepared material supplied, carry out all the operations involved in making the door up to the wedging up stage.

    (d) Wedge up, and clean off the door on both faces.

    (e) Fit and hang the door into a prepared opening.

    (f) Fit and fix the necessary door furniture.

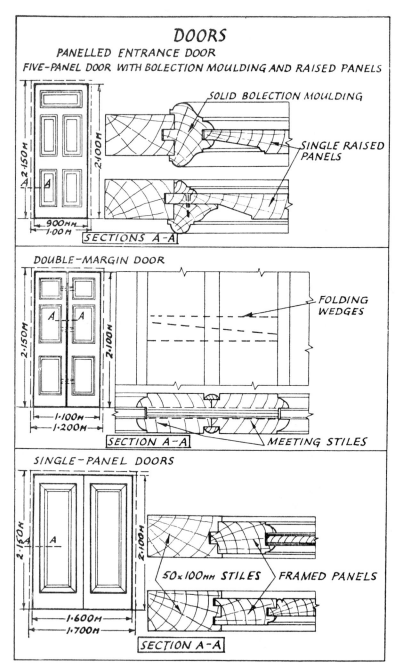

DOORS

PANELLED ENTRANCE DOOR
FIVE-PANEL DOOR WITH BOLECTION MOULDING AND RAISED PANELS

SOLID BOLECTION MOULDING

SINGLE RAISED PANELS

2·150M
2·100M

900MM
1·00 M

SECTIONS A-A

DOUBLE-MARGIN DOOR

FOLDING WEDGES

2·150M
2·100M

1·100M
1·200M

SECTION A-A

MEETING STILES

SINGLE-PANEL DOORS

2·150M
2·100M

50×100MM STILES   FRAMED PANELS

1·600M
1·700M

SECTION A-A

DOORS

SOLID BOLECTION MOULDING

METHOD OF JOINTING

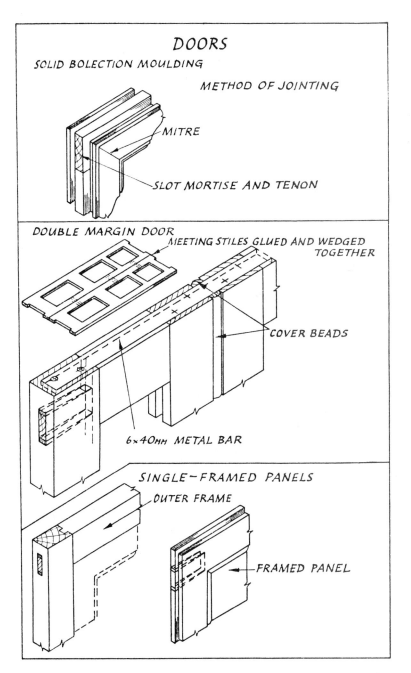

MITRE

SLOT MORTISE AND TENON

DOUBLE MARGIN DOOR

MEETING STILES GLUED AND WEDGED TOGETHER

COVER BEADS

6×40ᴍᴍ METAL BAR

SINGLE-FRAMED PANELS

OUTER FRAME

FRAMED PANEL

DOORS

GLAZED ENTRANCE DOORS

SINGLE DOOR GLAZED WITH BEADS

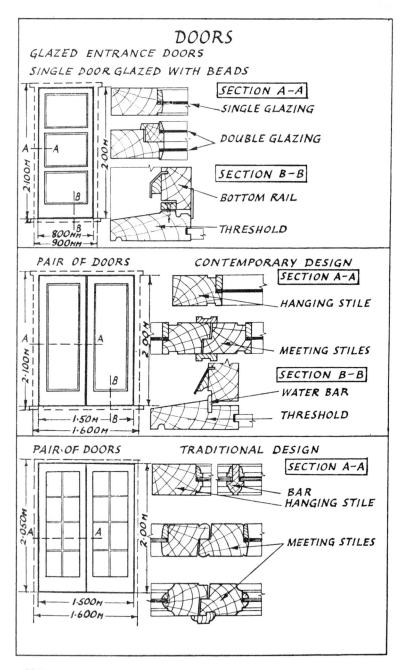

SECTION A-A
SINGLE GLAZING

DOUBLE GLAZING

SECTION B-B
BOTTOM RAIL

THRESHOLD

2·100M
2·00M
800MM
900MM

PAIR OF DOORS

CONTEMPORARY DESIGN
SECTION A-A
HANGING STILE

MEETING STILES

SECTION B-B
WATER BAR

THRESHOLD

2·100M
2·00M
1·50M
1·600M

PAIR·OF DOORS

TRADITIONAL DESIGN
SECTION A-A
BAR
HANGING STILE

MEETING STILES

2·050M
2·00M
1·500M
1·600M

DOORS

DOUBLE GLAZING

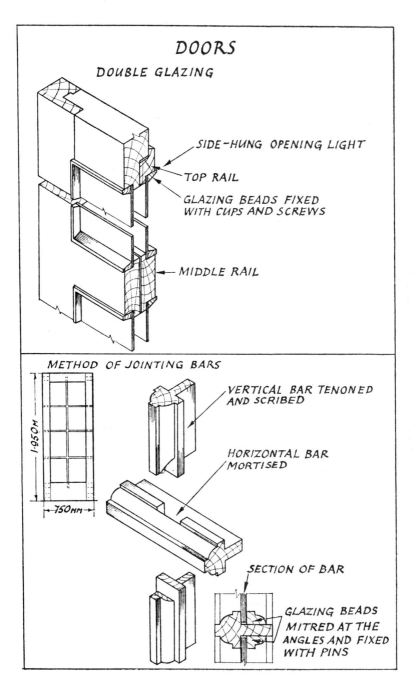

SIDE-HUNG OPENING LIGHT

TOP RAIL

GLAZING BEADS FIXED
WITH CUPS AND SCREWS

MIDDLE RAIL

METHOD OF JOINTING BARS

1·950M

750MM

VERTICAL BAR TENONED
AND SCRIBED

HORIZONTAL BAR
MORTISED

SECTION OF BAR

GLAZING BEADS
MITRED AT THE
ANGLES AND FIXED
WITH PINS

DOORS

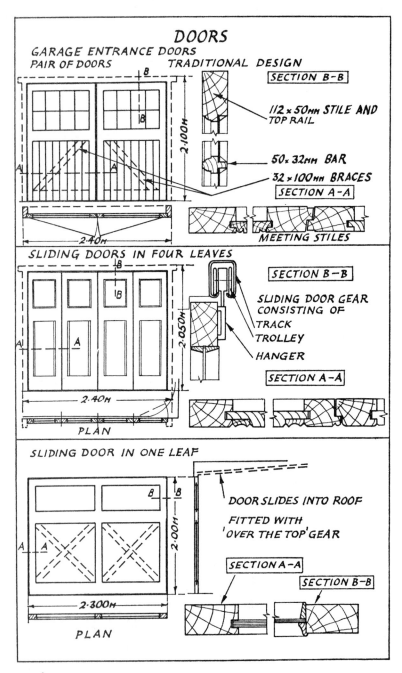

GARAGE ENTRANCE DOORS
PAIR OF DOORS   TRADITIONAL DESIGN

SECTION B-B

112 x 50mm STILE AND TOP RAIL

50 x 32mm BAR

32 x 100mm BRACES

SECTION A-A

2·100m

2·40m

MEETING STILES

SLIDING DOORS IN FOUR LEAVES

SECTION B-B

SLIDING DOOR GEAR CONSISTING OF
TRACK
TROLLEY
HANGER

SECTION A-A

2·050m

2·40m

PLAN

SLIDING DOOR IN ONE LEAF

DOOR SLIDES INTO ROOF

FITTED WITH 'OVER THE TOP' GEAR

SECTION A-A

SECTION B-B

2·00m

2·300m

PLAN

DOORS

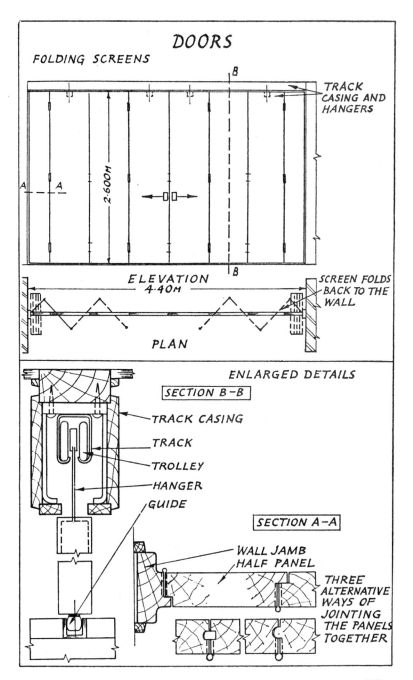

FOLDING SCREENS

B

TRACK
CASING AND
HANGERS

A | A

2·600M

ELEVATION
4·40M

SCREEN FOLDS
BACK TO THE
WALL

B

PLAN

ENLARGED DETAILS

SECTION B–B

TRACK CASING

TRACK

TROLLEY

HANGER

GUIDE

SECTION A–A

WALL JAMB
HALF PANEL

THREE
ALTERNATIVE
WAYS OF
JOINTING
THE PANELS
TOGETHER

DOORS

FITTING AND HANGING

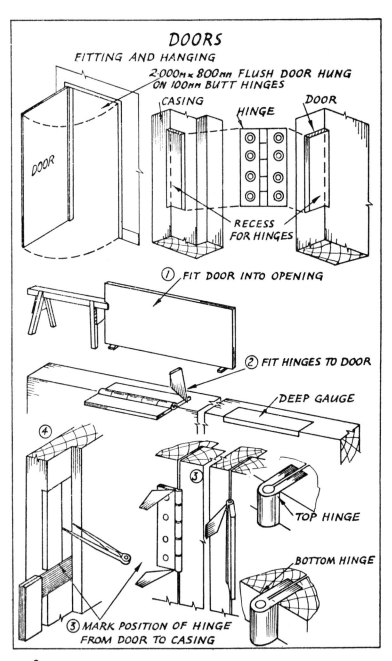

2·000m × 800mm FLUSH DOOR HUNG ON 100mm BUTT HINGES

CASING

HINGE

DOOR

DOOR

RECESS FOR HINGES

① FIT DOOR INTO OPENING

② FIT HINGES TO DOOR

DEEP GAUGE

④

③

TOP HINGE

BOTTOM HINGE

③ MARK POSITION OF HINGE FROM DOOR TO CASING

When they are being set in walls thicker than 225 mm it is usual to *frame and panel* the door linings. This is in order to minimise the effects of shrinkage. Each lining consists of two framed and panelled jambs tongued into a framed and panelled head. In good-class work the linings are fixed to framed grounds. Details of the linings are given on page 112.

The plan and elevation of a 375 mm lining set in 350 mm brickwork are shown at the top of page 112. The jamb lining consists of two stiles, rails to match the rails in the door, and raised panels. The head lining consists of two stiles, two rails, and a raised panel. A section through the jambs, grounds, and architraves is shown (A–A).

Details of a 500 mm lining, and an enlarged section showing the formation of rebates, the framed grounds, and built-up architraves, are shown at the foot of page 112.

Splayed door linings are often used to form a finish to openings in thick walls. The plan, elevation, and enlarged details of a 100 × 125 mm door frame finished on both sides with 25 mm splayed linings are shown on page 113 (top). The linings are tongued into the frame and fixed to the grounds. The jambs may be tongued or dovetailed into the head lining.

Semicircular linings for the heads of semicircular frames may be veneered and staved, built up of laminates, or they may consist of a thin facing glued to a hollow framing. Details of the lining are shown on page 113 (foot). The section A–A shows both the solid and the hollow frame constructions. The section B–B shows laminated and staved constructions.

It is usual to make the circular head as a separate unit when door openings are wider than 1·065 m. The joints between the head and the jambs are made in the springing. The lining must be made identical in shape and size to the head. To form it an assembly jig in the shape of a centre is needed (see page 115—top).

Semicircular splayed linings are in fact cone-shaped, and the shape of the circular head forms part of the curved surface of the cone. The circular head may be laminated or consist of a hollow frame with a thin facing. Details of the lining are given on page 114. The enlarged detail of section A–A shows a 25 mm lining tongued into the frame and finished with architraves fixed to the grounds. A jig which is the exact size and shape of the lining (shown on page 115 —foot) is required for its assembly. *Semicircular splayed linings* are often *panelled* when the walls are wide. The panels on the jamb linings are usually made to correspond with the panels in the doors. The plan and elevation views of the lining are shown on page 114 (foot), with an enlarged detail of the splayed lining tongued into the frame, the 31 mm moulded stiles, and the 9 mm plywood panels.

Practice lessons

1 Working from the information given:

   (a) Draw to a 1:20 scale, the plan and elevation of a 375 mm framed and panelled lining.

   (b) Draw to a 1:5 scale, an horizontal section through the lining.

2 *(a)* Draw, to a 1:20 scale, the plan and elevation of a semi-circular splayed lining, illustrated on page 114.

   (b) Draw, to a 1:4 scale, an horizontal section of the lining, showing the door frame, the architrave, and the grounds.

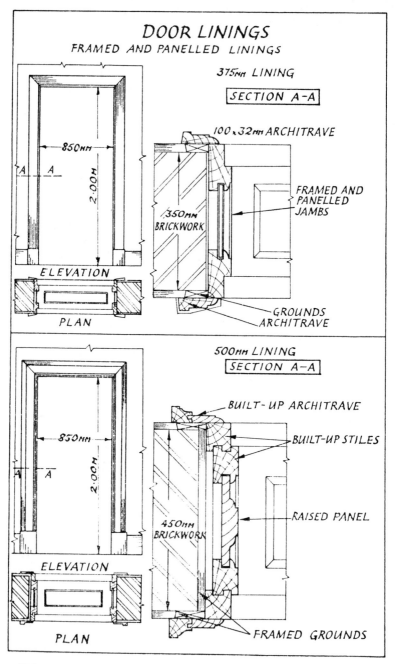

DOOR LININGS
FRAMED AND PANELLED LININGS

375mm LINING

SECTION A-A

100 x 32mm ARCHITRAVE

FRAMED AND PANELLED JAMBS

350mm BRICKWORK

850mm

2.00m

A   A

ELEVATION

PLAN

GROUNDS
ARCHITRAVE

500mm LINING
SECTION A-A

BUILT-UP ARCHITRAVE

BUILT-UP STILES

RAISED PANEL

450mm BRICKWORK

850mm

2.00m

A   A

ELEVATION

PLAN

FRAMED GROUNDS

DOOR LININGS

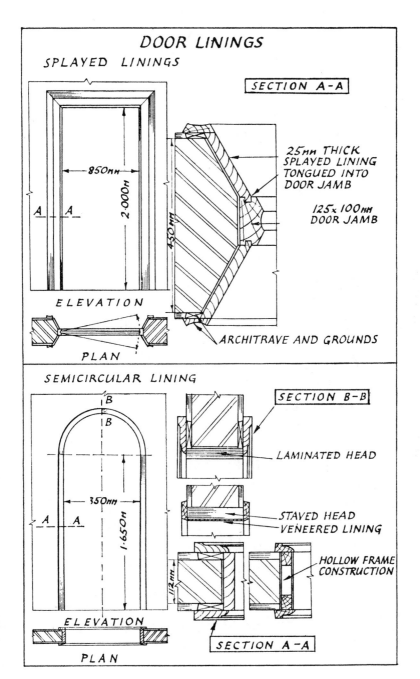

SPLAYED LININGS

SECTION A-A

850mm

2·000m

450mm

25mm THICK
SPLAYED LINING
TONGUED INTO
DOOR JAMB

125 x 100mm
DOOR JAMB

ELEVATION

PLAN

ARCHITRAVE AND GROUNDS

SEMICIRCULAR LINING

SECTION B-B

LAMINATED HEAD

350mm

1·650m

STAVED HEAD
VENEERED LINING

112mm

HOLLOW FRAME
CONSTRUCTION

ELEVATION

PLAN

SECTION A-A

DOOR LININGS

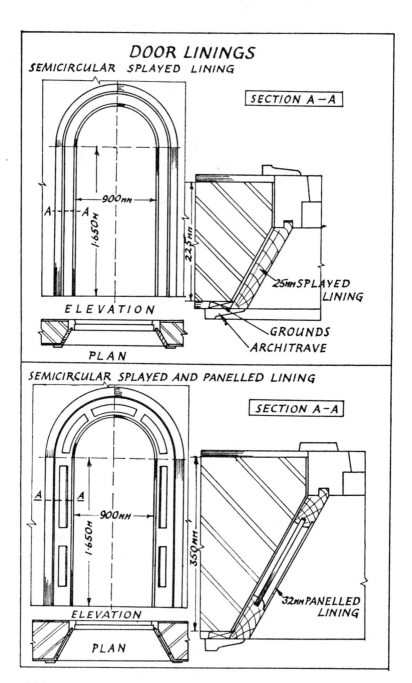

SEMICIRCULAR SPLAYED LINING

SECTION A–A

900ᴍᴍ

1·650ᴍ

225ᴍᴍ

A ─── A

ELEVATION

PLAN

25ᴍᴍ SPLAYED LINING

GROUNDS

ARCHITRAVE

SEMICIRCULAR SPLAYED AND PANELLED LINING

SECTION A–A

900ᴍᴍ

1·650ᴍ

350ᴍᴍ

A ── A

ELEVATION

PLAN

32ᴍᴍ PANELLED LINING

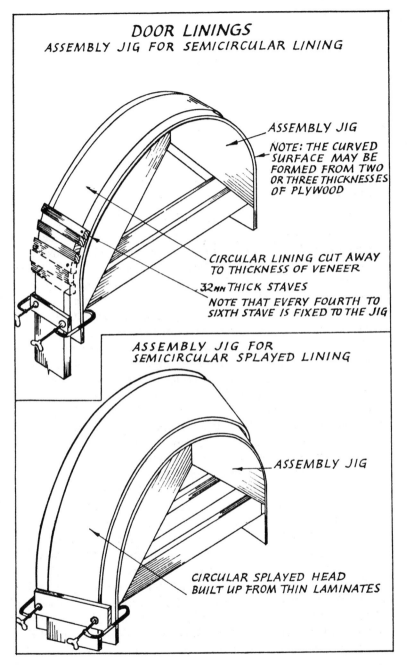

DOOR LININGS
ASSEMBLY JIG FOR SEMICIRCULAR LINING

ASSEMBLY JIG

NOTE: THE CURVED SURFACE MAY BE FORMED FROM TWO OR THREE THICKNESSES OF PLYWOOD

CIRCULAR LINING CUT AWAY TO THICKNESS OF VENEER

32MM THICK STAVES

NOTE THAT EVERY FOURTH TO SIXTH STAVE IS FIXED TO THE JIG

ASSEMBLY JIG FOR SEMICIRCULAR SPLAYED LINING

ASSEMBLY JIG

CIRCULAR SPLAYED HEAD BUILT UP FROM THIN LAMINATES

10 | Windows

Sash windows

Windows with box frames fitted with vertical sliding sashes are made with square, segmental, or semicircular heads. Those with segmental and semicircular heads will be discussed in Book 3.

The *square-headed* windows are of two main types—the ordinary sash window and the venetian window, which has three lights.

The ordinary double-hung sash window consists of a box frame fitted with a pair of vertically sliding sashes. This is illustrated on page 126 (top), with enlarged details of the members.

The frame for a double-hung sash window consists of a pair of pulley stiles 32 mm thick, a pulley head, and a solid sill. The box is formed from linings 18–25 mm thick, fixed on both sides of the frame. These are called inside and outside linings. The sashes, which are 40–56 mm thick, consist of stiles, top rails, meeting rails, bottom rails, and bars. Beads, which can easily be removed, are used to keep the sashes in position. The parting beads are grooved into the pulley stiles and head, and the staff beads screwed or nailed into the inside linings and sill (see page 133).

The methods of jointing the frames and sashes are shown on page 127 (top). The housing joint is extensively used for the frame. The pulley stiles may be trenched or tongued into the head, and trenched and wedged into the sill. The sashes are mortised and tenoned together. Details of the special construction necessary for the meeting rails are given on page 127 (foot).

The *venetian window* consists of a box frame containing two solid mullions and three pairs of sashes. The centre pair of sashes are hung, and the sashes in the side lights are fixed. This window is shown on page 126 (foot), with enlarged details of sections of the box jambs, the solid mullion, the solid head, meeting rails, and sill.

The frame of a venetian window consists of a pair of pulley stiles, two solid mullions 40–50 mm thick, a 75 mm solid head, and a solid sill. Outside linings are required on the jambs, the mullions, and the head, but inside linings are necessary on the jambs only.

The window is jointed together in the same way as the ordinary sash window, with the addition that the mullions are trenched into the head and sill, as is shown on page 127 (middle).

Operations involved in making sash windows

It is usual to complete the making of both frame and sashes in the joiner's shop. This includes the fitting of the sashes into the frames, and the fitting of parting and staff beads. After priming (painting with lead paint) the frames only are delivered to the building site for building in or fixing. The sashes are retained for glazing, and are delivered to the job when required.

The sequence of operations is as follows:

NOTE   It is assumed that the work is to be carried out in a well-equipped machine shop.

1   From the drawings, specification, and bill of quantities, set out the height and width rods, and prepare the cutting list.

The height and width rods are shown on page 128. It is most important that the rods should be accurately drawn and allowances made for planing. The bars should be accurately spaced out, and the squares for glass made equal. It is necessary to figure on the rod the overall sizes so that the dimensions of the work may be easily identified by other operatives, such as machinists.

2   From the cutting list, cut out and plane up all members.

3   Mark out the frame and sashes for machining.

Provided the height and width rods have been accurately set out, each member can be marked out from the rods. If this has not been done only the overall or clearance lines can be taken from them.

The marking out of the pulley stiles with the positions of the pockets and the pulleys is shown on page 129 (top). The sill and the pulley head are also shown. Notice that the sill and head sections are marked on the face side of each member. The marking out of the vertical members of the sashes, consisting of two pairs of stiles and two upright bars, is given in the middle of the page. The rails, bars, and meeting rails are shown at the foot of the page. In practice one pattern only is required for all members of the same shoulder length.

4 Machine all the members.

In a well-organised shop the joiner is not concerned with the machining operations. Provided the work has been marked out correctly, all the machining would be executed by machinists, and the work returned to the joiner only for assembly and finishing.

5 Prepare the members for assembly. The pocket pieces must be cut out and fixed in the pulley stiles, and the pulleys fitted. These two operations are shown on page 130.

6 Assemble and finish frame and sashes. The method of assembling the frame is shown on page 131.

With the sill on the bench, wedge and nail the two pulley stiles, into the sill, then nail on the pulley head as shown on page 131 (top).

To fix the linings the frame is laid on the bench with the inside face upwards. A bearer, about 50×50 mm in section, is firmly fixed to the bench. The frame is fixed to this bearer at the sill end, so that the frame can be squared, as illustrated in the second drawing on the page.

Next fix the inside linings and then add the squaring strips (see the third drawing).

Turn the frame over and add the outside linings, as shown at the foot of page 131. The assembly and finishing of the sashes is shown on page 132 (foot).

In well-organised machine shops only minor adjustments are needed before the work is assembled, but in the smaller shops a number of operations may have to be done by hand. One such operation is the working of the horns on the stiles, and this is illustrated at the top of the page.

7 Fit the sashes into the frame, and fit the beads and the backings to the jambs.

The method of jointing the beads is shown on page 133 (top). A method of fastening the cord to the sash and the fixing of the backing is shown at the foot of the page.

8 Hang the sashes.

The sashes are hung with cords or lines carried over pulleys to balancing weights. Flax lines are mainly used on domestic work, but metal chains are required for the heavier sashes used in public buildings. Details of the position of the weights, lines, and pulleys in an ordinary sash window and a venetian window are given on page 134.

The operations involved in threading the cords and hanging the sashes are explained on page 135. The cords are threaded over the pulleys and attached to the weights. They are cut to the required lengths, and knotted to prevent their slipping back to the box. After the pocket pieces have been refixed the cords are fixed to the sashes. The flax lines can be attached with clout nails, or knotted and screwed to the stiles of the sashes. The chains are usually screwed on. The weights must hang clear of the sill and pulley ends of the box if the sashes are to work properly.

The weights may be made of cast iron or lead. If they are cast iron they are round; and if they are lead they are square. The weight of the two balancing weights should approximately equal the weight of one sash, but in practice 250 g is added to the weights carrying the top sash, and 250 g deducted from those carrying the bottom sash so that the sashes will stay in position.

Solid frames with casements opening outwards

A single-glazed window, with details of the meeting and hanging stiles, is shown on page 136 (top). As with glazed doors, double glazing will considerably reduce the heat loss which takes place at single-glazed windows, and is extensively used in Europe and Scandinavia. Two techniques of double glazing have been developed. With one method two casements are hinged together and fitted into the frame as a single unit. This is illustrated in the middle of page 136, where are shown the meeting stiles, framing, and hanging stile. The other method uses single-glazed casements on the outside with glazed shutters on the inside. This is shown at the foot of page 136.

Solid frames with casements opening inwards

When windows have casements opening inwards it is extremely difficult to make them weather-proof at the sill. To overcome this difficulty, specially designed water bars are introduced. Three illustrations of casements opening inwards are given on page 137.

Details of a *single-glazed window*, with sections of the meeting stiles (A–A) and the bottom rail and sill (B–B), are given at the top of page 137. Notice the weather strip and the metal water bar.

The second drawing shows a *double-glazed window* with a special construction at the sill end.

Details of a *window with glazed shutters*, showing the special shape of the bottom rail and the water bar, are given on page 137 (foot).

Bay windows

The majority of bay windows are of the casement type. The casements are made of wood and metal, and usually open outwards. The window consists of a series of frames, made up of one or more lights, coupled together. The front window is usually three lights wide, and the returns are one light wide.

The windows may be classified according to their shape in plan. They may be square bays, having a 90° return angle, cant bays with a return splay of 45° or 60°, or windows with five or more sides.

The sills may be jointed at the angles with handrail bolts and dowels, or halved together and screwed. The heads can be mitred and bolted together or tenoned into the angle posts and wall jambs. The angle posts may be made solid or built up in two or more pieces which are glued together to make a solid post.

It is usual to finish the windows with a fascia and soffit, and to cover it with a flat or pitched roof.

A *cant bay window* with a 45° splay is illustrated on page 138. A plan and elevation view giving the position of the window in the brickwork opening are shown at the top of page 138. The enlarged details give the section size and shape of the members. Section B–B shows the sill, casement head, and cornice; section A–A shows the jambs, and also the solid and built-up angle posts.

The cant bay window shown on page 139 has a 60° splay on the returns, with a transom and a built-up cornice. The window is set on to the face of the brickwork, and the wall jambs are bevelled to fit. The enlarged details show alternative methods of building up the angle posts.

A *five-sided bay window* is shown on page 140. The plan and elevation views; enlarged details with the shape and size of the wall jambs; and the solid angle posts and the split casements are given.

Pivot-hung windows

Centre, or pivot-hung, windows are of three main types—single-light, square-headed frames; single-light fanlights; and bull's-eye windows. Fanlights and bull's-eye windows will be dealt with in Book 3.

A *single-pane window of traditional design* is shown on page 141. This may be single or double glazed. The window consists of a solid frame into which a casement is fitted and hung on pivots in the centre. Beads must be fitted to the frame and casement in order to make the window weather-proof.

A plan, elevation, and section view of the window are shown at the top of page 141. In order for the window to open the beads must be cut, and the method of obtaining the position and angle of the cut is shown on the enlarged detail at the foot of the page. The detail gives a vertical section through the frame, showing the casement in an open position. The path of the bead rotates from the centre marked P. The longest point of the cut is marked A, and the angle of the cut is at a tangent to the path of the bead.

A modern *single-glazed window* is shown on page 142. The window consists of a 63 × 125 mm frame, 56 mm thick casement, and wood or metal beads. The enlarged details give horizontal and vertical sections for alternative methods of construction. Above the pivot the beads are fixed to the frame, and below the pivot to the casement. The wood beads round the casement are mitred. If metal beads are used they are fixed to the face of the frame above the pivot and to the face of the casement below the pivot.

A modern, *double-glazed, picture window* is illustrated on page 143. The window consists of a built-up frame into which the double casement is fitted and centre-hung on specially designed pivots which enable the casement to be turned into the room.

A plan, elevation, and vertical section of the window are shown at the top of the page. The enlarged details show the vertical section B–B with a built-up head, double top rail, bottom rail, and a built-up sill. The section A–A shows the jambs, beads, and casement stiles. Notice that below the pivot the bead is fixed to the frame, and above the pivot it is fixed to the casement. Note also the construction for making the frame draughtproof.

Windows of this type are usually made under licence, and because the construction is complex are best manufactured by highly skilled operatives.

Louvre ventilators

Louvre ventilators are made up of louvre boards pitched at 30°–45° or 60°, housed into an outer frame.

The ventilators are classified according to their shape. The most common types are pitched louvre frames, circular-headed louvre frames, and gothic-headed louvre frames. These are illustrated on page 144. The first drawing shows the elevation and section of a small pitched louvre, equilateral in shape. The second drawing shows a circular-headed frame with 25 mm louvre boards pitched at 45°. A gothic-headed frame is shown at the foot of the page.

The operations involved in making *pitched louvre frames* are shown on page 145. The true shape of the louvre boards and the housings in the frame are obtained by setting out the frame to full size. The method of finding the true shape of the boards is shown at the top of page 145. The marking out of the housings in the frame is given in the middle drawing. The pitched heads marked out in pairs, and the sill marked out for mortising and sinking, are shown at the foot of page 145.

The procedure in making louvre frames is the same as that for making windows. First mark out the frame; next prepare the frame and cut the louvre boards true to size and shape; then clean up all visible surfaces, assemble the frame, and fix the louvre boards.

Circular-headed louvre frames are more difficult to make than pitched frames, and special care must be taken with the setting out and the cutting of the housings in the circular heads.

The method of setting out the frame and louvres is shown on page 146. The first drawing shows how the true shape of the boards is obtained. Notice that the true face of the board is projected from the section. The method of marking out the housings in the circular head is shown in the second drawing. Notice the use of the square frame with the louvres marked on it, and the straight edge for marking the position of the grooves on both surfaces of the frame. The third drawing shows the use of a pitched block for marking the grooves on the inside edge of the frame.

The procedure for making this frame is the same as that for making the pitched louvre frame.

The *gothic-headed frame* is set out in the same way as the circular-headed frame.

Metal casements

During the transitional period from imperial to metric measure metal windows, of imperial size, will be required on a wide range of repair, and reconstruction, work.

A range of standard metal casements, in imperial and metric sizes, are given on page 147.

As mentioned earlier, the British Standards Institution recommend that the overall metric size of components should be multiples of a 300 mm module, with 300 mm as the first preference measurement, and 100 mm as the second.

A range of metal casements, in wood surrounds, set out on a 300 mm planning grid, are illustrated on page 148.

An enlarged sectional detail of the metal casements, and surrounds, is given at the foot of the page.

The frames are rebated to receive the casements, which are bedded in mastic and fixed with screws. Special attention must be paid to the rebate size of the frame so that the metal casements will fit accurately.

The enlarged details show the head, sill, jamb, and mullion of the surrounds, and a section view of the opening and fixed casements. The framing is usually mortised and tenoned, and wedged and pinned together.

European softwood is chiefly used for the framing (jambs, head, and mullions), and English oak for the sills.

For high-quality work a durable hardwood such as teak would be specified for the whole of the surround.

Practice lessons

1 Working from the information given:

   (a) Draw to a 1:20 scale the plan and elevation of the two-light window, with casements opening outwards, shown on page 136.

   (b) Draw (full size) section details of the frame, showing the jambs, stile, and meeting stiles.

2 *(a)* Draw to a 1:20 scale the plan and elevation of the two-light with casements opening inwards, shown on page 137.

   (b) Draw (full size) details of the frame showing the jamb, the meeting stiles, and the sill sections.

3 *(a)* Draw to a 1:20 scale the plan of the cant bay window illustrated on page 138.

   (b) Draw (full size) four methods of building up the angle posts on 45° and 60° angles.

4 *(a)* Set out a workshop rod for the pivot-hung window illustrated on page 141.

   (b) Prepare a cutting list for one frame.

   (c) From the prepared material supplied, carry out all the operations involved in making the frame and casement.

   (d) Fit and hang the casement into the frame, and cut and fit the beads.

   (e) Fit and fix the necessary ironmongery.

5 Working from the instructions given on pages 144 and 145:

   (a) Set out a workshop rod for the pitched louvre frame.

    (b) From the prepared material supplied, carry out all the operations involved in making the frame.

6 Working from the instructions given:

    (a) Set out a workshop rod for the sash window illustrated on page 126, to any convenient size.

    (b) From the prepared material supplied, carry out all the operations involved in making the box frame and sashes.

    (c) Fix the frame into a prepared opening in brickwork.

    (d) Fit and hang the glazed sashes, and fit and fix the ironmongery.

WINDOWS

CASED FRAMES FITTED WITH SLIDING SASHES

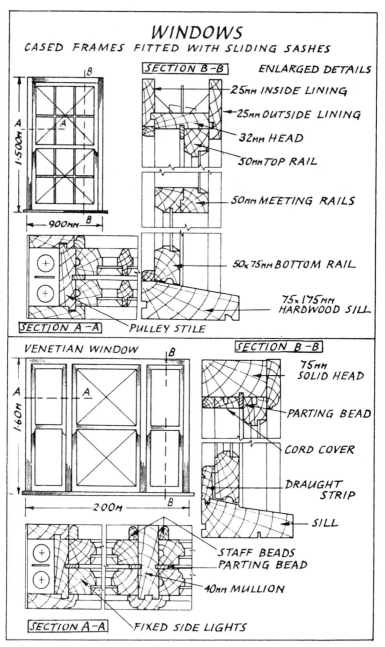

SECTION B-B   ENLARGED DETAILS

25mm INSIDE LINING

25mm OUTSIDE LINING

32mm HEAD

50mm TOP RAIL

50mm MEETING RAILS

50 x 75mm BOTTOM RAIL

75 x 175mm HARDWOOD SILL

1.500M

900mm

SECTION A-A   PULLEY STILE

VENETIAN WINDOW   SECTION B-B

75mm SOLID HEAD

PARTING BEAD

CORD COVER

DRAUGHT STRIP

SILL

1.60M

2.00M

STAFF BEADS
PARTING BEAD

40mm MULLION

SECTION A-A   FIXED SIDE LIGHTS

WINDOWS

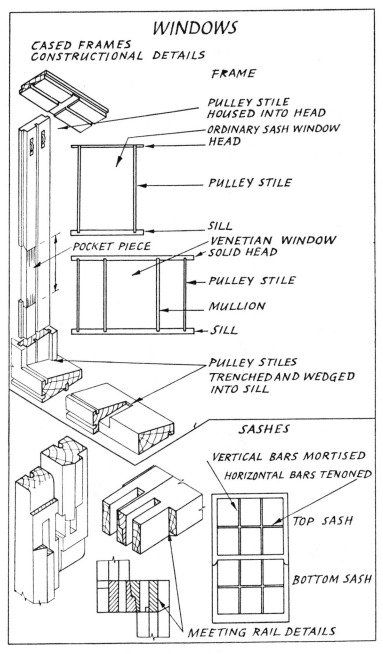

CASED FRAMES
CONSTRUCTIONAL DETAILS

FRAME

PULLEY STILE
HOUSED INTO HEAD

ORDINARY SASH WINDOW
HEAD

PULLEY STILE

SILL

POCKET PIECE

VENETIAN WINDOW
SOLID HEAD

PULLEY STILE

MULLION

SILL

PULLEY STILES
TRENCHED AND WEDGED
INTO SILL

SASHES

VERTICAL BARS MORTISED

HORIZONTAL BARS TENONED

TOP SASH

BOTTOM SASH

MEETING RAIL DETAILS

WINDOWS

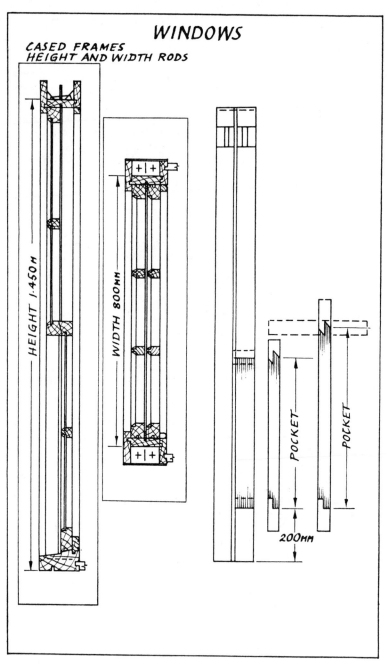

HEIGHT 1·450 M

WIDTH 800 MM

POCKET

POCKET

200 MM

128

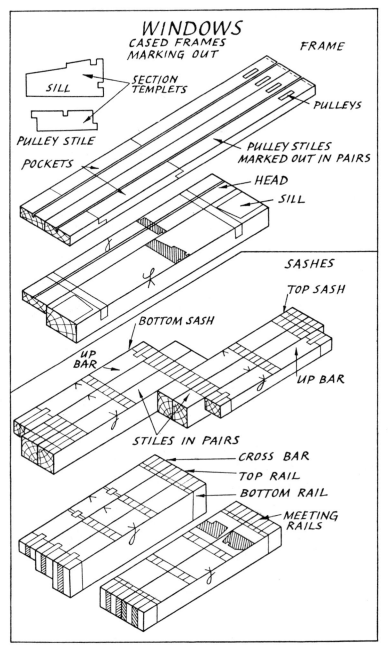

WINDOWS
CASED FRAMES
MARKING OUT

FRAME

SILL

SECTION
TEMPLETS

PULLEY STILE

PULLEYS

POCKETS

PULLEY STILES
MARKED OUT IN PAIRS

HEAD

SILL

SASHES

TOP SASH

BOTTOM SASH

UP
BAR

UP BAR

STILES IN PAIRS

CROSS BAR

TOP RAIL

BOTTOM RAIL

MEETING
RAILS

WINDOWS
CASED FRAMES
POCKET AND PULLEYS

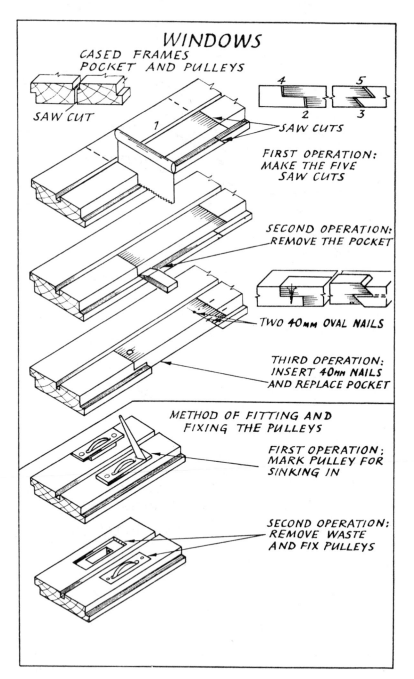

SAW CUT

4   5

2   3

SAW CUTS

FIRST OPERATION:
MAKE THE FIVE
SAW CUTS

SECOND OPERATION:
REMOVE THE POCKET

TWO 40mm OVAL NAILS

THIRD OPERATION:
INSERT 40mm NAILS
AND REPLACE POCKET

METHOD OF FITTING AND
FIXING THE PULLEYS

FIRST OPERATION:
MARK PULLEY FOR
SINKING IN

SECOND OPERATION:
REMOVE WASTE
AND FIX PULLEYS

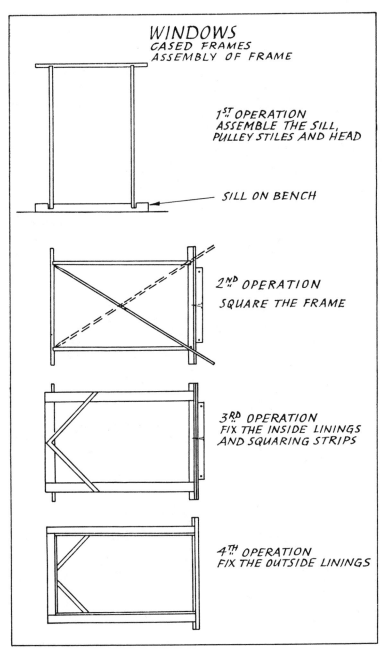

WINDOWS
CASED FRAMES
ASSEMBLY OF FRAME

1ST OPERATION
ASSEMBLE THE SILL,
PULLEY STILES AND HEAD

SILL ON BENCH

2ND OPERATION
SQUARE THE FRAME

3RD OPERATION
FIX THE INSIDE LININGS
AND SQUARING STRIPS

4TH OPERATION
FIX THE OUTSIDE LININGS

WINDOWS

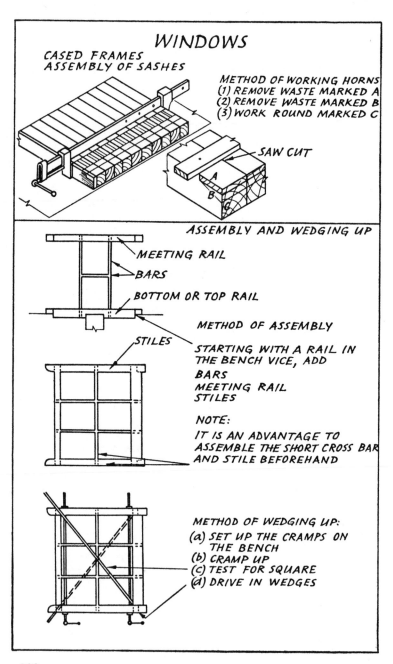

CASED FRAMES
ASSEMBLY OF SASHES

METHOD OF WORKING HORNS
(1) REMOVE WASTE MARKED A
(2) REMOVE WASTE MARKED B
(3) WORK ROUND MARKED C

SAW CUT

A
B
C

ASSEMBLY AND WEDGING UP

MEETING RAIL

BARS

BOTTOM OR TOP RAIL

METHOD OF ASSEMBLY

STARTING WITH A RAIL IN
THE BENCH VICE, ADD
BARS
MEETING RAIL
STILES

STILES

NOTE:

IT IS AN ADVANTAGE TO
ASSEMBLE THE SHORT CROSS BAR
AND STILE BEFOREHAND

METHOD OF WEDGING UP:
(a) SET UP THE CRAMPS ON
    THE BENCH
(b) CRAMP UP
(c) TEST FOR SQUARE
(d) DRIVE IN WEDGES

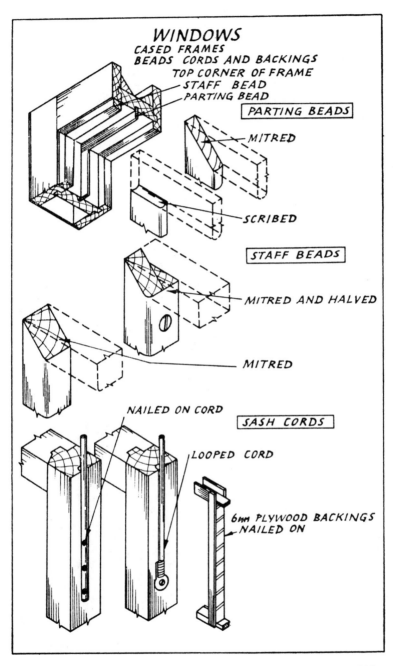

WINDOWS
CASED FRAMES
BEADS CORDS AND BACKINGS

TOP CORNER OF FRAME

STAFF BEAD
PARTING BEAD

PARTING BEADS

MITRED

SCRIBED

STAFF BEADS

MITRED AND HALVED

MITRED

NAILED ON CORD

SASH CORDS

LOOPED CORD

6ᴹᴹ PLYWOOD BACKINGS
NAILED ON

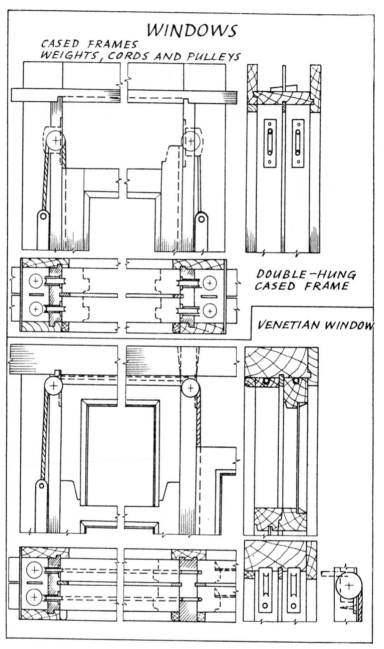

WINDOWS

CASED FRAMES
WEIGHTS, CORDS AND PULLEYS

DOUBLE—HUNG
CASED FRAME

VENETIAN WINDOW

WINDOWS

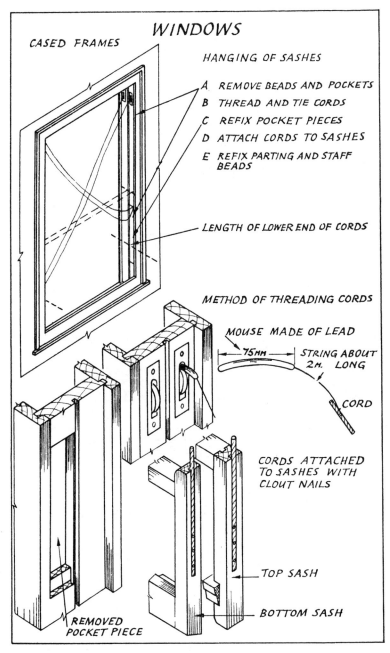

CASED FRAMES

HANGING OF SASHES

A REMOVE BEADS AND POCKETS

B THREAD AND TIE CORDS

C REFIX POCKET PIECES

D ATTACH CORDS TO SASHES

E REFIX PARTING AND STAFF BEADS

LENGTH OF LOWER END OF CORDS

METHOD OF THREADING CORDS

MOUSE MADE OF LEAD

75MM

STRING ABOUT 2M. LONG

CORD

CORDS ATTACHED TO SASHES WITH CLOUT NAILS

TOP SASH

BOTTOM SASH

REMOVED POCKET PIECE

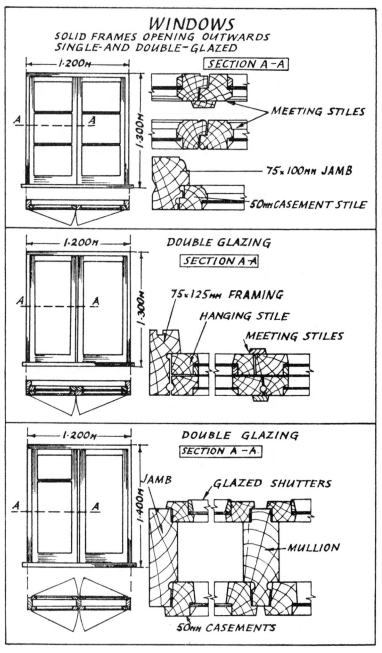

WINDOWS
SOLID FRAMES OPENING OUTWARDS
SINGLE- AND DOUBLE-GLAZED

1·200m

1·300m

SECTION A–A

MEETING STILES

75 × 100mm JAMB

50mm CASEMENT STILE

DOUBLE GLAZING

SECTION A–A

1·200m

1·300m

75 × 125mm FRAMING

HANGING STILE

MEETING STILES

DOUBLE GLAZING

SECTION A–A

1·200m

1·400m

JAMB

GLAZED SHUTTERS

MULLION

50mm CASEMENTS

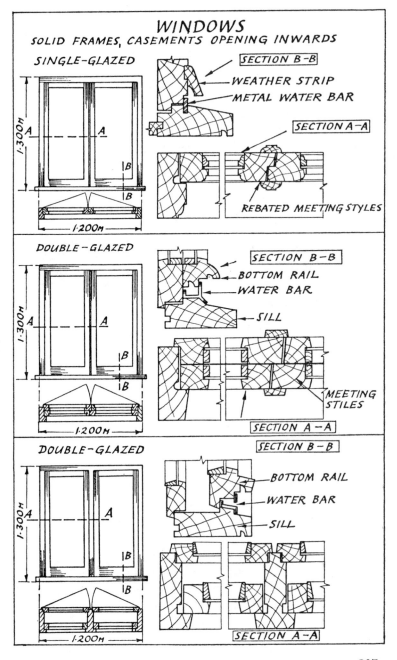

WINDOWS
SOLID FRAMES, CASEMENTS OPENING INWARDS

SINGLE-GLAZED

1·300M

A————A

|B
|B

1·200M

SECTION B-B
WEATHER STRIP
METAL WATER BAR

SECTION A-A

REBATED MEETING STYLES

DOUBLE-GLAZED

1·300M

A————A

|B
|B

1·200M

SECTION B-B
BOTTOM RAIL
WATER BAR
SILL

MEETING STILES

SECTION A-A

DOUBLE-GLAZED

1·300M

A————A

|B
|B

1·200M

SECTION B-B
BOTTOM RAIL
WATER BAR
SILL

SECTION A-A

WINDOWS

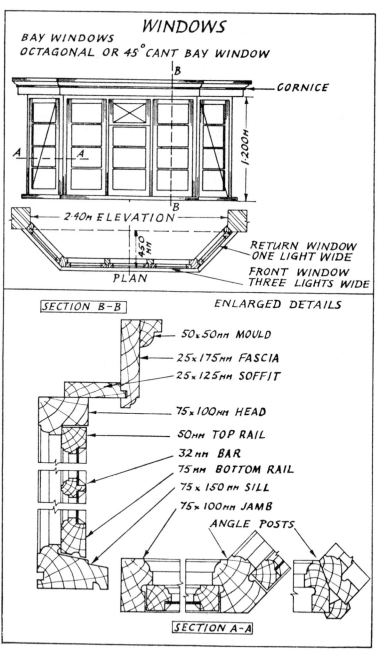

BAY WINDOWS
OCTAGONAL OR 45° CANT BAY WINDOW

CORNICE

1·200H

A — A

2·40M ELEVATION

RETURN WINDOW
ONE LIGHT WIDE

FRONT WINDOW
THREE LIGHTS WIDE

450 MM

PLAN

SECTION B-B

ENLARGED DETAILS

50 x 50MM MOULD

25 x 175MM FASCIA

25 x 125MM SOFFIT

75 x 100MM HEAD

50MM TOP RAIL

32MM BAR

75MM BOTTOM RAIL

75 x 150MM SILL

75 x 100MM JAMB

ANGLE POSTS

SECTION A-A

138

WINDOWS

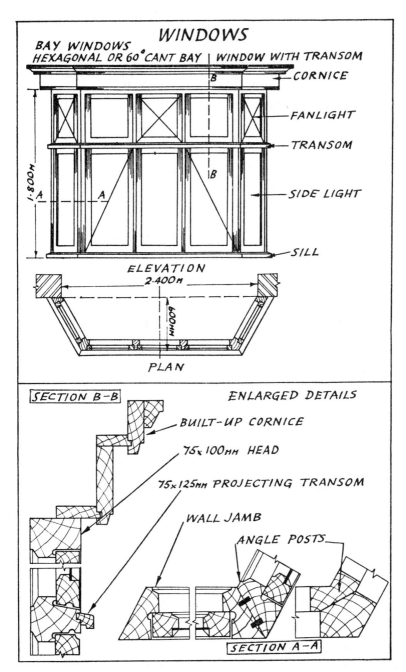

BAY WINDOWS
HEXAGONAL OR 60° CANT BAY | WINDOW WITH TRANSOM

CORNICE

FANLIGHT

TRANSOM

SIDE LIGHT

SILL

1·800M

A — A

B

B

ELEVATION
2·400M

600MM

PLAN

SECTION B-B   ENLARGED DETAILS

BUILT-UP CORNICE

75×100MM HEAD

75×125MM PROJECTING TRANSOM

WALL JAMB

ANGLE POSTS

SECTION A-A

WINDOWS

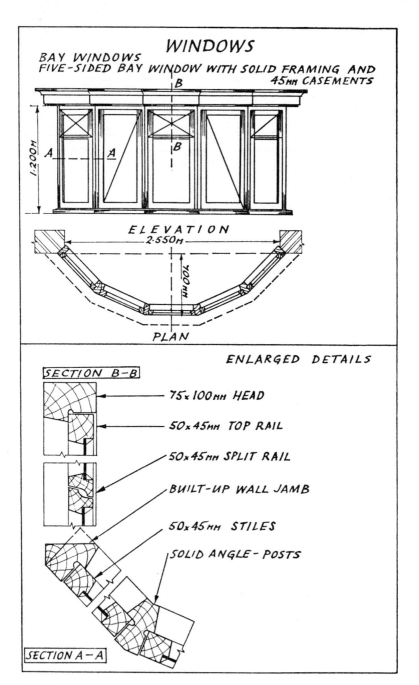

BAY WINDOWS
FIVE-SIDED BAY WINDOW WITH SOLID FRAMING AND 45ᴍᴍ CASEMENTS

1·200ᴍ

E L E V A T I O N

2·550ᴍ

700ᴍᴍ

P L A N

ENLARGED DETAILS

SECTION B-B

75 × 100ᴍᴍ HEAD

50 × 45ᴍᴍ TOP RAIL

50 × 45ᴍᴍ SPLIT RAIL

BUILT-UP WALL JAMB

50 × 45ᴍᴍ STILES

SOLID ANGLE-POSTS

SECTION A-A

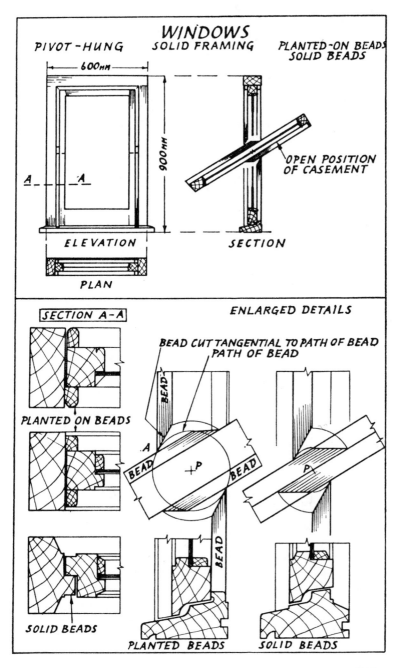

WINDOWS
SOLID FRAMING

PIVOT-HUNG

PLANTED-ON BEADS
SOLID BEADS

600mm

900mm

A — A

OPEN POSITION
OF CASEMENT

ELEVATION

SECTION

PLAN

SECTION A-A

ENLARGED DETAILS

BEAD CUT TANGENTIAL TO PATH OF BEAD
PATH OF BEAD

PLANTED ON BEADS

BEAD

BEAD

A

BEAD

BEAD

+P

P

SOLID BEADS

PLANTED BEADS

SOLID BEADS

141

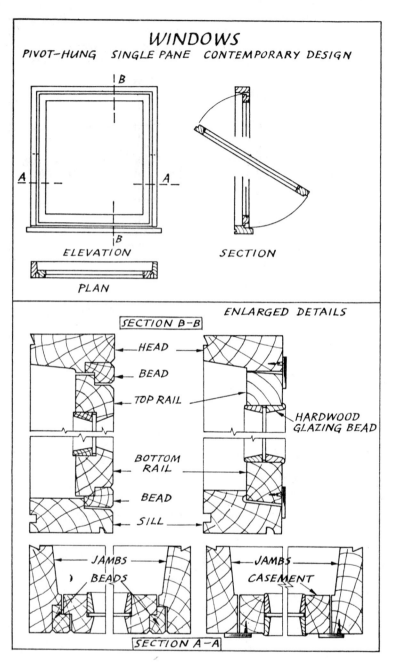

WINDOWS

PIVOT-HUNG SINGLE PANE CONTEMPORARY DESIGN

B

A —————— A

B

ELEVATION

SECTION

PLAN

ENLARGED DETAILS

SECTION B-B

HEAD

BEAD

TOP RAIL

HARDWOOD
GLAZING BEAD

BOTTOM
RAIL

BEAD

SILL

JAMBS

BEADS

JAMBS

CASEMENT

SECTION A-A

WINDOWS

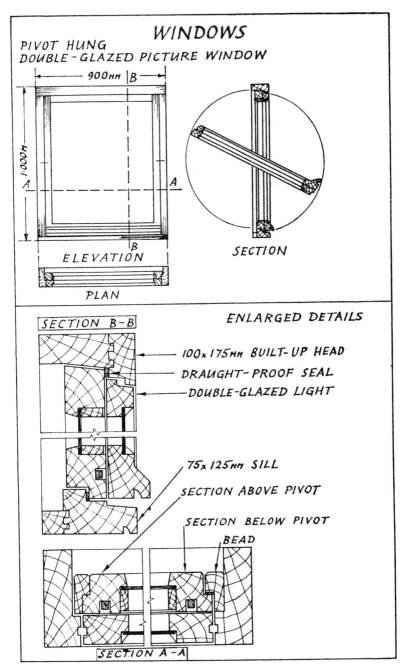

PIVOT HUNG
DOUBLE-GLAZED PICTURE WINDOW

900мм |B

1·000м

A —— A

ELEVATION

|B

PLAN

SECTION

ENLARGED DETAILS

SECTION B-B

100×175мм BUILT-UP HEAD
DRAUGHT-PROOF SEAL
DOUBLE-GLAZED LIGHT

75×125мм SILL

SECTION ABOVE PIVOT

SECTION BELOW PIVOT

BEAD

SECTION A-A

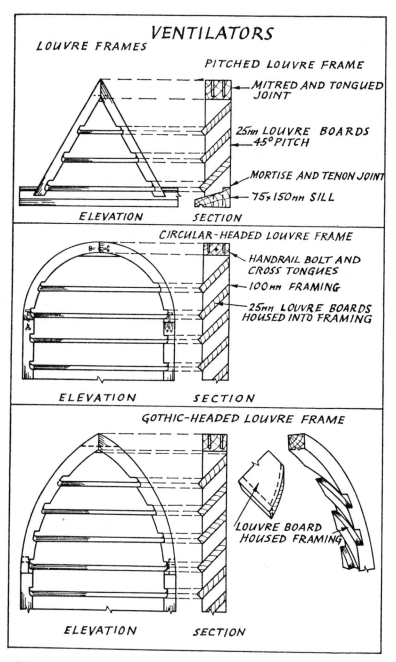

VENTILATORS

LOUVRE FRAMES

PITCHED LOUVRE FRAME

MITRED AND TONGUED JOINT

25mm LOUVRE BOARDS 45° PITCH

MORTISE AND TENON JOINT

75×150mm SILL

ELEVATION   SECTION

CIRCULAR-HEADED LOUVRE FRAME

HANDRAIL BOLT AND CROSS TONGUES

100mm FRAMING

25mm LOUVRE BOARDS HOUSED INTO FRAMING

ELEVATION   SECTION

GOTHIC-HEADED LOUVRE FRAME

LOUVRE BOARD HOUSED FRAMING

ELEVATION   SECTION

144

VENTILATORS

PITCHED LOUVRE FRAME
PRACTICAL METHOD OF MARKING OUT LOUVRE BOARDS & FRAME

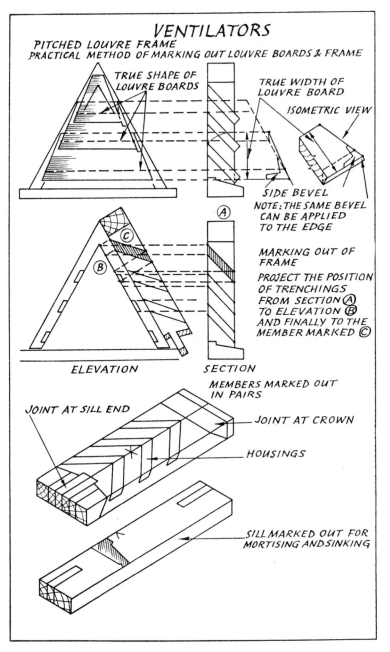

TRUE SHAPE OF
LOUVRE BOARDS

TRUE WIDTH OF
LOUVRE BOARD

ISOMETRIC VIEW

SIDE BEVEL

NOTE: THE SAME BEVEL
CAN BE APPLIED
TO THE EDGE

MARKING OUT OF
FRAME

PROJECT THE POSITION
OF TRENCHINGS
FROM SECTION Ⓐ
TO ELEVATION Ⓑ
AND FINALLY TO THE
MEMBER MARKED Ⓒ

Ⓐ

Ⓒ

Ⓑ

ELEVATION

SECTION

MEMBERS MARKED OUT
IN PAIRS

JOINT AT SILL END

JOINT AT CROWN

HOUSINGS

SILL MARKED OUT FOR
MORTISING AND SINKING

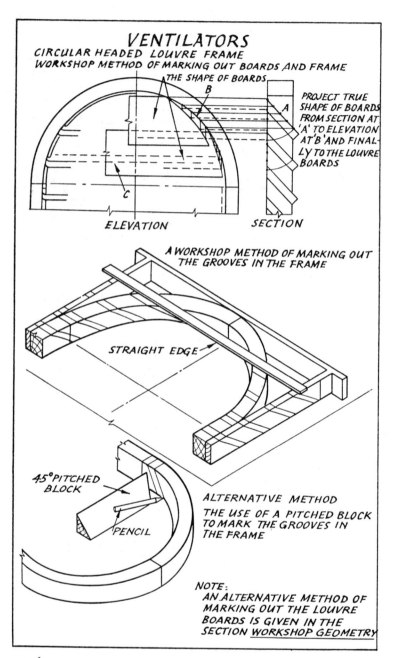

VENTILATORS

CIRCULAR HEADED LOUVRE FRAME
WORKSHOP METHOD OF MARKING OUT BOARDS AND FRAME
THE SHAPE OF BOARDS

B

A

PROJECT TRUE
SHAPE OF BOARDS
FROM SECTION AT
'A' TO ELEVATION
AT 'B' AND FINAL-
LY TO THE LOUVRE
BOARDS

C

ELEVATION

SECTION

A WORKSHOP METHOD OF MARKING OUT
THE GROOVES IN THE FRAME

STRAIGHT EDGE

45°PITCHED
BLOCK

PENCIL

ALTERNATIVE METHOD
THE USE OF A PITCHED BLOCK
TO MARK THE GROOVES IN
THE FRAME

NOTE:
AN ALTERNATIVE METHOD OF
MARKING OUT THE LOUVRE
BOARDS IS GIVEN IN THE
SECTION WORKSHOP GEOMETRY

146

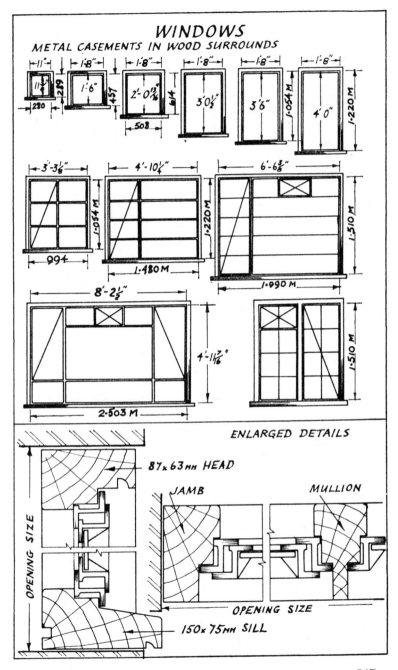

WINDOWS
METAL CASEMENTS IN WOOD SURROUNDS

11″ · 1·3″ · 289
11½″ · 280

1·8″ · 457
1·6″

1·8″ · 2·0⅞″ · 614
508

1·8″
3·0½″

1·8″ · 1·054 M
3·6″

1·8″ · 1·220 M
4·0″

3·3⅜″ · 1·054 M
994

4·10¼″ · 1·220 M
1·480 M

6·6⅜″ · 1·510 M
1·990 M

8·2½″ · 4·11⁷⁄₁₆″
2·503 M

1·510 M

ENLARGED DETAILS

OPENING SIZE

87 × 63 mm HEAD

JAMB

MULLION

OPENING SIZE

150 × 75 mm SILL

147

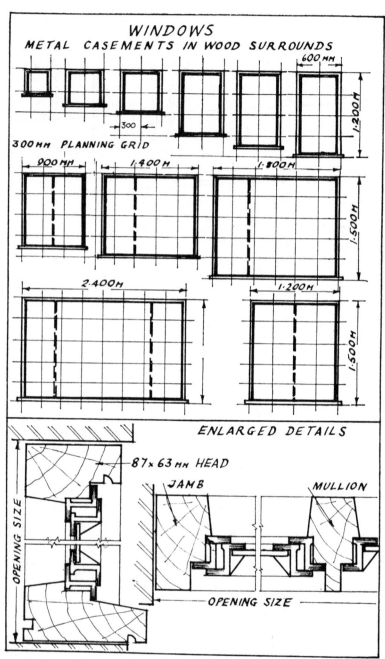

WINDOWS
METAL CASEMENTS IN WOOD SURROUNDS

600 MM

1·200 M

300

300 MM PLANNING GRID

900 MM

1·400 M

1·800 M

1·500 M

2·400 M

1·200 M

1·500 M

ENLARGED DETAILS

87 × 63 MM HEAD

JAMB

MULLION

OPENING SIZE

OPENING SIZE

Types of gate

Entrance gates forming part of a boundary fence or wall are made either in pairs or as single gates. They are usually hung to open inwards. It is usual for the gates to be similar in design to the boundary fence, especially if this is paled. They generally have either a ledged-and-braced or a framed-and-braced construction.

Single gates should be wide enough to allow for the free passage of goods and people. They are usually between 760 mm and 1·065 m wide.

A *paled gate* hung to 125 × 125 mm gateposts and hinged to open inwards is shown on page 152 (top). The gate consists of 25 × 75 mm pales, 32 × 100 mm rails, and 32 × 75 mm braces. The enlarged details show the method of fixing the pales to the ledges. This is done by screwing ledges to pales, and nailing pales to ledges. Note the position of the nails and how they are clinched.

When the gate is framed (shown on the second plan drawing) it is usual to tenon the rails into the stiles and pin the joint, as shown in the enlarged detail.

The gateposts, usually made of oak, should have their butt ends charred by fire, liberally tarred, and embedded in concrete to a depth of at least 600 mm. The posts are usually finished with a cap, details of which are given in the middle of page 152.

The *framed-and-panelled gate* illustrated at the foot of page 152 has 50 × 100 mm framing, 18 mm match-boards in the lower panel, and slats in the upper space. The enlarged details show the rails tenoned, wedged and pinned into the stiles. A cross-section of the stile and boards is also shown. The top edges of the rails and the horns are chamfered.

Pairs of gates should not be less than 2·1 m wide and 1·065 m high.

A typical pair of entrance gates is illustrated on page 153 (top). The gates consist of framing 63 mm thick, lower panels of 18 mm match-boards placed diagonally, and upper panels which are slatted. The enlarged details show the joints and the shape of the horns, together with sections of the hanging stile, muntin, slat, and meeting stiles.

Factory entrance gates are similar in construction to framed, ledged, and braced doors, but the top rails are finished with a capping and the stiles have moulded horns. The height and width of the gates depends on the type of factory. Most factories would require gates at least 2·7 m wide and 2·1–2·4 m high. It is usual to incorporate a wicket gate in one of the gates, so that it is possible to enter the premises without having to open the main gates.

Each gate consists of framing 63–75 mm thick, mortised and tenoned, wedged and pinned together, and sheeted with 25 mm match-boards. It is essential to brace each door with braces placed at an angle of not less than 45° to the bottom and middle rail.

A typical pair of factory entrance gates is shown at the foot of page 153. The small drawings show a plan and elevation view of the gates, and give the position of the wicket and braces. The section C–C shows the top rail and capping. Section B–B gives details of the meeting stiles and wicket gate, with the position of the boards on the wicket. The section A–A shows the hanging stile and boards.

Materials for gates

Softwoods from America and Europe and English oak are extensively used in gate construction. The softwood gates are usually finished with paint, but they may alternatively be treated with a preservative. The surface of oak gates can be treated with raw linseed oil or with a varnish, but when the gates form part of an oak fence the finish should match that of the fence.

It used to be common practice to paint all joints on external joinery such as entrance gates, factory and garage doors with a lead paint, in order to protect them against the weather. This no longer needs to be done, because of the introduction of waterproof adhesives.

Practice lessons

1 Working from the information given:

   (a) Draw to a 1:20 scale the plan and elevation of a framed-and-panelled gate 900 mm wide.
   (b) Prepare full-size section details of the framing and match-board panel.

2 (a) Set out a workshop rod for a single framed-and-panelled entrance gate 700 mm wide.
   (b) Prepare a cutting list for one gate.
   (c) From the prepared material supplied, carry out all the operations involved in making the gate up to the wedging up stage.
   (d) Assemble and finish the gate.
   (e) Hang the gate to fixed posts, and fit and fix the gate ironmongery.

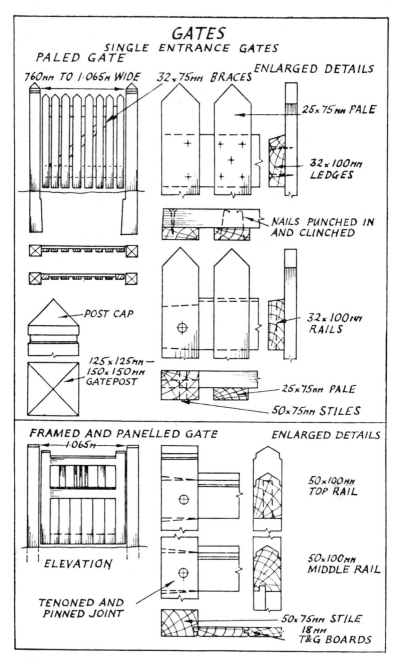

GATES

SINGLE ENTRANCE GATES

PALED GATE

760mm TO 1·065m WIDE

32 × 75mm BRACES

ENLARGED DETAILS

25 × 75mm PALE

32 × 100mm LEDGES

NAILS PUNCHED IN AND CLINCHED

32 × 100mm RAILS

POST CAP

125 × 125mm — 150 × 150mm GATEPOST

25 × 75mm PALE

50 × 75mm STILES

FRAMED AND PANELLED GATE

1·065m

ELEVATION

TENONED AND PINNED JOINT

ENLARGED DETAILS

50 × 100mm TOP RAIL

50 × 100mm MIDDLE RAIL

50 × 75mm STILE

18mm T&G BOARDS

GATES

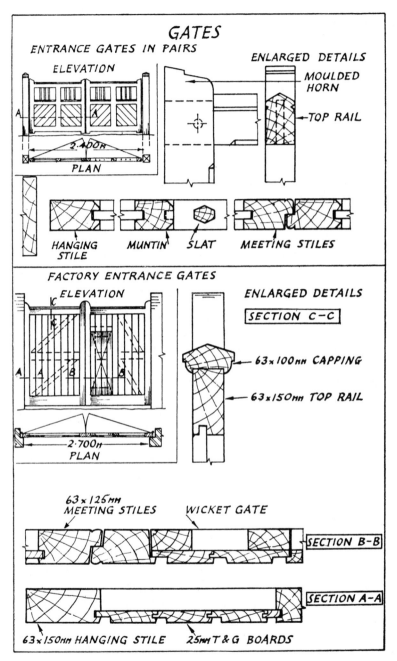

ENTRANCE GATES IN PAIRS

ELEVATION

ENLARGED DETAILS

MOULDED HORN

TOP RAIL

A A

2.400m

PLAN

HANGING STILE   MUNTIN   SLAT   MEETING STILES

FACTORY ENTRANCE GATES

ELEVATION

ENLARGED DETAILS

SECTION C-C

C C

A A B B

2.700m

PLAN

63×100mm CAPPING

63×150mm TOP RAIL

63×125mm MEETING STILES   WICKET GATE   SECTION B-B

SECTION A-A

63×150mm HANGING STILE   25mm T & G BOARDS

New building regulations

New safety regulations relating to stairways came into operation in Feburary 1966.

The main improvements relate to the pitch of private and common (public) stairways, the going and proportion of tapered steps, and the guarding of stairways.

The regulations state that:

The pitch of a *private stairway* must not be more than 42°.

The rise per step not more than 200 mm.

The going per step not less than 212 mm.

The pitch of a *common stairway* must not be more than 38°.

The rise per step not more than 190 mm.

The going per step not less than 225 mm.

The sum of the going of a parellel step plus twice its rise should be not less than *570 mm* and not more than *625 mm* as illustrated on page 162.

Illustrations showing the width of parallel steps, tapered steps, and the notional width of tapered steps (winders) are given at the foot of page 162.

Tapered steps

The regulations state that the least going of tapered steps, or winders, should be not less than 75 mm and that the greatest and least going of consecutive tapered steps must be uniform.

The regulation concerning the going of tapered steps states that the going and pitch of tapered steps shall be measured in the vertical plane of the pitch lines connecting the nosings of consecutive steps at a distance of *265 mm* from the extremities of the width of such steps, and the sum of the going plus twice the rise shall be—

(a) Not less than *572 mm* and (b) not more than *635 mm* (where the angle of taper is 10° or less) or *710 mm* (in any other case).

The interpretation of this regulation is illustrated on page 163. Tapered steps, with an angle on plan of over *20°*, are shown at the top of the page, and steps with an angle on plan of *12°* are shown at the foot of the page.

Notice that the traditional arrangement of three winders on the quarter-turn do not meet the requirements of this regulation.

Two practical applications of the regulation are given on page 164. The first shows a quarter-turn of winders for a private stairway *900 mm* wide, and the second a quarter-turn of winders for a common stairway *1·35 m* wide.

Guarding of stairways

The regulations state that all stairways shall be guarded on each side by a wall, screen, or balustrade, as illustrated on page 165.

Any flight of steps, in a private stairway or common stairway, with an aggregate rise of more than *600 mm*, shall have a continous handrail fixed securely at a height of not less than *840 mm* nor more than *1 m* measured vertically above the pitch lines—

(a) on each side of the stairway, if the least width is *1·07 m* or more; or

(b) on one side of the stairway, in any other case (as illustrated on page 165).

In well-designed stairs the straight flight should not be more than sixteen steps long. To change the direction of the stairs or gain headroom it is necessary to introduce landings or winders.

Landings

Landings may be quarter- or half-space. Examples of the way these landings are used in different stair designs are shown on page 166.

A *quarter-space landing* in a flight of stairs is illustrated at the top of page 166. The landing consists of 15 mm boards jointed together and fixed to 63 × 125 mm joists with buttons. The section A–A gives details of the nosing and buttons.

Two quarter-space landings used in open newel stairs are shown in the middle of page 166. The enlarged detail shows the landing riser, the nosing, the 25 mm tongued-and-grooved boards, and the 63 × 150 mm trimmer into which the three landing joists are framed.

A *half-space landing* used in dog-leg stairs is shown in the next drawing. The plan gives the position of the landing joists, and the enlarged detail shows the riser, nosing, floor boards laid on 12 mm insulating board, the trimmer, and the carriage piece.

Fly landings, illustrated at the foot of page 166, are necessary in straight flights having more than sixteen steps.

Winders

The use of winders as an alternative to landings should be avoided if at all possible. When they are used they should be placed at the bottom of the stairs to reduce the risk of accidents.

All winders must be planned to conform with the 1966 regulations given, in detail, at the beginning of this chapter.

A stairway containing a quarter-turn of four winders is illustrated on page 167 (top). The method of cutting out and building up the winders from 225 to 275 mm boards is also shown. Notice that the grain is parallel to the nosing, and notice too that the allowance for housing into the string.

It is necessary to set out the winders to full size, and also to mark clearly the face of treads and the position of the risers.

A half-turn of eight winders is shown in the second drawing. The enlarged details show the newels, the face of the treads, and the position of the risers. A section of the tread and riser is also shown.

The stairs shown in the next drawing have four winders in the quarter-turn and a circular wall string. The wall string is usually laminated, or veneered, and staved at the back. The marking out of the winders is also shown.

Details of a *geometrical stair* containing eight winders and a circular wall string is shown at the foot of page 167. The enlarged detail shows the circular wreath (twisted) string and the position of the treads and risers.

Balustrades

Balustrades may be classified as open or solid.

Open balustrades usually consist of balusters, which are fixed at the top into a groove in the underside of the handrail, and are housed into the string capping at the bottom. Details of the fixing of the balusters are shown on page 168 (top).

A *panelled balustrade* is shown at the foot of page 168. The framed panelling is grooved into the handrail, and fixed by means of fillets to the capping and newels.

Bottom steps

The bottom step of a flight of stairs is usually finished in a special way with either a bull-nose or a round-end step. The step consists of a tread, rounded at the newel end, a riser which is cut away to a veneer thickness, a block, built up in three thicknesses and shaped to the required curve, and a scotia board which fits underneath the tread.

NOTE   The bent veneered riser is made tight by wedging.

A *bull-nose step* is shown on page 169 (top). Details of the riser cut away to veneer thickness, the built-up block, and the scotia board are given.

A *round-end step* is illustrated in the middle of page 169. Sketches of the riser, built-up block, and the scotia board formed in two pieces are given.

A *large round-end step* is shown at the foot of page 169, with details of the setting out, the shape of the built-up block, and the wedges.

Operations involved in building open newel stairs

The work involves the setting out, the working, the fitting up, and the assembly of all the component parts. These include the strings, treads, risers, newels, handrails, balusters, bull-nose step, and the spandrel framing to the lower flight.

The plan and elevation of the stairs and the dimensions of each member are shown on page 170 (top). An enlarged plan and elevation with a section view of the treads and risers are given at the foot of page 170.

It is necessary to check all the dimensions from the actual building before beginning work on the stairs. The rise from floor to floor and the exact size and shape of the stair well are required. From this information the storey rod can be marked out, showing the position of each tread and the landing. The pitchboard, tread-and-riser sticks, and the margin templet can then be made. The pitchboard and the tread-and-riser sticks may be cut from 6 mm plywood, aluminium or plastic sheet. The templets, especially the pitchboard, must be accurately made.

NOTE   The bull-nose step is the only member which needs to be set out full size.

The *timber-cutting list* consists of six strings, thirteen treads, sixteen risers, three nosings, four newels, one half-newel, four handrails, capping, balusters, and the spandrel framing (the traingular-shaped panelling under the stairs).

It is common practice, in a fully mechanised shop, for the joiner to receive all the timber planed up to size and ready to be marked out for jointing. It is usual to mark out the strings first, and then the treads and risers, newels and handrails.

The *marking out of the strings* is shown on page 171. The wall string and the outer string to the lower flight, which contains seven steps, are shown at the top of page 171. Notice the easings for the skirtings on the wall string, and the tenons at each end of the outer string. The marking out of the strings on the return flight, which contains only two treads, and the marking out of the strings in the top flight, which has four treads, are shown in the next two drawings. For machine working only, one tread and one riser require marking out for tonguing and grooving, and this is shown at the foot of page 171.

The *marking out of the four newels and one half-newel* is given on page 172. Notice the marking out of the mortises for the strings and handrails. The caps, which form the finish to the top of the newels, the floor line, and the pendants or droppers, which finish the lower ends of hanging newels, should also be noted. In this case these are needed for the fourth newel and for the fifth, which is a half-newel. The methods of forming the housings for the steps and working the newel cap are shown at the foot of page 172.

The *marking out of the handrails* from the strings is illustrated on page 173. Notice the allowances made for housing the handrails into the newels.

When all the machining has been completed the *main joints* can be fitted together. These include the joints connecting the strings to the newels and the handrails to the newels.

The method of assembling these is illustrated on page 173 (foot). Note the use of the pitchboard to find the correct angle for the joints.

The making of the *bull-nose step* involves a certain amount of preparatory work before assembly. A plan, front, and isometric view of the step, together with the scotia board and the built-up block, are shown on page 174 (top).

NOTE   The scotia board and block must be accurately made, especially on the curved surfaces.

The riser and block must be assembled very carefully. The method of marking the amount of riser to be cut away is shown on page 174 (middle). The block templet, or the block itself, is rolled on the riser so that the length of riser to be cut to veneer thickness can be measured. To this length must be added the thickness of the folding wedges. Next, the block is glued and screwed to the riser marked A on page 174, and is rolled once more to position B. The wedges are then inserted and the block screwed to the riser. The finished operation is shown on page 174 (foot). The tread may be fixed to the riser with slot screws or by screws inserted through the block.

In high-class work it is usual to assemble the stairs in the shop. The joints between the strings and the newels are temporarily held with draw bore pins so that the spandrel framing and balustrades can be fitted accurately.

The method of marking out and assembling the *spandrel framing* is shown on page 175. The members are held in position for marking out with three gee-cramps. Notice the use of wedges to hold up the shoulders of the halved joints.

When the spandrel framings are large and have numerous panels it is better to rebate the framing to receive the panels, which are then fixed from the back with fillets.

Practice lessons

1 Working from the information given, make neat sketches to explain the following stair-building terms:

  (a) Private and common stairways.
  (b) Parallel and tapered steps.
  (c) Pitch line.
  (d) Notional width.

2 Set out a quarter-turn of winders from the following particulars (scale 1:20):

  Rise per step 200 mm
  Going per step 225 mm
  Notional width 900 mm.

3 *(a)* Set out a workshop rod for the first three steps of the open newel stairs illustrated on page 170, showing a panelled balustrade, newel, and bull-nose step.
  (b) Make all the necessary templets for making the stairs.

4 *(a)* From the material supplied, carry out all the operations involved in making the newel, steps, strings, and handrail.
  (b) Carry out all the operations involved in making the bull-nose step.
  (c) Carry out all the operations involved in making the spandrel framing.
  (d) Assemble, and finish, the stair units.

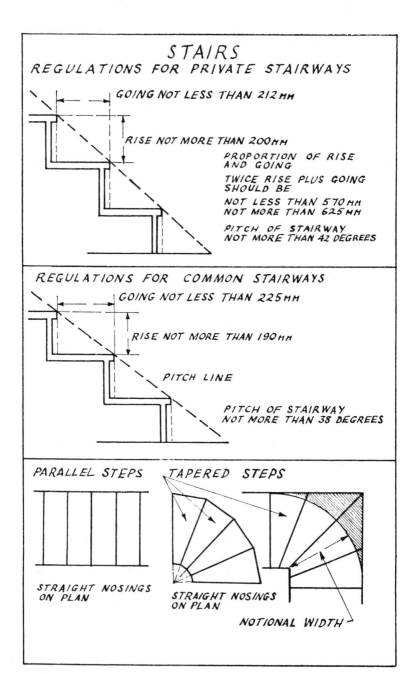

STAIRS
REGULATIONS FOR PRIVATE STAIRWAYS

GOING NOT LESS THAN 212 MM

RISE NOT MORE THAN 200MM

PROPORTION OF RISE AND GOING

TWICE RISE PLUS GOING SHOULD BE

NOT LESS THAN 570 MM
NOT MORE THAN 625 MM

PITCH OF STAIRWAY NOT MORE THAN 42 DEGREES

REGULATIONS FOR COMMON STAIRWAYS

GOING NOT LESS THAN 225 MM

RISE NOT MORE THAN 190 MM

PITCH LINE

PITCH OF STAIRWAY NOT MORE THAN 38 DEGREES

PARALLEL STEPS   TAPERED STEPS

STRAIGHT NOSINGS ON PLAN

STRAIGHT NOSINGS ON PLAN

NOTIONAL WIDTH

162

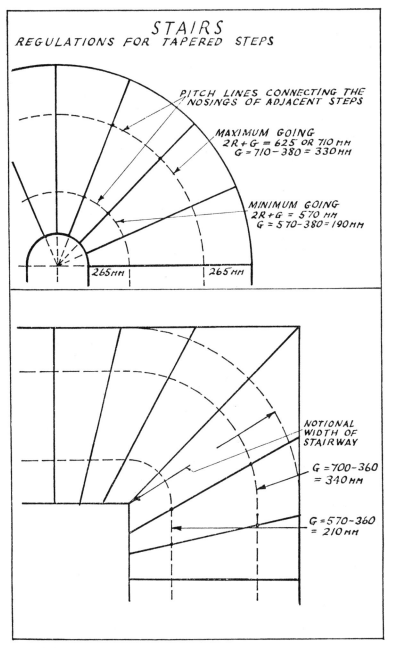

STAIRS
REGULATIONS FOR TAPERED STEPS

PITCH LINES CONNECTING THE
NOSINGS OF ADJACENT STEPS

MAXIMUM GOING
2R + G = 625 OR 710 MM
G = 710 - 380 = 330 MM

MINIMUM GOING
2R + G = 570 MM
G = 570 - 380 = 190 MM

265 MM | 265 MM

NOTIONAL
WIDTH OF
STAIRWAY

G = 700 - 360
= 340 MM

G = 570 - 360
= 210 MM

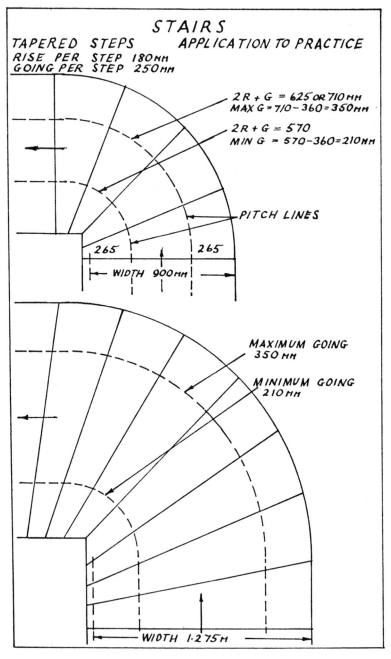

STAIRS

TAPERED STEPS **APPLICATION TO PRACTICE**

RISE PER STEP 180mm
GOING PER STEP 250mm

2R + G = 625 OR 710mm
MAX G = 710 − 360 = 350mm

2R + G = 570
MIN G = 570 − 360 = 210mm

PITCH LINES

265   265

WIDTH 900mm

MAXIMUM GOING
350mm

MINIMUM GOING
210mm

WIDTH 1·275m

STAIRS
GUARDING OF STAIRWAYS

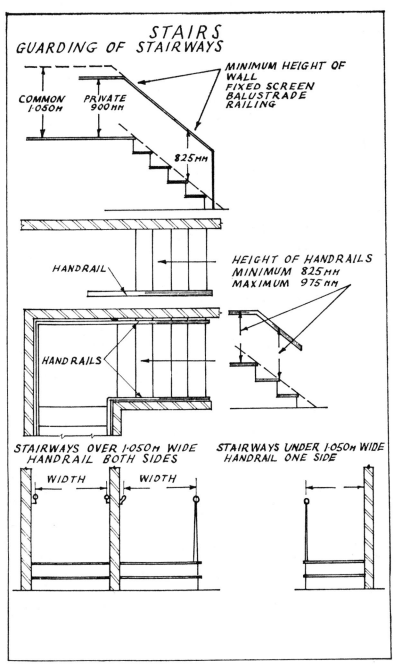

MINIMUM HEIGHT OF
WALL
FIXED SCREEN
BALUSTRADE
RAILING

COMMON
1·050M

PRIVATE
900MM

825MM

HANDRAIL

HEIGHT OF HANDRAILS
MINIMUM 825MM
MAXIMUM 975MM

HANDRAILS

STAIRWAYS OVER 1·050M WIDE
HANDRAIL BOTH SIDES

WIDTH   WIDTH

STAIRWAYS UNDER 1·050M WIDE
HANDRAIL ONE SIDE

STAIRS

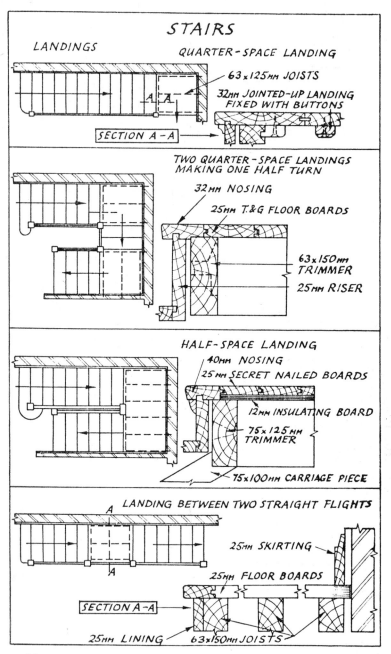

LANDINGS

QUARTER-SPACE LANDING

63 × 125ʜʜ JOISTS

32ʜʜ JOINTED-UP LANDING FIXED WITH BUTTONS

SECTION A-A

TWO QUARTER-SPACE LANDINGS MAKING ONE HALF TURN

32ʜʜ NOSING

25ʜʜ T.&G FLOOR BOARDS

63 × 150ʜʜ TRIMMER

25ʜʜ RISER

HALF-SPACE LANDING

40ʜʜ NOSING

25ʜʜ SECRET NAILED BOARDS

12ʜʜ INSULATING BOARD

75 × 125ʜʜ TRIMMER

75 × 100ʜʜ CARRIAGE PIECE

LANDING BETWEEN TWO STRAIGHT FLIGHTS

25ʜʜ SKIRTING

25ʜʜ FLOOR BOARDS

SECTION A-A

25ʜʜ LINING

63 × 150ʜʜ JOISTS

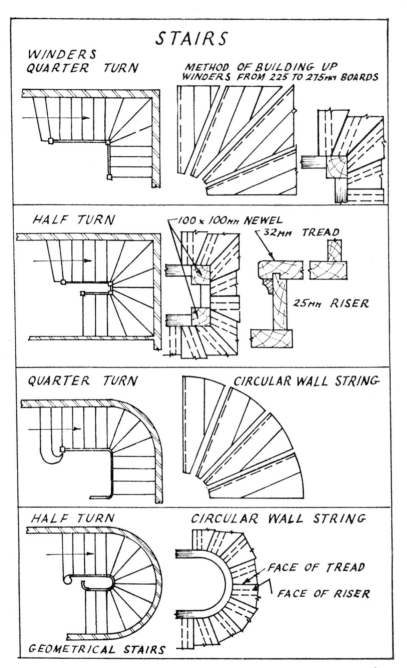

STAIRS

WINDERS
QUARTER TURN

METHOD OF BUILDING UP
WINDERS FROM 225 TO 275mm BOARDS

HALF TURN

100 x 100mm NEWEL

32mm TREAD

25mm RISER

QUARTER TURN

CIRCULAR WALL STRING

HALF TURN

CIRCULAR WALL STRING

FACE OF TREAD

FACE OF RISER

GEOMETRICAL STAIRS

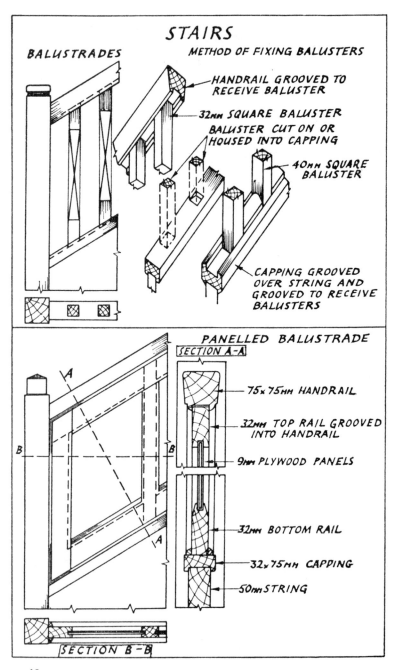

STAIRS

BALUSTRADES

METHOD OF FIXING BALUSTERS

HANDRAIL GROOVED TO RECEIVE BALUSTER

32мм SQUARE BALUSTER

BALUSTER CUT ON OR HOUSED INTO CAPPING

40мм SQUARE BALUSTER

CAPPING GROOVED OVER STRING AND GROOVED TO RECEIVE BALUSTERS

PANELLED BALUSTRADE

SECTION A-A

75 x 75мм HANDRAIL

32мм TOP RAIL GROOVED INTO HANDRAIL

9мм PLYWOOD PANELS

32мм BOTTOM RAIL

32 x 75мм CAPPING

50мм STRING

SECTION B-B

STAIRS

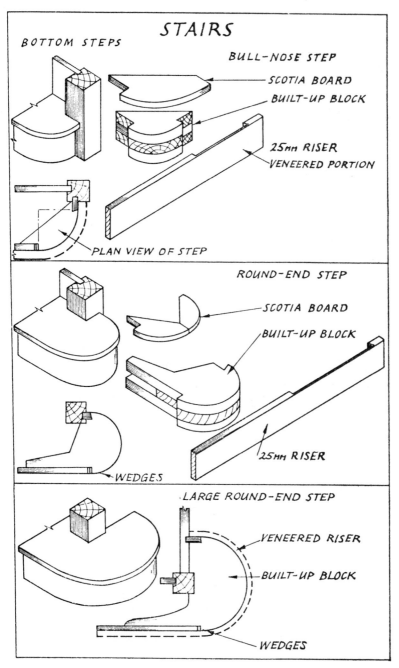

BOTTOM STEPS

BULL-NOSE STEP

— SCOTIA BOARD

— BUILT-UP BLOCK

25mm RISER
VENEERED PORTION

PLAN VIEW OF STEP

ROUND-END STEP

— SCOTIA BOARD

— BUILT-UP BLOCK

25mm RISER

WEDGES

LARGE ROUND-END STEP

VENEERED RISER

BUILT-UP BLOCK

WEDGES

STAIRS

OPEN NEWEL STAIRS

MEMBER SIZES
32mm TREADS
25mm RISERS
40mm WALL STRINGS
50mm OUTER STRINGS
40x75mm CAPPINGS
75x75mm HANDRAILS
100x100mm NEWELS
25x50mm BALUSTERS
32mm SPANDREL FRAMING

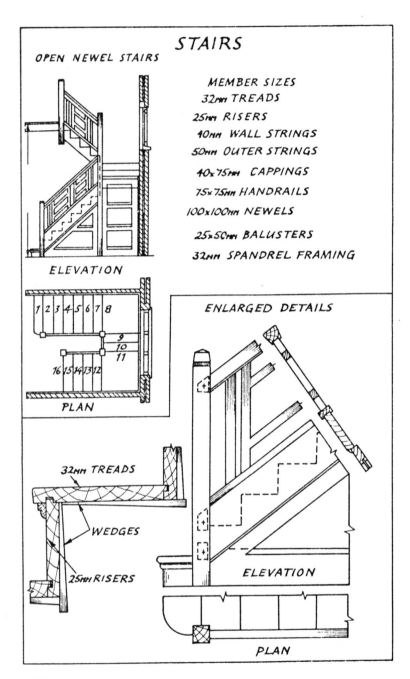

ELEVATION

PLAN

ENLARGED DETAILS

32mm TREADS

WEDGES

25mm RISERS

ELEVATION

PLAN

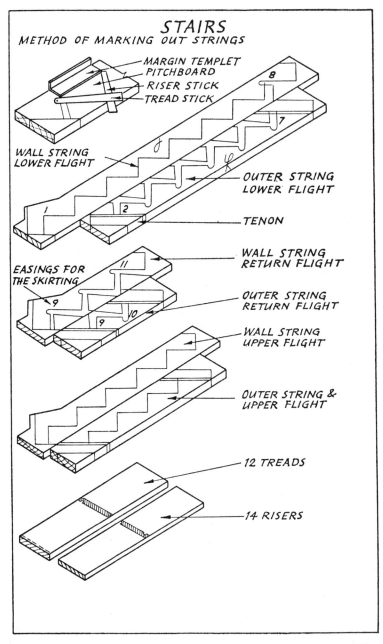

STAIRS
METHOD OF MARKING OUT STRINGS

MARGIN TEMPLET
PITCHBOARD
RISER STICK
TREAD STICK

WALL STRING
LOWER FLIGHT

OUTER STRING
LOWER FLIGHT

TENON

WALL STRING
RETURN FLIGHT

EASINGS FOR
THE SKIRTING

OUTER STRING
RETURN FLIGHT

WALL STRING
UPPER FLIGHT

OUTER STRING &
UPPER FLIGHT

12 TREADS

14 RISERS

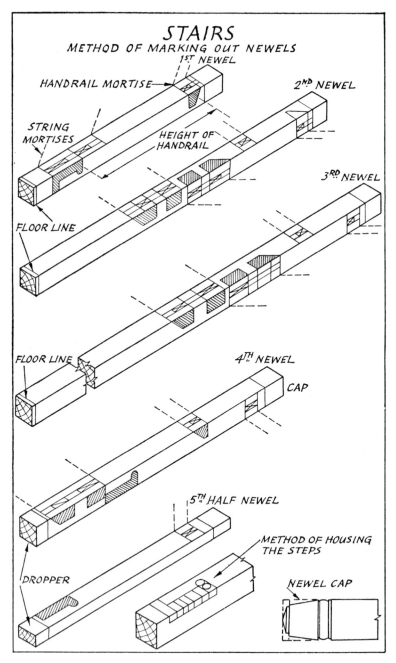

STAIRS
METHOD OF MARKING OUT NEWELS

1ST NEWEL

HANDRAIL MORTISE

2ND NEWEL

STRING MORTISES

HEIGHT OF HANDRAIL

3RD NEWEL

FLOOR LINE

FLOOR LINE

4TH NEWEL

CAP

5TH HALF NEWEL

METHOD OF HOUSING THE STEPS

NEWEL CAP

DROPPER

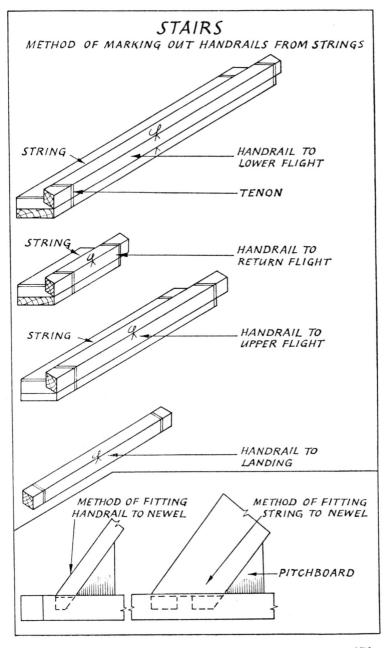

STAIRS
METHOD OF MARKING OUT HANDRAILS FROM STRINGS

STRING

HANDRAIL TO
LOWER FLIGHT

TENON

STRING

HANDRAIL TO
RETURN FLIGHT

STRING

HANDRAIL TO
UPPER FLIGHT

HANDRAIL TO
LANDING

METHOD OF FITTING
HANDRAIL TO NEWEL

METHOD OF FITTING
STRING TO NEWEL

PITCHBOARD

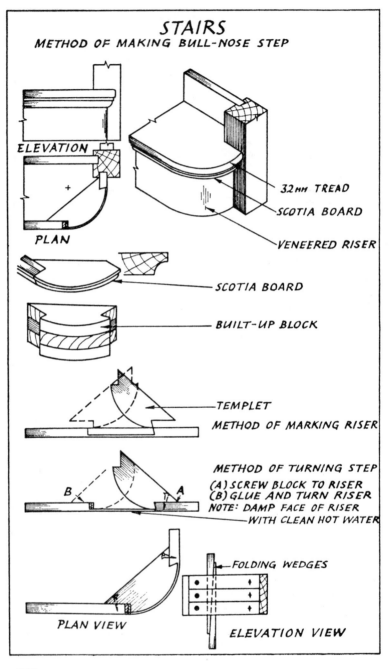

STAIRS
METHOD OF MAKING BULL-NOSE STEP

ELEVATION

PLAN

32 MM TREAD

SCOTIA BOARD

VENEERED RISER

SCOTIA BOARD

BUILT-UP BLOCK

TEMPLET

METHOD OF MARKING RISER

METHOD OF TURNING STEP
(A) SCREW BLOCK TO RISER
(B) GLUE AND TURN RISER
NOTE: DAMP FACE OF RISER
WITH CLEAN HOT WATER

B   A

FOLDING WEDGES

PLAN VIEW

ELEVATION VIEW

174

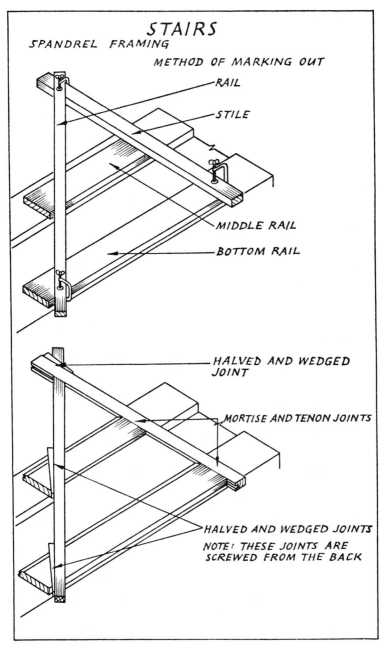

STAIRS
SPANDREL FRAMING

METHOD OF MARKING OUT

RAIL

STILE

MIDDLE RAIL

BOTTOM RAIL

HALVED AND WEDGED JOINT

MORTISE AND TENON JOINTS

HALVED AND WEDGED JOINTS

NOTE: THESE JOINTS ARE SCREWED FROM THE BACK

Internal fittings are of two main types: built-in fittings and unit fitments.

Three methods of construction are used: framed-and-panelled construction, hollow-frame flush construction, and solid-core flush construction.

Built-in fittings

Built-in fittings include all permanent fixtures, such as cupboards and wardrobes, built into recesses.

A typical *built-in cupboard* of traditional design is illustrated on page 179 (top). The cupboard fits into an alcove and has two pairs of doors and two drawers. Six shelves, supported on bearers firmly fixed to the wall, provide the storage space. The drawing shows a plan, the front elevation, and a section view of the cupboard. The enlarged details give the section shape of the main members.

A *built-in wardrobe* of modern design is given at the foot of page 179. The frame is made of solid timber, and the doors are of blockboard 25 mm thick. The scale drawings show a plan, the front elevation, and a section view of the wardrobe. The enlarged details show the section sizes of the frame members and the blockboard doors. Notice the special shape of the frame sill, which makes cleaning easy.

It is usual in the smaller workshops to cut the door panels from stock-size blockboards, but in workshops equipped with suitable presses the blockboard panels can be made to suit the door size. This results in a considerable saving in production costs.

Unit fitments

Unit fitments include cabinets, cupboards, and dressers made as detachable units. They are of two main types—those made as pieces of furniture, such as kitchen cabinets, dressers, bathroom fittings, etc., and those fittings made as units but fixed permanently, such as modern kitchen fittings and shop and office fittings.

A plan, elevation, and section view of a *kitchen dresser* fitted into the corner of a room are shown on page 180 (top). The enlarged vertical and horizontal sections give details of the shelves, the doors, and the solid sides.

The *kitchen cupboards* illustrated at the foot of page 180 are of modern design. The floor fitting consists of four drawers and one cupboard. The wall fitting has two shelves and a pair of doors. The fitting has a skeleton frame construction, with a 6 mm plywood facing. The drawings show the plan, elevation, and section views of each fitting, together with enlarged details of the doors and drawers.

The production of fitments for a wide range of purposes has now become a highly developed industry. Many firms, indeed, produce catalogues of their unit furniture, and it is completely finished and ready for use.

Examples of such modern kitchen fitments are illustrated on page 181. Sink units, wall cupboards, and storage fitments are shown.

Modern bedroom fitments (wardrobes) are shown on page 182.

Practice lessons

1 Working from the information given:

    (a) Draw to a 1:20 scale the plan and elevation of the built-in fitting illustrated on page 179.

    (b) Draw (full size) the section details of the blockboard doors and framing.

2 *(a)* Set out a workshop rod for part of the drawer fitting illustrated at the foot of page 180.

    (b) Prepare a cutting list for one drawer, two stiles, and two rails of the carcase to contain the drawer.

    (c) From the prepared material supplied, make the carcase, and fit the drawer front into its opening.

    (d) Using a dovetailed method of construction, carry out all the operations involved in making and finishing the drawer.

INTERNAL FITTINGS

BUILT-IN CUPBOARDS

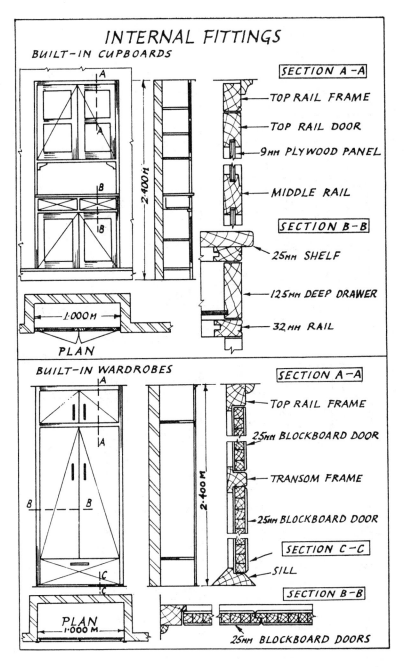

SECTION A-A

TOP RAIL FRAME

TOP RAIL DOOR

9 MM PLYWOOD PANEL

MIDDLE RAIL

SECTION B-B

25 MM SHELF

125 MM DEEP DRAWER

32 MM RAIL

2·400 M

1·000 M

PLAN

BUILT-IN WARDROBES

SECTION A-A

TOP RAIL FRAME

25 MM BLOCKBOARD DOOR

TRANSOM FRAME

25 MM BLOCKBOARD DOOR

SECTION C-C

SILL

SECTION B-B

25 MM BLOCKBOARD DOORS

2·400 M

PLAN
1·000 M

INTERNAL FITTINGS

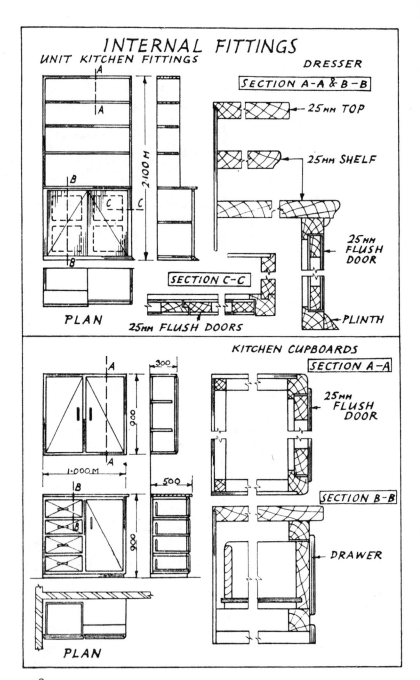

UNIT KITCHEN FITTINGS

DRESSER

SECTION A-A & B-B

25mm TOP

25mm SHELF

25mm FLUSH DOOR

PLINTH

2100 H

B

C

PLAN

SECTION C-C

25mm FLUSH DOORS

KITCHEN CUPBOARDS

SECTION A-A

25mm FLUSH DOOR

SECTION B-B

DRAWER

300

900

1.000 M

500

900

PLAN

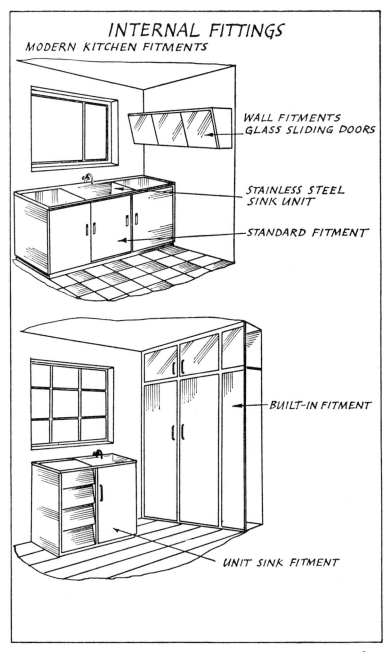

INTERNAL FITTINGS

MODERN KITCHEN FITMENTS

WALL FITMENTS
GLASS SLIDING DOORS

STAINLESS STEEL
SINK UNIT

STANDARD FITMENT

BUILT-IN FITMENT

UNIT SINK FITMENT

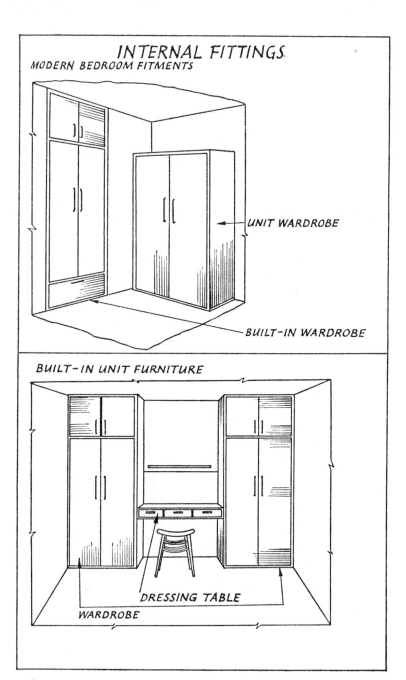

INTERNAL FITTINGS

MODERN BEDROOM FITMENTS

UNIT WARDROBE

BUILT-IN WARDROBE

BUILT-IN UNIT FURNITURE

DRESSING TABLE

WARDROBE

Centres are wood structures which are used as temporary supports for arches during the construction. Arches are constructed mainly in brickwork, masonry, or concrete, and they may be flat, segmented, or semicircular in shape. These forms are illustrated on page 187.

Centres consist of one or more ribs which support laggings. *Laggings* are cut to a length equal to the thickness of the wall. The type of lagging used depends on the size of the arch bricks and the thickness of the mortar joints. Small arch bricks with wide mortar joints require solid laggings. Masonry arch stones need at least two laggings for support, and folding, or easing, wedges for the setting of heavy stones. Details of the laggings needed on centres for both brick and masonry arches are given on page 188.

The centres are supported on vertical props. Folding wedges are necessary to permit a slight vertical adjustment of levels. The wedges also allow the centre to be eased, or lowered, and then removed. This operation is called *easing* and *striking*.

The shape and construction of the centre is governed by the shape and size of the arch to be supported.

Centres for small arches

A *flat arch* needs only a turning piece. Elevation and vertical section views of a solid turning piece supporting a flat arch are shown on page 189 (top).

A *segmental arch* of 50 mm rise or less may need only a turning piece, but most will require a centre consisting of two curved ribs to span the width of the opening, and to which laggings are nailed. Details of a segmental centre with 25 mm ribs, 19 × 32 mm lagging, and 50 × 175 mm props are shown in the middle of the page. Notice the slow-driving folding wedges.

A *small semicircular arch* is supported on a centre consisting of two built-up ribs which are prevented from spreading by the introduction of a tie. The laggings are made of 19 × 32 mm laths or plywood. The centre is supported on 50 × 175 mm props. This is shown at the foot of the page.

A *bull's-eye window* in brickwork, with a centre identical in size and shape to that of the semicircular arch just dealt with, is shown on page 191 (top). Notice that two independent centres are used: one to support the relieving arch and the other for the face brick-work.

Centres for large arches

Braced or trussed centres are needed for arches with a span greater than 1·2 m.

A *semicircular centre* of 2·4 m span is given on page 190 (top). The centre consists of two built-up braced ribs with laggings securely nailed to their curved edges. The centre is supported on 75 × 100 mm props.

A *semi-elliptical arch and centre* are illustrated in the middle of the page. The construction is identical to that for the semicircular centre above.

A four-centre arch in 350 mm brickwork is shown at the foot of the page. The centre for this is similar in construction to the other centres, but the laggings are made of two layers of plywood.

A *semicircular masonry arch and centre* are shown on page 191 (foot). Notice that in this case the built-in door frame acts as a centre for the relieving arch.

Operations involved in making centres

It is necessary to set out all centres accurately and to full size. The marking out of a solid turning piece is given on page 192 (top). Notice how a radius rod and a bradawl are used for marking out the curve. The second drawing shows the setting out of a segmental centre. The method of setting out the turning pieces for sawing is shown in the middle of the page. With the pieces marked out as shown, they can be cut on a band saw with the minimum amount of waste. The setting out of the ribs for a segmental centre is also given on page 192.

The drawing at the foot of the page shows a complete segmental centre supported on 50 × 175 mm props. Notice that the easing wedges are slow-driving and do not taper right down to a point. This saves the end of the wedge from being crushed as it is slackened. The method of spacing out the laggings with a spacing piece is also shown.

The setting out and making of a *semicircular centre* is shown on page 193. The outline of the arch is drawn with the aid of a radius rod, and the proper position and size of the ribs and the tie are found. Each braced or main rib of the centre is built up of two layers. The first layer, shown in the second drawing, is made up of a tie and five segments (three ribs and two half-ribs). The second layer consists of four segments of approximately equal length which are butt-jointed to form the whole rib. The two layers should be securely nailed together and then the struts and the vertical tie added. The top end of these members should be nailed to the first layer of ribs, and the bottom end nailed to the tie. The centre is completed by adding the lagging and bearers.

Details of the supports are given at the foot of the page, where are shown the laggings, bearers, easing wedges, and the props.

Material used for centres

European softwood, in standard sizes, is extensively used for centering, but any inexpensive timber is suitable provided it is sound. 75 × 150 to 100 × 225 mm deals are required for the solid turning pieces; 25 × 150, 175 or 225 mm for the ribs of segmental centres, and 19 × 150 to 25 × 225 mm for semicircular centres up to 2·4 m in span.

Practice lessons

1 Working from the information given:
   (a) Draw to a 1:20 scale the elevation and section view of a centre to support a segmental arch in 225 mm brickwork. Span 900 mm.
   (b) Make neat sketches to show the types of laggings that are used to support brick and stonework arches

2 *(a)* Set out a workshop rod for a centre to support a semicircular arch in brickwork 225 mm thick. Span 900 mm.
   (b) From suitable materials, carry out all the operations involved in making the two ribs of the centre.
   (c) Complete the construction of the centre by adding the laggings and bearers.
   (d) Set up the centre in the brickwork opening, to enable the bricklayer to build the arch.

CENTERING

BRICK ARCHES

FLAT OR SEGMENTAL ARCH

PRE-CAST R.C. LINTEL

BUILT-IN JOINERY WORK

BRICK FACINGS

SOLID TURNING PIECE

SEGMENTAL CENTRE

SEMICIRCULAR OR
SEMI-ELLIPTICAL ARCH

TWO-RING RELIEVING ARCH
CENTRE BUILT UP OF TWO
RIBS AND LAGGINGS

BRICK FACINGS

CENTRE FORMED
WITH ONE RIB AND
PLYWOOD OR FIBRE-
BOARD LAGGING

STONE ARCHES

SEGMENTAL SEMICIRCULAR
OR ELLIPTICAL ARCHES

BUILT-IN JOINERY WORK

BRICK RELIEVING ARCH
STONE FACINGS

CENTRE BUILT
UP OF TWO
RIBS AND
LAGGINGS

187

CENTERING

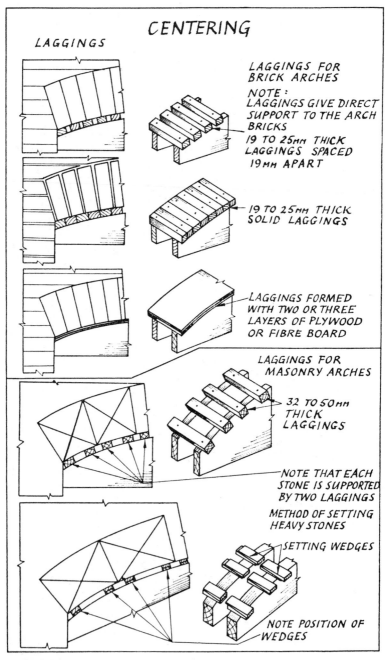

LAGGINGS

LAGGINGS FOR BRICK ARCHES

NOTE:
LAGGINGS GIVE DIRECT SUPPORT TO THE ARCH BRICKS

19 TO 25mm THICK LAGGINGS SPACED 19mm APART

19 TO 25mm THICK SOLID LAGGINGS

LAGGINGS FORMED WITH TWO OR THREE LAYERS OF PLYWOOD OR FIBRE BOARD

LAGGINGS FOR MASONRY ARCHES

32 TO 50mm THICK LAGGINGS

NOTE THAT EACH STONE IS SUPPORTED BY TWO LAGGINGS

METHOD OF SETTING HEAVY STONES

SETTING WEDGES

NOTE POSITION OF WEDGES

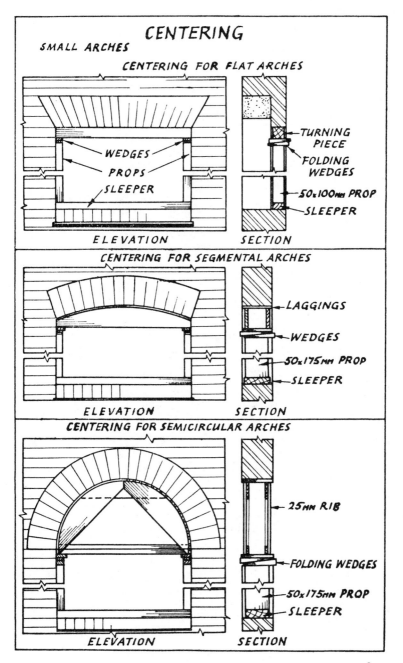

CENTERING

SMALL ARCHES

CENTERING FOR FLAT ARCHES

WEDGES
PROPS
SLEEPER

ELEVATION

TURNING PIECE
FOLDING WEDGES
50x100mm PROP
SLEEPER

SECTION

CENTERING FOR SEGMENTAL ARCHES

LAGGINGS
WEDGES
50x175mm PROP
SLEEPER

ELEVATION

SECTION

CENTERING FOR SEMICIRCULAR ARCHES

25mm RIB
FOLDING WEDGES
50x175mm PROP
SLEEPER

ELEVATION

SECTION

189

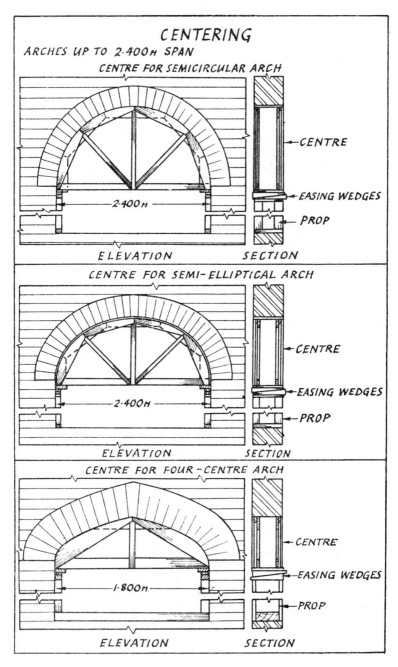

CENTERING

ARCHES UP TO 2·400m SPAN

CENTRE FOR SEMICIRCULAR ARCH

2·400 m

ELEVATION

SECTION

CENTRE

EASING WEDGES

PROP

CENTRE FOR SEMI-ELLIPTICAL ARCH

2·400 m

ELEVATION

SECTION

CENTRE

EASING WEDGES

PROP

CENTRE FOR FOUR-CENTRE ARCH

1·800 m

ELEVATION

SECTION

CENTRE

EASING WEDGES

PROP

CENTERING

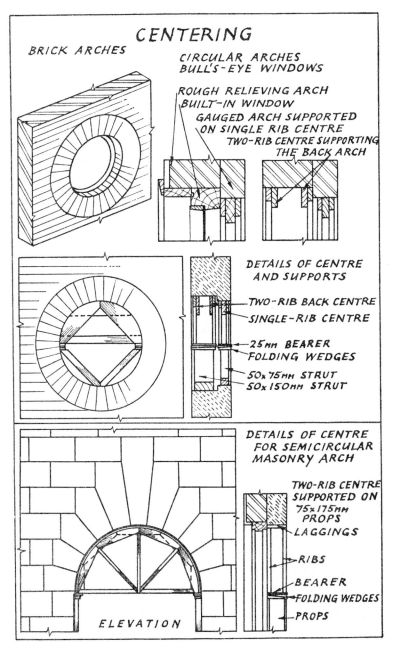

BRICK ARCHES

CIRCULAR ARCHES
BULL'S-EYE WINDOWS

ROUGH RELIEVING ARCH
BUILT-IN WINDOW
GAUGED ARCH SUPPORTED
ON SINGLE RIB CENTRE
TWO-RIB CENTRE SUPPORTING
THE BACK ARCH

DETAILS OF CENTRE
AND SUPPORTS

TWO-RIB BACK CENTRE
SINGLE-RIB CENTRE

25mm BEARER
FOLDING WEDGES

50 x 75mm STRUT
50 x 150mm STRUT

DETAILS OF CENTRE
FOR SEMICIRCULAR
MASONRY ARCH

TWO-RIB CENTRE
SUPPORTED ON
75 x 175mm
PROPS
LAGGINGS

RIBS

BEARER
FOLDING WEDGES
PROPS

ELEVATION

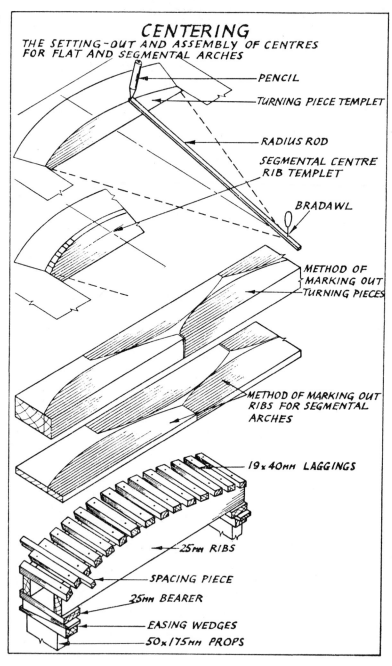

CENTERING

THE SETTING-OUT AND ASSEMBLY OF CENTRES
FOR FLAT AND SEGMENTAL ARCHES

PENCIL

TURNING PIECE TEMPLET

RADIUS ROD

SEGMENTAL CENTRE RIB TEMPLET

BRADAWL

METHOD OF MARKING OUT TURNING PIECES

METHOD OF MARKING OUT RIBS FOR SEGMENTAL ARCHES

19 x 40mm LAGGINGS

25mm RIBS

SPACING PIECE

25mm BEARER

EASING WEDGES

50 x 175mm PROPS

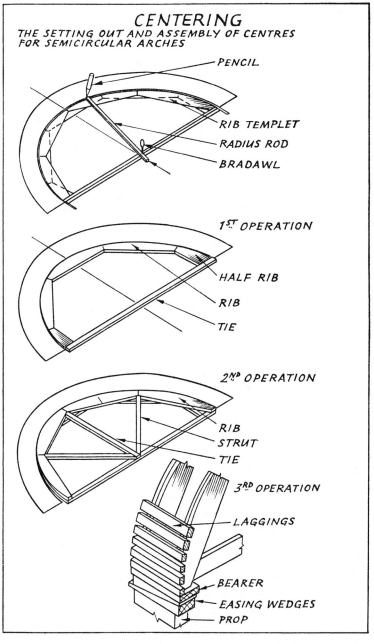

CENTERING

THE SETTING OUT AND ASSEMBLY OF CENTRES FOR SEMICIRCULAR ARCHES

PENCIL

RIB TEMPLET
RADIUS ROD
BRADAWL

1ST OPERATION

HALF RIB
RIB
TIE

2ND OPERATION

RIB
STRUT
TIE

3RD OPERATION

LAGGINGS

BEARER
EASING WEDGES
PROP

The design and construction of formwork for reinforced concrete structures was briefly dealt with in *Carpentry and Joinery : Book 1*. Beams cast *in situ* and floor slabs were discussed, and an account given of the various types of materials used for shuttering and their surface finishes. The following chapter deals more fully with this complex subject.

Over the past twenty-five years there have been great changes in the design and methods of construction for reinforced concrete buildings. As a result, new ideas and techniques have had to be introduced for formwork to enable it to cope with the demands made on it. Its function, however, remains the same—to provide moulds of the desired shape into which the wet concrete can be poured and left to set. It is essential that they should remain rigid and stable until the concrete has thoroughly hardened.

Common faults in formwork

Formwork is subjected to pressures from two distinct sources—dead loads and live or constructional loads. *Dead loads* are the result of the weight of the wet concrete and its steel reinforcement; while *live loads* are caused by the movement of workmen and equipment as the concrete is poured into position. They include the weight of hoisting equipment, conveyors, chutes, runways and vibrating equipment.

The *intensity of pressure* in the wet concrete increases with its thickness or depth, and the points of maximum pressure occur at the bases of walls, beams, and columns. Badly designed formwork will tend to become very distorted at these points of failure, and this may cause them to collapse.

Concrete foundation work includes stanchions, bases and footings, and can be relatively large. It is important that the formwork should be stable enough to hold the concrete until it has set properly. Diagrams indicating various situations where formwork may fail because it is not sufficiently strong are given on page 200.

The first illustration shows how thin profiles supported on widely spaced stakes will tend to bulge under the lateral, or sideways, pressure exerted by the wet concrete.

The diagram in the middle of the page shows the formwork to a retaining wall. As you will see, the concrete exerts its maximum pressure on the formwork at its base. Because the form is badly anchored and is not supported by enough struts, it has lifted and bulged so that the concrete is able to escape at the foot of the wall.

At the foot of page 200 is shown how structural faults in the formwork may cause a box mould to a stanchion base to fail.

The illustrations on page 201 indicate other common situations where instability may cause formwork to fail. The first drawing shows formwork for a *suspended floor*. This may have to carry a dead load—the weight of the wet concrete and its steel reinforcement—of up to 1000 kg/m² super, in addition to the constructional loads. It is vital that it should be able to do this and still remain rigid, since the whole of the floor decking must remain stable and flat throughout the casting operation. Its stability is often impaired because the shuttering used is too thin, the decking timbers (joists) too small, and the supports for these too widely spaced. These faults and their consequences are all shown at the top of page 201.

The form for a *large column* may fail because of the intense pressure at its base. It must be very securely anchored to prevent it from lifting and, allowing the wet concrete to escape (see the foot of page 201). In addition, it must be held together along its length by yokes: and if these are too widely spaced, bulging may occur. The same is true of formwork for beams.

Formwork for columns

Two important factors have to be considered when formwork for columns is being designed—the size of the section and the length.

The drawing at the top of page 202 shows a column form, which can be up to 2·7 m long: the wet concrete can be poured in from the top and consolidated with a vibrator. All four sides can be prefabricated and set up in position as shown.

Forms for columns longer than 2·7 m, however, cannot be filled from the top because it is difficult to place and consolidate the wet concrete satisfactorily. For this reason, three sides of the form are set up in position, and the fourth added in single boards as the concrete is being poured in. Details of this type of column form are given at the foot of page 202.

Column clamps or *yokes* should be made up of interchangeable components which are easy to dismantle or set up in position on the form. Two types are illustrated on page 203.

The traditional type of clamp shown in the pictorial view at the top of page 203 is already in position. An enlarged detail is also given of the threaded rod, with its washers and wing nuts.

A modern type of metal column clamp is illustrated at the foot of the page. The clamps are again shown in position on the column form, and there is also an enlarged view of the corner and the wedge device which is used to tighten up the form.

Formwork for walls

Details of the formwork required for a reinforced concrete wall 225 mm thick are given at the top of page 204. The shuttering consists of horizontal boarding 32 mm thick, which is formed into panels with 50 × 100 mm verticals spaced at centres of 450 to 600 mm.

The oblique sectional view shows the shuttering firmly fixed to the kicker wall, and the positions and sizes of the walings, struts, runners, and pegs. An enlarged detail which shows the way the panels are connected together is given in the middle of page 204.

Details of the formwork to a reinforced concrete string course cast *in situ* are given at the foot of page 204. The pictorial view shows the constructional details for the framed brackets, props and shuttering, and a sectional view of the string course is also given.

Formwork for cavity walls

Concrete cavity walls can be constructed as two separate walls, and the details of the formwork that will be required are given at the foot of page 205. Here, both inner and outer walls are 225 mm thick, and the cavity between them is 100 mm wide. The walls are cast in 1·2 m lifts, and three lifts of the inner wall must be completed before work can start on the outer wall.

A system of *climbing formwork* is used for this construction. The formwork to the inner wall is identical on both faces, but this is not so for the outer wall: steel shuttering is used in the cavity and timber shuttering on the face side. 18 mm rod ties are used to secure the form, and both ties and timber components are interchangeable.

The sectional view of the wall on page 205 shows the formwork in position, and the elevations give the sizes and distances apart of the timbers.

Trofdek plywood shutter panels can be used for wall formwork as shown on page 205. A pictorial view of the corner of a wall is given with the shutter panels set vertically and supported by rod wall ties. A sectional view of the 1·2 m wide shutter panel is also shown, together with an enlarged detail of the 400 mm trough.

Beam formwork: clamps and brackets

The traditional clamps and brackets used to hold together timber formwork for beams are now being superseded by metal varieties which can be adjusted by means of screws. Two examples of the modern clamp are illustrated on page 206.

At the top of page 206 is illustrated a *synchronised, screw-type clamp* which is used for large beams.

A *light-weight clamp* for beams up to 600 mm wide is shown in the middle of page 206.

A modern type of *hanger* for beam formwork is shown at the foot of page 206: this is one of a wide range of accessories available from the manufacturers of metal formwork.

Many of the modern hangers and wall ties are designed in two parts. The first is the inner section, which is embedded in the concrete and becomes a permanent part of the structure. The other part is made up of the standard screw fittings which support the formwork: as you will realise, these are withdrawn when the formwork is stripped.

Floor centres

Three typical examples of floor centring are given on page 207. The illustration at the top of the page shows the traditional style of work, where the floor slab decking and the beam formwork are supported on timber hangers. This method has now been superseded by more practical systems.

The *patent telescopic centres* shown in the middle of page 207 are extensively used in modern building practice. The beams are supported at each end by the top flange of the main floor beams, and are spaced out to receive standard-sized steel shuttering panels.

The *patent forms of panels* illustrated at the foot of page 207 consist of three basic parts:

1   A standard-sized channel-section steel frame with a reversible plywood top
2   An H-section support beam
3   An adjustable prop.

This system of formwork is simple in design, the components are automatically located, and it can be stripped with ease.

Practice lessons

1 Working from the information given:

   (a) Make neat diagrams to illustrate the pressure of wet concrete on—
      (i) Foundation formwork
      (ii) Beam formwork
      (iii) Column formwork.
   (b) Explain the need for the good anchorage of column formwork.

2 *(a)* Make neat isometric drawings to show the construction of—
      (i) A short column form
      (ii) A long column form.
   (b) Make neat sketches of two types of column clamps.

3 *(a)* Draw, to any convenient scale, details of the wall formwork illustrated on page 204.
   (b) Make neat sketches to explain the following terms:
      (i) Kicker wall.
      (ii) Telescopic centres.
      (iii) Panel forms.
      (iv) Adjustable props.

FORMWORK

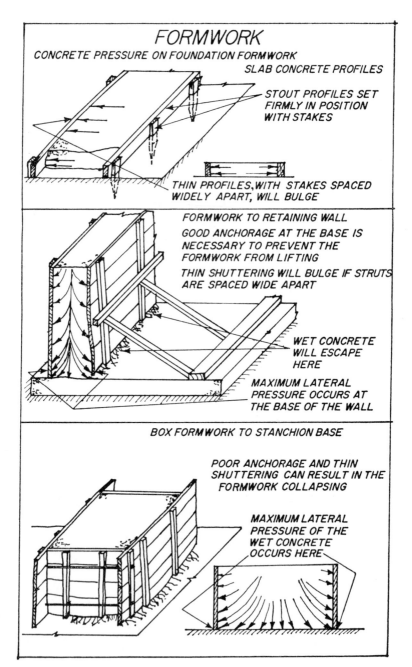

CONCRETE PRESSURE ON FOUNDATION FORMWORK

SLAB CONCRETE PROFILES

STOUT PROFILES SET FIRMLY IN POSITION WITH STAKES

THIN PROFILES, WITH STAKES SPACED WIDELY APART, WILL BULGE

FORMWORK TO RETAINING WALL

GOOD ANCHORAGE AT THE BASE IS NECESSARY TO PREVENT THE FORMWORK FROM LIFTING

THIN SHUTTERING WILL BULGE IF STRUTS ARE SPACED WIDE APART

WET CONCRETE WILL ESCAPE HERE

MAXIMUM LATERAL PRESSURE OCCURS AT THE BASE OF THE WALL

BOX FORMWORK TO STANCHION BASE

POOR ANCHORAGE AND THIN SHUTTERING CAN RESULT IN THE FORMWORK COLLAPSING

MAXIMUM LATERAL PRESSURE OF THE WET CONCRETE OCCURS HERE

FORMWORK

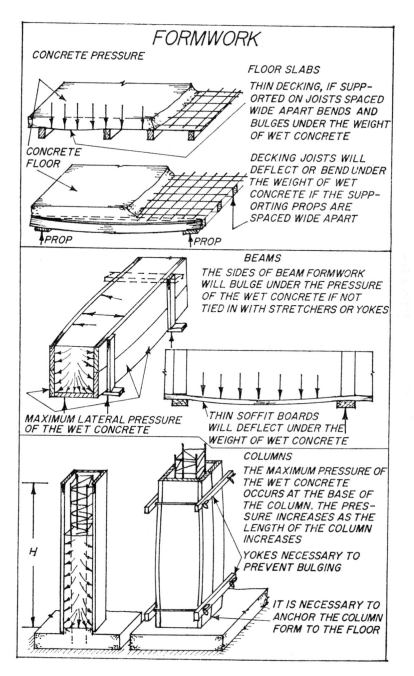

CONCRETE PRESSURE

FLOOR SLABS

THIN DECKING, IF SUPPORTED ON JOISTS SPACED WIDE APART BENDS AND BULGES UNDER THE WEIGHT OF WET CONCRETE

CONCRETE FLOOR

DECKING JOISTS WILL DEFLECT OR BEND UNDER THE WEIGHT OF WET CONCRETE IF THE SUPPORTING PROPS ARE SPACED WIDE APART

PROP   PROP

BEAMS

THE SIDES OF BEAM FORMWORK WILL BULGE UNDER THE PRESSURE OF THE WET CONCRETE IF NOT TIED IN WITH STRETCHERS OR YOKES

MAXIMUM LATERAL PRESSURE OF THE WET CONCRETE

THIN SOFFIT BOARDS WILL DEFLECT UNDER THE WEIGHT OF WET CONCRETE

COLUMNS

THE MAXIMUM PRESSURE OF THE WET CONCRETE OCCURS AT THE BASE OF THE COLUMN. THE PRESSURE INCREASES AS THE LENGTH OF THE COLUMN INCREASES

YOKES NECESSARY TO PREVENT BULGING

H

IT IS NECESSARY TO ANCHOR THE COLUMN FORM TO THE FLOOR

201

FORMWORK

TYPES OF COLUMN FORMS

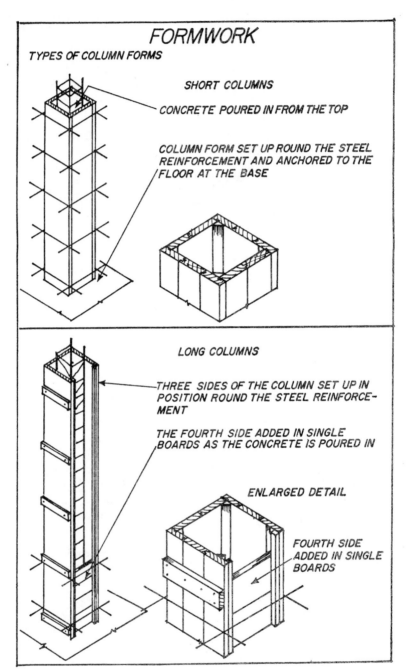

SHORT COLUMNS

CONCRETE POURED IN FROM THE TOP

COLUMN FORM SET UP ROUND THE STEEL REINFORCEMENT AND ANCHORED TO THE FLOOR AT THE BASE

LONG COLUMNS

THREE SIDES OF THE COLUMN SET UP IN POSITION ROUND THE STEEL REINFORCEMENT

THE FOURTH SIDE ADDED IN SINGLE BOARDS AS THE CONCRETE IS POURED IN

ENLARGED DETAIL

FOURTH SIDE ADDED IN SINGLE BOARDS

202

FORMWORK

TYPES OF COLUMN CLAMPS

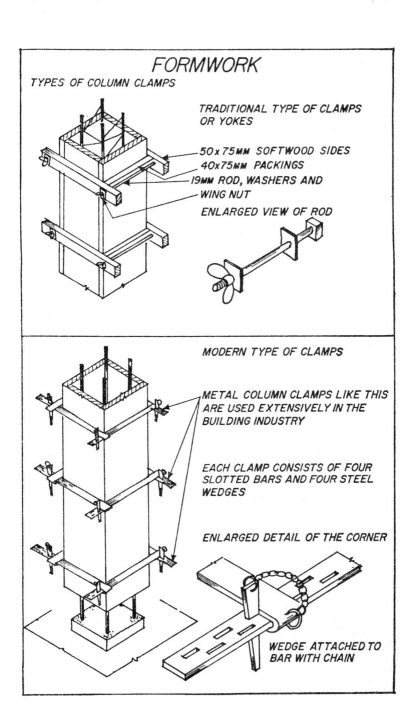

TRADITIONAL TYPE OF CLAMPS
OR YOKES

50x75MM SOFTWOOD SIDES
40x75MM PACKINGS
19MM ROD, WASHERS AND
WING NUT

ENLARGED VIEW OF ROD

MODERN TYPE OF CLAMPS

METAL COLUMN CLAMPS LIKE THIS
ARE USED EXTENSIVELY IN THE
BUILDING INDUSTRY

EACH CLAMP CONSISTS OF FOUR
SLOTTED BARS AND FOUR STEEL
WEDGES

ENLARGED DETAIL OF THE CORNER

WEDGE ATTACHED TO
BAR WITH CHAIN

FORMWORK

WALL FORMWORK – CONSTRUCTIONAL DETAILS

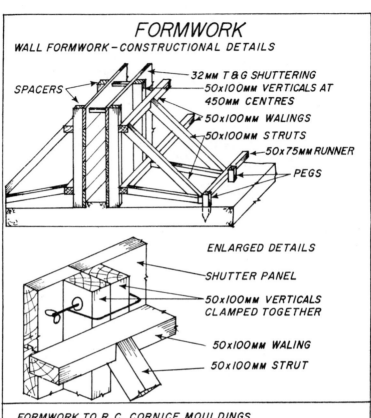

SPACERS

32MM T & G SHUTTERING

50×100MM VERTICALS AT 450MM CENTRES

50×100MM WALINGS

50×100MM STRUTS

50×75MM RUNNER

PEGS

ENLARGED DETAILS

SHUTTER PANEL

50×100MM VERTICALS CLAMPED TOGETHER

50×100MM WALING

50×100MM STRUT

FORMWORK TO R.C. CORNICE MOULDINGS AND STRING COURSES

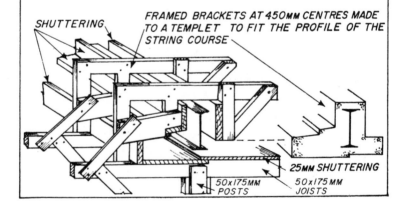

SHUTTERING

FRAMED BRACKETS AT 450MM CENTRES MADE TO A TEMPLET TO FIT THE PROFILE OF THE STRING COURSE

25MM SHUTTERING

50×175MM POSTS

50×175MM JOISTS

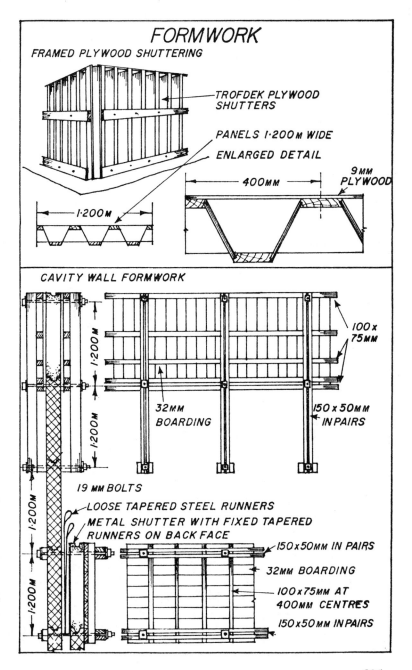

FORMWORK

FRAMED PLYWOOD SHUTTERING

TROFDEK PLYWOOD SHUTTERS

PANELS 1·200 M WIDE

ENLARGED DETAIL

9 MM PLYWOOD

400MM

1·200 M

CAVITY WALL FORMWORK

1·200 M

1·200 M

100 x 75MM

32MM BOARDING

150 x 50MM IN PAIRS

1·200 M

19 MM BOLTS

LOOSE TAPERED STEEL RUNNERS

METAL SHUTTER WITH FIXED TAPERED RUNNERS ON BACK FACE

150 x 50MM IN PAIRS

32MM BOARDING

100 x 75MM AT 400MM CENTRES

1·200 M

150 x 50 MM IN PAIRS

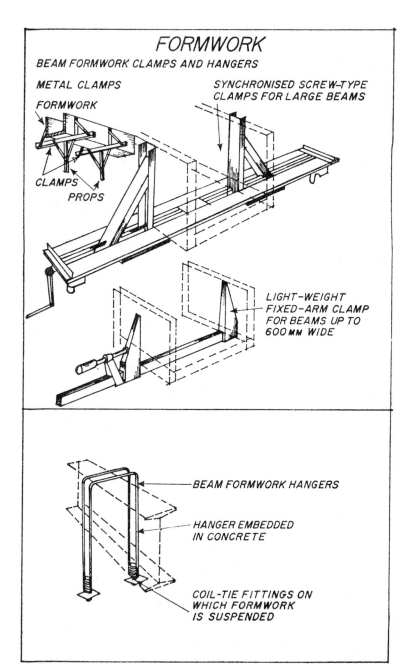

FORMWORK

BEAM FORMWORK CLAMPS AND HANGERS

METAL CLAMPS

FORMWORK

CLAMPS

PROPS

SYNCHRONISED SCREW-TYPE
CLAMPS FOR LARGE BEAMS

LIGHT-WEIGHT
FIXED-ARM CLAMP
FOR BEAMS UP TO
600 MM WIDE

BEAM FORMWORK HANGERS

HANGER EMBEDDED
IN CONCRETE

COIL-TIE FITTINGS ON
WHICH FORMWORK
IS SUSPENDED

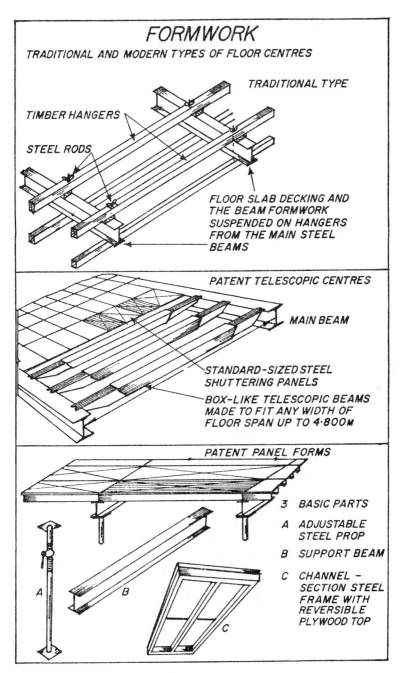

FORMWORK
TRADITIONAL AND MODERN TYPES OF FLOOR CENTRES

TRADITIONAL TYPE

TIMBER HANGERS

STEEL RODS

FLOOR SLAB DECKING AND
THE BEAM FORMWORK
SUSPENDED ON HANGERS
FROM THE MAIN STEEL
BEAMS

PATENT TELESCOPIC CENTRES

MAIN BEAM

STANDARD-SIZED STEEL
SHUTTERING PANELS

BOX-LIKE TELESCOPIC BEAMS
MADE TO FIT ANY WIDTH OF
FLOOR SPAN UP TO 4·800M

PATENT PANEL FORMS

3   BASIC PARTS

A   ADJUSTABLE
    STEEL PROP

B   SUPPORT BEAM

C   CHANNEL –
    SECTION STEEL
    FRAME WITH
    REVERSIBLE
    PLYWOOD TOP

A

B

C

207

Saw milling for the building industry includes all the sawing operations necessary to bring timber to a convenient size for carpentry or joinery work. The operations involved in saw milling may be classified as felling, transportation, and conversion.

Felling

The best-quality timber is obtained from trees which are felled as soon as possible after reaching maturity. The time taken for various types of trees to reach maturity depends on their size and rate of growth; for example, the large trees of America take longer to mature than do the small softwoods of Europe. However, it is true to say that if a tree keeps free from disease it will continue to grow for several hundreds of years, and when felled will produce many times the normal amount of first-quality timber.

Trees are best felled during the winter period, when they contain relatively little sap. Moreover, during this period the evaporation of moisture is slight, so that the shrinkage which occurs in the log will also be comparatively small. The operations involved and the tools and equipment used in the felling and transportation of the timber depend on the size of the logs, the number of trees to be felled, and the siting of the saw mills.

Trees used to be felled with the axe and cross-cut saws, but today the lumber industry is highly mechanised and specially designed portable power saws are used instead.

Transportation of logs to the mills

Logs are conveyed from the forest areas to the saw mills by road, by railway, or by being floated along suitable waterways. Each timber-producing country has developed a system of transportation to suit its own particular conditions. In Britain, with the exception of parts of Scotland, the trees are grown in hedgerows or small woodlands, and the logs are taken on special timber carriers to the nearest sawmill.

In the northern areas of Scandinavia the logs are stacked during the winter on the banks of the great network of lakes and rivers. In the spring they are floated down to the sawmills which have been set up where the timber can conveniently be loaded into ships for export. In Switzerland much of the timber is conveyed down the mountain slopes by cable railway; the logs are put into bundles and attached to the cable. In America many of the saw-mills and woodworking factories are situated in or near the great forest areas. For reasons of economy it is better to take the sawmill to the timber than the timber to the sawmill, where this is possible.

Conversion

The conversion of timber means the sawing of logs into planks, deals, battens, boards, and scantlings. This process is followed by the re-sawing of the sawn timber into exact sizes for specific purposes.

The machines used for the conversion of logs into square sections are of three main types—the circular-saw mill, the horizontal and vertical log band mill, and the frame saw.

The *circular-saw mill* or *rack-feed saw bench* is used only in the smaller sawmills. The machine consists of a vertical saw, 900 mm to 2·1 m in diameter, and a travelling table on to which the log is fastened. The timber is fed end-on into the rotating saw. A sketch of the machine is given on page 221 (top).

NOTE   The maximum feed speed is 12 m per minute.

The *horizontal log band mill* can convert logs up to 2·1 m in diameter. The bandsaw is from 150 to 250 mm wide and is mounted on two large pulleys which are 1·35 to 2·1 m in diameter. The log is supported on a travelling carriage, and is fed into the saw end-on as shown in the sketch at the foot of page 221.

The *vertical log band mill* consists of a wide bandsaw mounted vertically over two large pulleys, one above and one below the log. All the operations involved in placing the log on to the very large carriage and in sawing it are mechanically done. A sketch of a vertical log band mill is given on page 222 (top).

Both horizontal and vertical band mills are replacing the machines that were formerly used because of their high output, accuracy, and thin saw kerf.

The *frame saw* is used extensively in Scandinavia. It consists of a number of reciprocating saws set vertically in a frame. The log is fed end-on into the saws. Although the feed speeds are relatively low compared with those of band mills, the output can be very high, especially when logs are being converted into boards. A sketch of a frame saw is given at the foot of page 222.

DEFECTS AND SELECTION OF TIMBER

Defects in sawn timber originate mainly in changes in moisture content and in growth faults.

Changes in moisture content

Changes in moisture content cause defects such as those illustrated on page 223. Twisting, bowing, shrinkage away from the heart, square sections distorted by shrinkage, and end shakes are shown.

Any of these defects may develop in joinery work during or after its manufacture. Examples of defects in panelled joinery are given at the foot of the page. The first drawing shows grooves which have closed together, and which will therefore require easing. This frequently happens if joinery is left for some time before assembly. The second drawing shows panels of a finished piece of work which have shrunk clear of the grooves.

Growth defects

Growth defects which affect the quality of carpentry and joinery
work are illustrated on page 224.

A large proportion of *sapwood* and *waney edges* may occur in
deals cut from small softwood logs, and thus make this timber
unsuitable for good-class joinery work.

Cup or *ring shakes* are clefts between two annual rings. They
cause much waste, since the defective timber must be cut away.

Small dead knots situated near the centre of the log are caused
by the small branches of the early year's growth. The knots are
usually not more than 12 mm in diameter, and they can be cut out
without much waste.

Large knots are a source of weakness in wood. Timber containing them cannot be used for main structural members, and is
suitable only for being broken down into smaller sections.

Short grain is common in timber produced from home-grown
hardwoods. The affected timber should be avoided on any framed
joinery or structural work, since tenons in short-grain timber
break off easily, and structural members fail before the safe limited
stress of the material is reached.

Upsett occurs when the trunk is thrown violently on to its end.
This crushes the fibres, as is shown on page 224 (foot), and thus
cripples and buckles them. It happens particularly with the
mahoganies, and is the result of unskilled felling. When a tree that
has been damaged in this way is converted the affected parts break
easily.

Selection of timber for structural work

It is essential that all timber to be used as load-bearing timbers in
a structure should be graded for strength and quality, and used
accordingly. For example, the trimming timbers of a floor must be
sound, straight-grained timbers, free from large knots.

The cross-sections of three joists are given on page 225 (top).
A shows a first-quality joist with the annual rings running the deep
way of the joist. This gives a joist section of high strength. The
joist marked B is also of good quality, but because the annual rings
run the narrow way of the joist the joist has less strength. The joist

marked C has heart wood in the centre, and is therefore poor-quality timber. It will warp and shake badly.

The two joists illustrated in the second drawings show the importance of selecting straight-grained timber for main members which require mortising. Notice the large knots on the edges of the poor-quality joist, and those near the mortises. These will considerably affect the strength of the member.

Knots or short grain should be avoided in all framing joints. The two joists shown in the third drawings are tenoned at the ends. Notice how the strength of the lower joint is impaired by the large knot.

Selection of timber for floor covering

Floorboards should be free from all defects that affect the appearance and wearing qualities of the floor.

Three floorboards are shown on page 225 (foot). The first board is rift-sawn, straight grained, and free from all defects. The second board, which has a heart in the centre, has been cut from small timber. Consequently its wearing qualities are poor, and it is liable to shrink and warp. The timber in the third board is of very poor quality, and the large knots and short grain make it unsuitable for use in floor coverings.

Selection of timber for doors and panelled framing

With *hardwood joinery* it is important that the grain in panels should match, and that the heavy grain in the framing should be placed in the lower part of the frame. Knots and short grain should be avoided where mortises and tenons occur.

A panelled door, marked (A), made of carefully selected timber is illustrated on page 226 (top). A door (B) made without selection of timber is also shown. Notice the badly matched panels and the heavy grain in the upper part of the second door.

The method of cutting out hardwood door sections from waney-edged planks is illustrated on page 226 (foot). Notice that the sapwood and the heart-wood must be removed when first-quality timber is required.

In the manufacture of *softwood doors and panelling* it is best, where possible, to use deals which are the thickness of the framing and equal in width to the widest members, which are usually the rails. Thus two stiles 112 mm wide are obtained from a 225 mm wide deal. Sometimes, however, it is advisable to use deals wider than the two stiles so that the heart can be removed. Four 50 × 225 mm sections are shown on page 226 (middle). Two stiles are cut from the first section, and one wide rail from the second. The third drawing shows the removal of the heart-wood and the fourth the cutting of the panels.

Selection of timber for windows

A typical two-light casement window is shown on page 227 (top). The jambs, mullion, head, and casements are softwood, and the sill is oak.

The framing, which has a section of 75 × 100 mm, is cut from 75 × 200 mm deals. Notice that the heart-wood is removed with the rebating, and the that sapwood is placed to the back of the section (second drawing). Small sections containing a heart are unsuitable for joinery (third drawing), though the heart-wood can be removed from the wider deals. The method of removing the heart from 75 × 225 mm deals in order to obtain two good-quality 75 × 100 mm sections is shown in the fourth drawing.

The method of cutting out casement sections from 50 mm deals is also shown. Notice that four 50 × 50 mm sections are obtained from a 50 × 225 mm deal. The small scantling shown is unsuitable for joinery work.

The method of obtaining hardwood framing from through-and-through sawn planks is illustrated at the foot of page 227. Notice that most of the sapwood is removed.

Method of construction to minimise shrinkage and warping

The effect of warping and shrinkage that takes place in manu-factured timber can be minimised by taking precautions over
1   The arrangement of each member in the job
2   The width of each member
3   The design of the joints.

The arrangement of wide boards for jointing is shown on page 228 (top). Notice the positions of the heart sides of the boards.

Warping can be considerably reduced by building up wide boards from narrow widths. The boards illustrated are glue-jointed together. The warping and shrinkage of wide floorboards tongued and grooved together is shown in the second section. In contrast, the narrow boards hardly show warping at all.

Joints designed to cover up any shrinkage or movement of the boards are shown in the third section. Notice that when shrinkage occurs in the traditional vee-jointed match-board a gap develops. With the other two forms of joints, however, a cover of at least 9 mm is provided to disguise this.

Two types of laminated floorboards, which are not subject to warping, are shown at the foot of page 228.

TIMBER DISEASES

Decay in building timber is caused mainly by the attack of fungi and insects.

Dry rot

Dry rot is the most common fungoid disease of building timbers. It is highly infectious and, since the fungus actually feeds on wood, can cause a tremendous amount of destruction, especially in floor joists and wall plates, and floorboarding.

The appearance of the affected timbers varies with the extent and age of the disease. In the early stages the spores (germs or seeds) of the fungus throw out minute, hollow, silky threads which quickly develop into an interlaced network, grey in colour, and cover the timber. If the conditions are very damp, masses like white cottonwool may be formed; these patches later develop into brown or dark-red sponge-like growths called mushrooms, which often exceed 300 mm in diameter. The spores produced on the surface of the spongy growths can easily be carried by air currents, vermin, and insects to infect timber far away from the original site of the disease. The fungus may also spread over brickwork or plaster, and is often carried on tools and workmen's clothing.

Sound and seasoned timber having a moisture content of 20% or less is not likely to be attacked by the fungus. For this reason timber fixed in buildings must be kept dry. When ground floors are constructed in timber, effective damp-proof courses and site concrete must be provided.

Wall plates and the ends of floor joists should be properly treated with a suitable preservative. A free passage of fresh air round all timbers must be maintained, as stagnant moist air is favourable to the growth of the disease. Defective roof coverings, gutters, pipes, and so on should be repaired without delay. Details of the structural faults which contribute to the development of dry rot are given on page 229.

Depending upon its extent, the disease can be eradicated in various ways. All walls and floors affected by the fungus should be cleaned off with a wire brush, and a blow-lamp flame should be applied to the whole of the wall and floor surfaces in order to kill the spores. If the decay is extensive it is necessary to remove all the affected timber and burn it immediately.

Insect attack on wood

Insects are the cause of a considerable amount of damage to timber. The insects responsible for most of the damage are the death-watch beetle, the powder-post beetle, and the common furniture beetle. Illustrations of these are given on page 230.

The *death-watch beetle* attacks well-matured hardwood; the fine oak roofs of many of our churches and other ancient buildings are often badly infected with it. A drawing of a typical oak roof of the hammer-beam type is given on page 231 (top). Softwoods and recently seasoned hardwoods are rarely affected.

The beetles lay their eggs in holes and cracks in the wood. The white grubs or larvae which hatch out are about 6 mm long when fully grown. The grubs cause great destruction by boring innumerable tunnels, about 3 mm in diameter, converting the wood into dust in the process.

The conditions which encourage attack by the beetle are poor ventilation and dampness. To prevent it, provision of good ventilation is essential, and it is necessary to treat the new timber with several coats of creosote or one of the patent preservatives. All infected timber must be removed and replaced with sound wood free from sap.

Lyctus powder-post beetles cause damage to internal joinery such as panelling, built-in fittings, and furniture, and timber stacked in yards (see page 231—foot).

The eggs are laid in the pores of sapwood, and the grubs hatched from them form small holes (about 2 mm in diameter) on the surface of the wood. Small piles of dust are cast out from the holes and act as an indication that the timber is infected. The surface of such timber may be treated with a proprietary solution which will kill the grub as it emerges from the timber during the spring and summer.

NOTE The proper seasoning of timber will destroy any grubs which may be present.

The *common furniture beetle* or 'wood-worm' is the best known of the wood-boring beetles. It is a very small brown beetle, about 2 to 4 mm long, and it attacks old furniture. From June to August the beetles leave the wood and fly to other timber to lay a number of tiny white lemon-shaped eggs. The eggs hatch and the larvae, or worms, bore into the wood. The larva continues to bore for a year or more. A fully grown larva is about 6 mm long, white in colour, with a brown head and strong biting jaws. It then bores to within a short distance of the surface of the wood, and pupates. A few weeks later the beetle emerges and bores its way out of the timber, leaving a flight hole (about 2 mm in diameter) in the surface.

Because most wood-boring beetles can fly, it is best to kill them before they leave the timber and lay their eggs. This can be done by several applications of a preservative during the spring or early summer.

PRESERVATION OF TIMBER

Fungal and insect life must have a supply of food readily available. This can be poisoned by the application of a toxic liquid to the wood. The cellular structure of wood makes the process easy, since most cells are connected by pits through which the preservative liquid can pass. The sapwood, in which the pits are open, is more easily impregnated than the heart-wood, where many of the pits will have become closed.

Types of preservatives

Wood preservatives may be divided into three main groups:
(a)   Tar-oil type, e.g. creosote—the most commonly used preservative
(b)   Water solution type, e.g. sodium fluoride, zinc chloride
(c)   Organic solvent type, e.g. copper napthenate in white spirit.

It is very important that preservatives should be applied to the timber by the correct method; a first-class preservative can be made ineffective by incorrect application. The two methods of application in general use are non-pressure processes and pressure processes.

Non-pressure methods of application

Non-pressure methods include the application of a preservative by brush, spray dipping, and steeping. They are, in general, less effective than pressure methods, though with absorbent timbers the steeping (hot-and-cold bath) method is quite satisfactory for most purposes, especially since it can be completed in a day.

Preservative is very commonly applied by brush. The preservative should be liberally applied, and any shakes or cracks in the surface filled. Two or three coats are necessary, and each coat should be allowed to dry before the next is applied.

Dipping is the submerging of timber in a preservative tank for a short time. The size of the tank is governed by the size and shape of the timber units to be dipped. A typical cold dipping trough is shown on page 232 (top). Notice that after being dipped the units (fencing posts, floor joists, etc.) are placed on a draining rack, usually of corrugated sheeting.

Steeping consists of submerging timber in a tank of either hot or cold preservative for a period of two to four hours. Details of a steeping tank are given on page 231 (middle). The seasoned timber is placed in the tank and held in position with bars. Cold creosote is run into the tank to cover the timber, and is gradually heated to 94°C. After being maintained at this temperature for one to three hours, the heat is turned off and the preservative allowed to cool. The liquid is then pumped back to the storage tank and the timber removed.

The *butt treatment* of fence-posts and gateposts is usually carried out in a metal drum large enough to hold one to two dozen posts. The heat from the fire under the drum must be sufficient to bring the preservative to a temperature of about 94°C. After about one hour the fire is raked out and the liquid allowed to cool. Details of a typical butt tank are given on page 232 (foot).

Pressure methods of application

Pressure processes are the most effective for applying preservatives. They are generally used for treating large quantities of timber. Special pressure cylinders are used which are built to withstand the vacuum and liquid pressures employed. The cylinders vary in size from 15 to 30 m long and 1·8 to 2·1 m in diameter. The timber is loaded on to trolleys which are run into the cylinder on a track. Details of the pressure cylinders are given on page 233.

The *full-cell process* is known also as the Bethell process, after the inventor. The timber is loaded into the cylinder and the doors sealed. A vacuum is created in the cylinder, and sustained for fifteen minutes to one hour. The preservative is then introduced at a temperature of 60° to 82°C without breaking the vacuum. When the cylinder is full, pressure is applied at between 6,890 and 12,402 mbar. This pressure is maintained long enough to force the required amount of preservative into the timber.

NOTE   The purpose of the initial vacuum is to withdraw air and any surface moisture on the timber, since these are apt to obstruct the penetration of the preservative.

The *empty-cell process* obtains a good penetration yet leaves only a small amount of preservative in the timber. The process is so named because the surplus preservative is withdrawn from the cavities of the wood cells by the expansive force of compressed air, leaving the cell walls impregnated.

The timber in the cylinder is first subjected to an air pressure of about 2,756 mbar. With this pressure maintained, the hot preservative is pumped in and the cylinder completely filled. An additional air pressure of about 690 mbar is then applied for a short time. This causes the preservative to enter the wood cells and to compress the air already in them. The pressure is then released, so that the compressed air within the timber can expand. As it does so, it expels a quantity of the preservative from the cell cavities. A further amount of preservative is removed from the cells by the air pressure being reduced with a pump.

This process is ideal for the treatment of timber for building purposes; it is effective, and the wood so treated is relatively clean to handle. The process is comparatively cheap because of the small amount of preservative used.

Preparation of timber for treatment

All timbers which are to be treated with a preservative should be properly seasoned; if the cells of wood are filled with sap it is very difficult to force in more liquid. All shaping, boring, or cutting of any kind must be done before impregnation, irrespective of the treatment used.

Some timbers are resistant to impregnation by preservatives, and the pressure treatment may result in a small and uneven penetration. This difficulty may be overcome by a process called *incising*. The incising machine consists of four geared rollers, each fitted with adjustable steel teeth. Two of the rollers are placed in a horizontal position, and two in a vertical position. This arrangement makes it possible to make incisions on the four sides of a piece of timber in one operation. The steel teeth make slit-like incisions parallel with the grain of the timber. The incisions are about 16 mm deep, and they provide a means of entry from which the preservative can be forced to spread along the grain.

Diagrams showing the improvement in penetration after incising are given on page 234.

NOTE It has been shown by tests that the strength of structural members is not impaired by incising.

Practice lessons

1 Working from the information given:

   (a) Name, and briefly describe, the three main types of saw milling machines.

   (b) Make a neat sketch of one of the machines.

2 *(a)* Make neat diagrams to show the defects in sawn timber due to changes in moisture content.

   (b) Make neat diagrams to show the common growth defects in sawn timber.

3 *(a)* Illustrate, with neat sketches, the methods of selecting timber for:

     (i) Structural work.

     (ii) Joinery work.

   (b) Make neat sketches to show methods of construction that will minimise shrinkage and warping.

4 *(a)* Explain briefly the causes of dry rot in building timbers.

   (b) Name, and briefly describe, the life cycle of the wood-boring beetle which attacks well-matured hardwoods.

5 *(a)* Name, and briefly describe, two wood preservatives that are in common use.

   (b) Explain briefly the non-pressure and pressure methods of application.

TIMBER

LOG CONVERSION

CIRCULAR SAW MILL

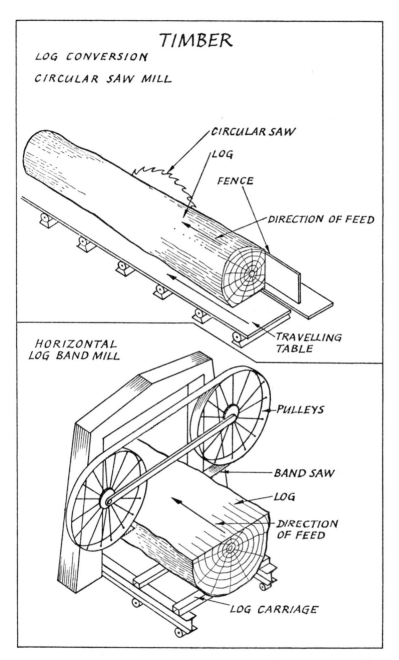

CIRCULAR SAW

LOG

FENCE

DIRECTION OF FEED

TRAVELLING TABLE

HORIZONTAL LOG BAND MILL

PULLEYS

BAND SAW

LOG

DIRECTION OF FEED

LOG CARRIAGE

TIMBER

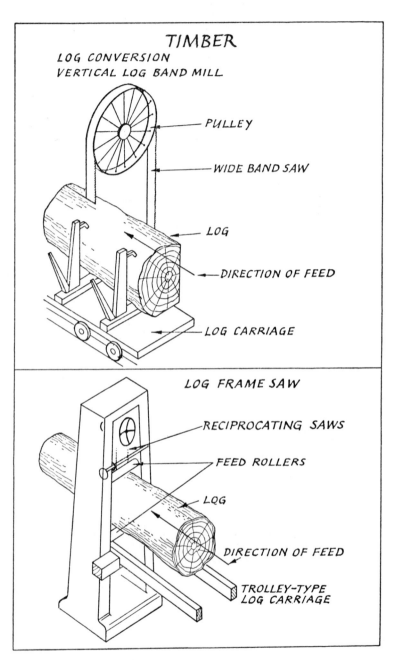

LOG CONVERSION
VERTICAL LOG BAND MILL

PULLEY

WIDE BAND SAW

LOG

DIRECTION OF FEED

LOG CARRIAGE

LOG FRAME SAW

RECIPROCATING SAWS

FEED ROLLERS

LOG

DIRECTION OF FEED

TROLLEY-TYPE
LOG CARRIAGE

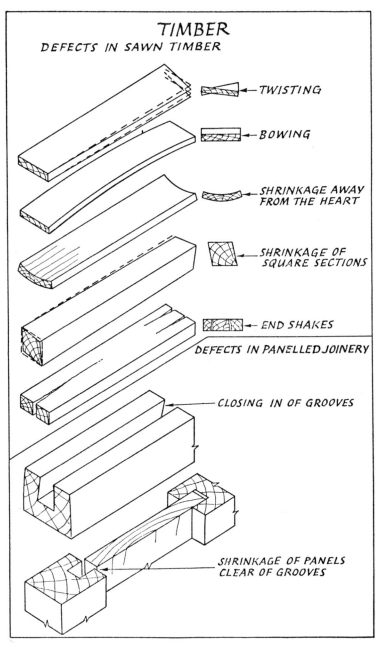

TIMBER
DEFECTS IN SAWN TIMBER

TWISTING

BOWING

SHRINKAGE AWAY FROM THE HEART

SHRINKAGE OF SQUARE SECTIONS

END SHAKES

DEFECTS IN PANELLED JOINERY

CLOSING IN OF GROOVES

SHRINKAGE OF PANELS CLEAR OF GROOVES

TIMBER

DEFECTS IN SAWN TIMBER

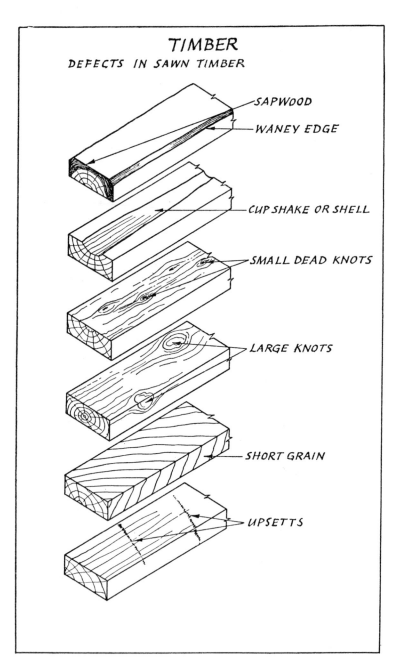

SAPWOOD

WANEY EDGE

CUP SHAKE OR SHELL

SMALL DEAD KNOTS

LARGE KNOTS

SHORT GRAIN

UPSETTS

TIMBER
SELECTION OF TIMBER FOR STRUCTURAL WORK
FLOOR TIMBERS

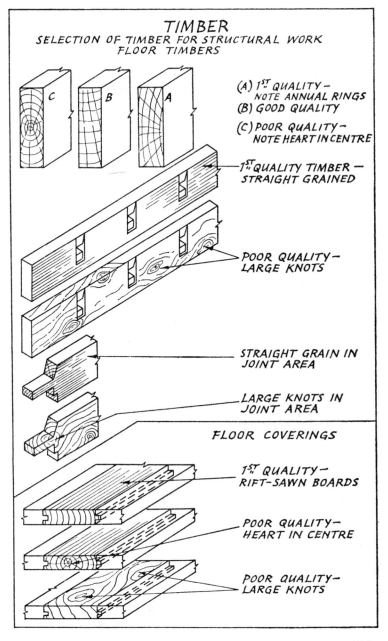

(A) 1ST QUALITY –
NOTE ANNUAL RINGS
(B) GOOD QUALITY

(C) POOR QUALITY –
NOTE HEART IN CENTRE

1ST QUALITY TIMBER –
STRAIGHT GRAINED

POOR QUALITY –
LARGE KNOTS

STRAIGHT GRAIN IN
JOINT AREA

LARGE KNOTS IN
JOINT AREA

FLOOR COVERINGS

1ST QUALITY –
RIFT-SAWN BOARDS

POOR QUALITY –
HEART IN CENTRE

POOR QUALITY –
LARGE KNOTS

225

TIMBER
THE SELECTION OF TIMBER FOR DOORS

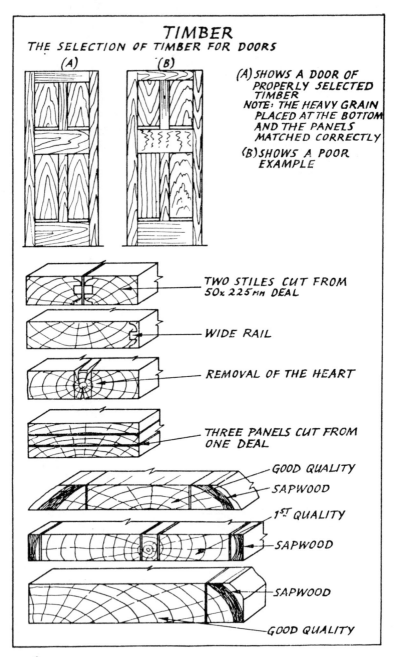

(A) SHOWS A DOOR OF PROPERLY SELECTED TIMBER
NOTE: THE HEAVY GRAIN PLACED AT THE BOTTOM AND THE PANELS MATCHED CORRECTLY

(B) SHOWS A POOR EXAMPLE

TWO STILES CUT FROM 50 x 225 mm DEAL

WIDE RAIL

REMOVAL OF THE HEART

THREE PANELS CUT FROM ONE DEAL

GOOD QUALITY

SAPWOOD

1ST QUALITY

SAPWOOD

SAPWOOD

GOOD QUALITY

TIMBER
SELECTION OF TIMBER FOR WINDOWS

75 x 100mm FRAMING
75 x 150mm SILLS
50mm CASEMENTS

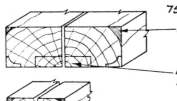

75 x 100mm FRAMING EX 75 x 200mm

— SAPWOOD

— HEARTWOOD REMOVED WITH REBATING

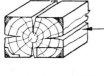

— UNSUITABLE FOR JOINERY

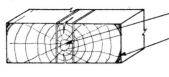

— HEARTWOOD

— SAPWOOD

50 x 50mm
SECTIONS EX 50 x 225mm

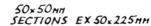

— HEARTWOOD

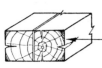

— UNSUITABLE FOR JOINERY

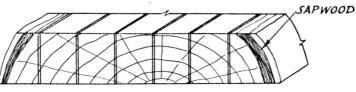

— SAPWOOD

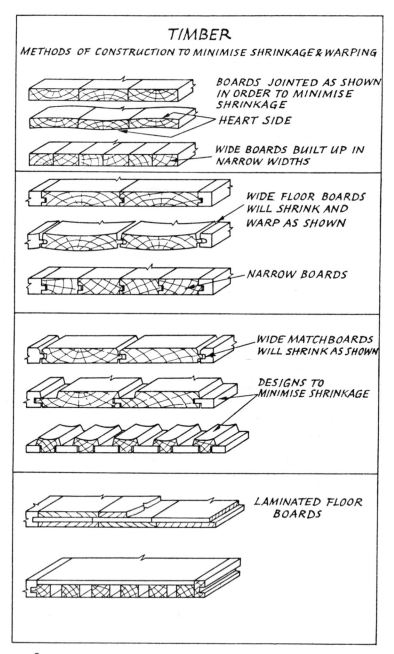

TIMBER

METHODS OF CONSTRUCTION TO MINIMISE SHRINKAGE & WARPING

BOARDS JOINTED AS SHOWN IN ORDER TO MINIMISE SHRINKAGE

HEART SIDE

WIDE BOARDS BUILT UP IN NARROW WIDTHS

WIDE FLOOR BOARDS WILL SHRINK AND WARP AS SHOWN

NARROW BOARDS

WIDE MATCHBOARDS WILL SHRINK AS SHOWN

DESIGNS TO MINIMISE SHRINKAGE

LAMINATED FLOOR BOARDS

TIMBER

DRY ROT
STRUCTURAL FAULTS IN FLOORS

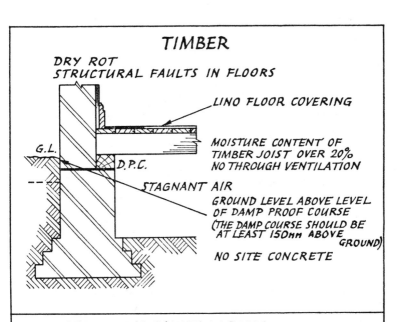

LINO FLOOR COVERING

MOISTURE CONTENT OF TIMBER JOIST OVER 20% NO THROUGH VENTILATION

G.L.

D.P.C.

STAGNANT AIR

GROUND LEVEL ABOVE LEVEL OF DAMP PROOF COURSE (THE DAMP COURSE SHOULD BE AT LEAST 150mm ABOVE GROUND)

NO SITE CONCRETE

STRUCTURAL FAULTS IN ROOFS

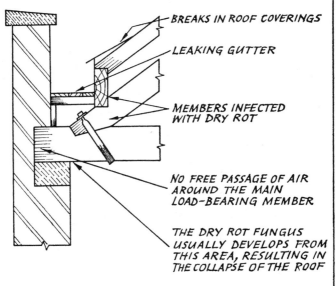

BREAKS IN ROOF COVERINGS

LEAKING GUTTER

MEMBERS INFECTED WITH DRY ROT

NO FREE PASSAGE OF AIR AROUND THE MAIN LOAD-BEARING MEMBER

THE DRY ROT FUNGUS USUALLY DEVELOPS FROM THIS AREA, RESULTING IN THE COLLAPSE OF THE ROOF

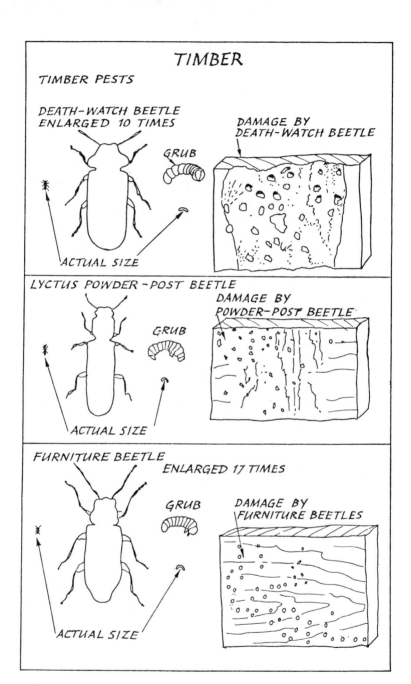

TIMBER

TIMBER PESTS

DEATH-WATCH BEETLE
ENLARGED 10 TIMES

GRUB

ACTUAL SIZE

DAMAGE BY
DEATH-WATCH BEETLE

LYCTUS POWDER-POST BEETLE

GRUB

ACTUAL SIZE

DAMAGE BY
POWDER-POST BEETLE

FURNITURE BEETLE
ENLARGED 17 TIMES

GRUB

ACTUAL SIZE

DAMAGE BY
FURNITURE BEETLES

TIMBER

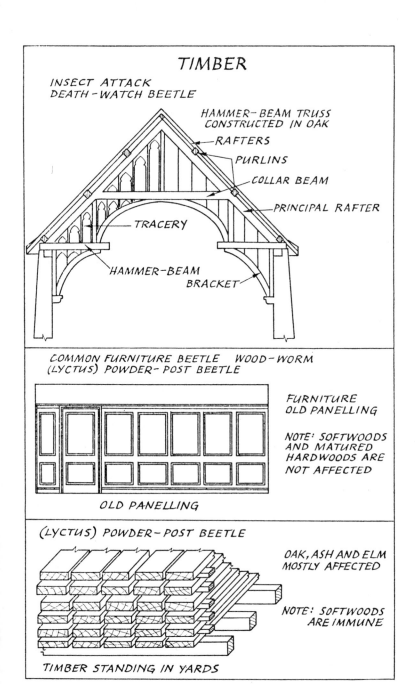

INSECT ATTACK
DEATH-WATCH BEETLE

HAMMER-BEAM TRUSS
CONSTRUCTED IN OAK

RAFTERS

PURLINS

COLLAR BEAM

PRINCIPAL RAFTER

TRACERY

HAMMER-BEAM
BRACKET

COMMON FURNITURE BEETLE   WOOD-WORM
(LYCTUS) POWDER-POST BEETLE

FURNITURE
OLD PANELLING

NOTE: SOFTWOODS
AND MATURED
HARDWOODS ARE
NOT AFFECTED

OLD PANELLING

(LYCTUS) POWDER-POST BEETLE

OAK, ASH AND ELM
MOSTLY AFFECTED

NOTE: SOFTWOODS
ARE IMMUNE

TIMBER STANDING IN YARDS

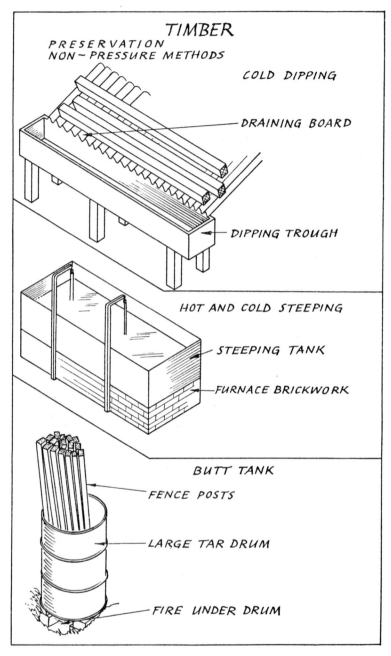

TIMBER

PRESERVATION
NON-PRESSURE METHODS

COLD DIPPING

DRAINING BOARD

DIPPING TROUGH

HOT AND COLD STEEPING

STEEPING TANK

FURNACE BRICKWORK

BUTT TANK

FENCE POSTS

LARGE TAR DRUM

FIRE UNDER DRUM

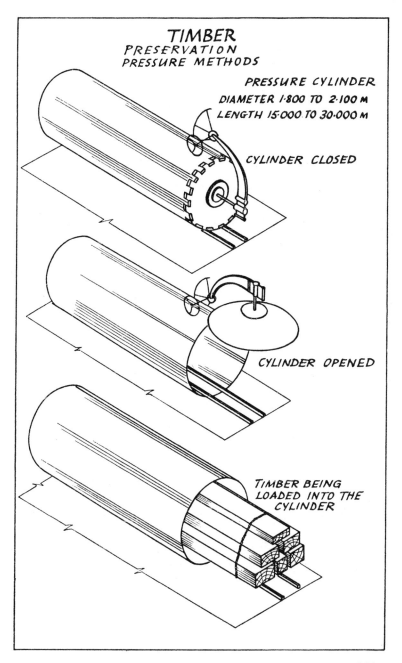

TIMBER
PRESERVATION
PRESSURE METHODS

PRESSURE CYLINDER
DIAMETER 1·800 TO 2·100 M
LENGTH 15·000 TO 30·000 M

CYLINDER CLOSED

CYLINDER OPENED

TIMBER BEING
LOADED INTO THE
CYLINDER

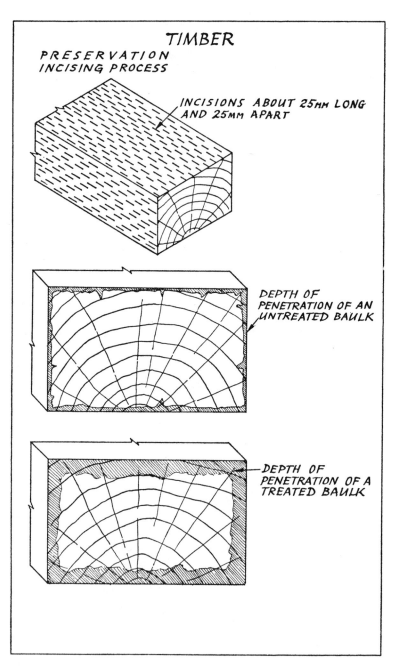

TIMBER

PRESERVATION
INCISING PROCESS

INCISIONS ABOUT 25mm LONG
AND 25mm APART

DEPTH OF
PENETRATION OF AN
UNTREATED BAULK

DEPTH OF
PENETRATION OF A
TREATED BAULK

234

A wide range of ironmongery is manufactured in Britain and many other countries to meet the requirements of builders. Cheap, good-quality fittings are mass-produced for the general building and woodworking trades, and more expensive, high-quality fittings are manufactured for the specialised industries such as ship-building.

A modern development in the production of ironmongery is the invention of designs which can be fitted by mechanical means. This is particularly advanced in Sweden, where joinery work is made mechanically from start to finish, thus eliminating all site work.

This chapter deals with two types of fittings; those which allow movement (hinges and pivots) and those which give security (bolts and locks).

Hinges

In addition to the three types described in Book 1, hinges can be obtained in a wide range of designs for special purposes.

A *brass butt hinge* fitted with steel washers is shown on page 240 (top). Hinges like these are used mainly on high-class hardwood joinery work.

A *rising butt hinge* is given in the middle of the page. Hinges of this type are used mainly on domestic work, since they will lift doors clear of thick floor coverings.

A *pin hinge* is illustrated at the foot of the page. This is used extensively in Europe, and is gaining popularity in Britain. The main advantage of this type is that the door can be taken off its hinges without the screws being removed. Enlarged details are given of the pin. Notice that it is clear of the face of the door.

Care must be taken when fitting all these hinges to keep the knuckle part of the hinge clear of the door surface, as is shown in the enlarged sections.

Parliament hinges are used where it is necessary for a door to fold back to the wall. These project from the face of the door, as illustrated on page 241. The first type is one used in Britain, and the second is a modern type made in Scandinavia.

Special hinges are sometimes used to enable the exterior of casement windows to be cleaned from the inside of the room. These are shown at the foot of page 241. One part of the hinge is fixed to the rebate of the sill or head, and the other to the face of the casement.

Flap hinges are used mainly on internal fittings. An ordinary back-flap hinge made in sizes from 25 to 75 mm is shown in the first drawing on page 242. A *counter-flap hinge* is illustrated in the middle of the page. Notice that when the hinge is closed it is flush with the counter-top surface with no projecting knuckle, as there is in the case of other flap hinges.

A *cabinet-flap hinge* is shown at the foot of page 242. This is used for doors that project 3 to 12 mm from the face of the framing.

Door pivot hinges

Swing doors may be hung with either pivoted floor springs or helical spring hinges.

A *pivoted floor spring* is given on page 243 (top), where are shown the box floor spring, the shoe, the top socket, and the top pivot, which is adjusted up and down by a screw. An adjustable pivot plate is fixed to the head of the frame. The lower pivot is attached to a spring and enclosed in a box sunk into the floor. The spring is fitted with an air check to slow down the swing of the door at the point at which it has about 150 mm to close. The lower pivot fits into a shoe at the bottom of the door, and the upper pivot into a socket at the top of the door.

Care must be taken when fitting and hanging swing doors. First the doors are fitted into the opening, allowing the minimum amount of play, and the box floor spring, pivots, and sockets are fixed. Then the door is hung by the pivot in the head of the frame, being screwed down to engage the socket in the top end of the door. A plan showing the pivot and the door in an open and closed position is given on page 243 (top).

A pair of *helical spring hinges* on a single swing door are given at the foot of page 243. Only the top hinges are sprung, and they are shown fitted to the edge of the door in the enlarged drawing. The spring is tightened or slackened by the turning of a bar inserted into the hole in the collar. When this has been done a locking pin is fitted.

A plan view of the hinge is given, showing the door in an open and closed position.

The operations involved in fitting and hanging the door are the same as those for doors fitted with butt hinges, but extra care is needed when the hinge is being fitted into the frame.

Casement light pivots

Pivots for centre-hung casement lights are of two main types: the ordinary pin-and-socket pivot, and the spring or friction pivot.

A *pin-and-socket pivot* used to hang the casement of a single-light window is shown on page 244 (top). The enlarged details show the fitting of the pivots. Notice the groove cut in the bead to the socket; this enables the casement to be removed for cleaning.

A pivot which is a type of pin and socket is shown fixed to the face of the frame and casement at the foot of page 244. All casement lights fitted with this type of pivot need a stay to hold them firm when they are open.

A *friction pivot* is shown on page 244 (middle), with sectional views of the spring and plate let into the casement stile, and the single plate let into the frame. This type of pivot will hold the casement firm in any position, and needs no stay.

Locks and bolts

Doors made in pairs and rebated together at the meeting stile as, for example, are entrance doors and french windows, are usually fitted with a rebated mortise lock and an espagnolette bolt.

A *rebated mortise lock* is shown on page 245 (top). The drawings show isometric views of the doors, the lock, and the striking plate. A plan is also shown of the rebated meeting stiles.

An *espagnolette bolt* consists of two long bolts, of which one secures the top of the door and the other the bottom. The bolts are operated simultaneously by a handle or lever being turned in the centre. The drawings on page 245 (foot) show a pair of doors fitted with an espagnolette bolt, and enlarged details of three different designs of bolts. Two of these are fitted to the face of the door, and the third is fitted to the edge, as is shown.

Cabinet locks

Cabinet locks are used for drawers, cupboards, and boxes.

A *drawer lock* is shown on page 246 (top). The lock is fitted to the inside face of the drawer front, and the bolt is operated with a key, which shoots into a striking plate.

A *cupboard lock* is illustrated in the middle of the page. This lock also is fitted to the inside face of the door, and the bolt shoots into a striking plate.

A *box* or *chest lock* is shown at the foot of page 246. The body of the lock is similar to that of a drawer lock, but the locking mechanism is different. The striking plate is attached to the lid, and has two hook-shaped projections. When the lid is closed these projections are engaged with a key-operated bolt to keep the box locked.

Practice lessons

1 Working from the information given:

   (a) Make neat sketches of two types of butt hinges, and show a section view of the hinges' position on the door and frame.

   (b) Draw an isometric view of a parliament hinge, and explain the reason for its use.

   (c) Make isometric sketches of two types of flap hinges.

2 *(a)* Make neat sketches of the following pivot hinges and state their uses:

     (i)   Pivoted floor springs.

     (ii) Socket pivots.

     (iii) Friction pivots.

   (b) Draw an isometric view of a rebated mortise lock and striking plate.

3 *(a)* Make a neat sketch of an espagnolette bolt, and explain its use.

   (b) Draw isometric views of a drawer and cupboard lock.

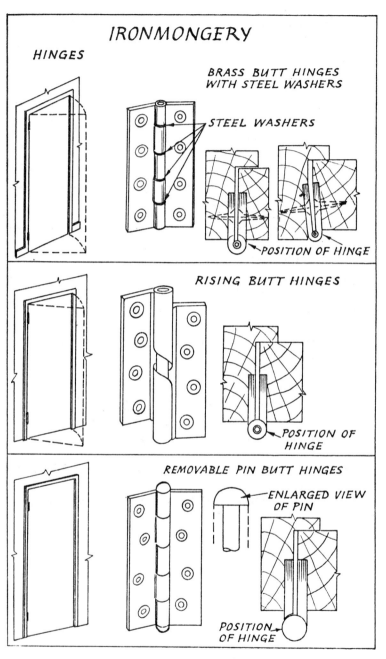

IRONMONGERY

HINGES

BRASS BUTT HINGES WITH STEEL WASHERS

STEEL WASHERS

POSITION OF HINGE

RISING BUTT HINGES

POSITION OF HINGE

REMOVABLE PIN BUTT HINGES

ENLARGED VIEW OF PIN

POSITION OF HINGE

IRONMONGERY

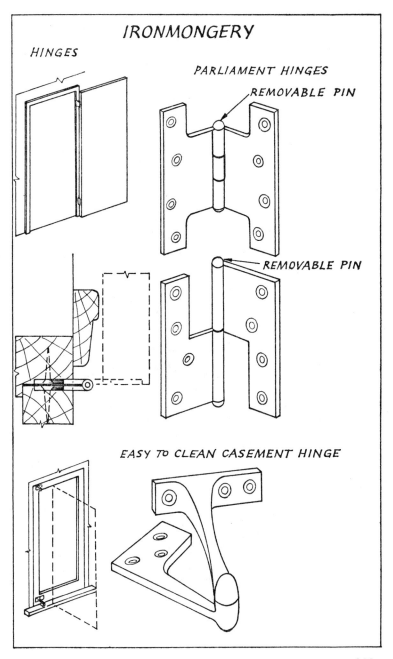

HINGES

PARLIAMENT HINGES

REMOVABLE PIN

REMOVABLE PIN

EASY TO CLEAN CASEMENT HINGE

IRONMONGERY

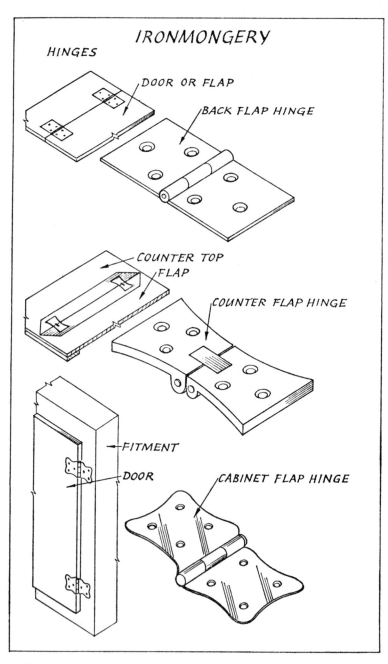

HINGES

DOOR OR FLAP

BACK FLAP HINGE

COUNTER TOP

FLAP

COUNTER FLAP HINGE

FITMENT

DOOR

CABINET FLAP HINGE

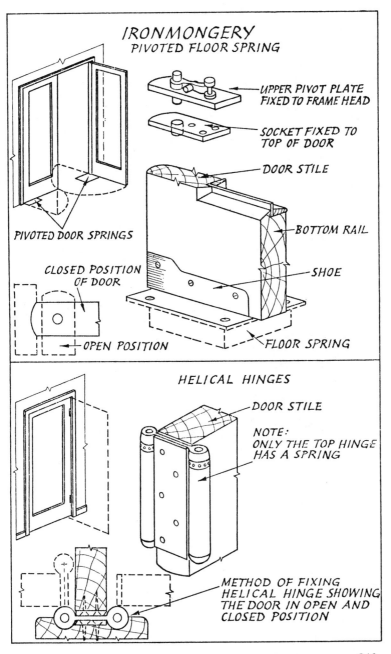

IRONMONGERY
PIVOTED FLOOR SPRING

UPPER PIVOT PLATE
FIXED TO FRAME HEAD

SOCKET FIXED TO
TOP OF DOOR

DOOR STILE

PIVOTED DOOR SPRINGS

BOTTOM RAIL

CLOSED POSITION
OF DOOR

SHOE

OPEN POSITION

FLOOR SPRING

HELICAL HINGES

DOOR STILE

NOTE:
ONLY THE TOP HINGE
HAS A SPRING

METHOD OF FIXING
HELICAL HINGE SHOWING
THE DOOR IN OPEN AND
CLOSED POSITION

243

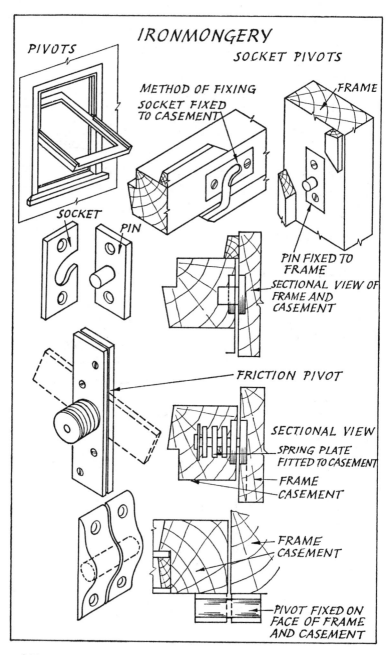

IRONMONGERY

SOCKET PIVOTS

PIVOTS

METHOD OF FIXING

SOCKET FIXED TO CASEMENT

FRAME

SOCKET

PIN

PIN FIXED TO FRAME

SECTIONAL VIEW OF FRAME AND CASEMENT

FRICTION PIVOT

SECTIONAL VIEW

SPRING PLATE FITTED TO CASEMENT

FRAME
CASEMENT

FRAME
CASEMENT

PIVOT FIXED ON FACE OF FRAME AND CASEMENT

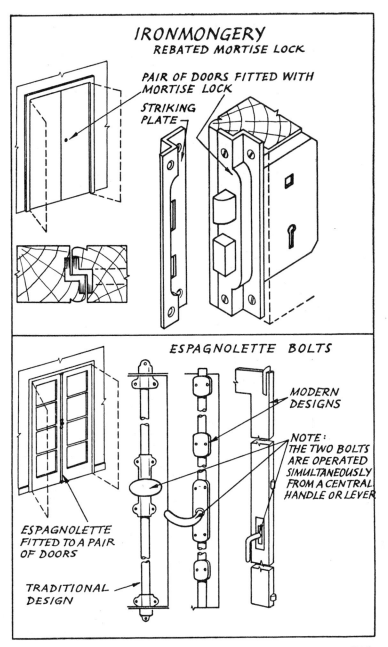

IRONMONGERY
REBATED MORTISE LOCK

PAIR OF DOORS FITTED WITH
MORTISE LOCK

STRIKING
PLATE

ESPAGNOLETTE BOLTS

MODERN
DESIGNS

NOTE:
THE TWO BOLTS
ARE OPERATED
SIMULTANEOUSLY
FROM A CENTRAL
HANDLE OR LEVER

ESPAGNOLETTE
FITTED TO A PAIR
OF DOORS

TRADITIONAL
DESIGN

245

IRONMONGERY

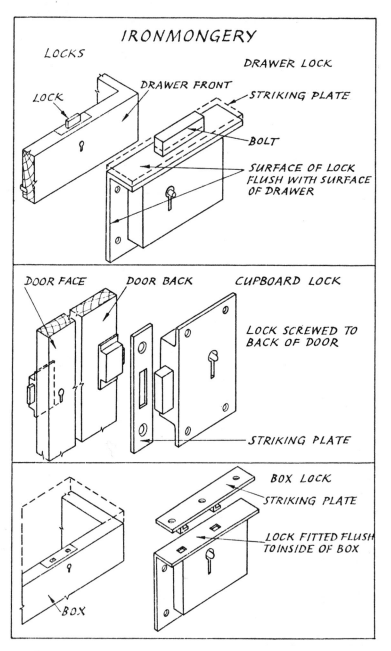

LOCKS

DRAWER LOCK

LOCK

DRAWER FRONT

STRIKING PLATE

BOLT

SURFACE OF LOCK FLUSH WITH SURFACE OF DRAWER

DOOR FACE   DOOR BACK   CUPBOARD LOCK

LOCK SCREWED TO BACK OF DOOR

STRIKING PLATE

BOX LOCK

STRIKING PLATE

LOCK FITTED FLUSH TO INSIDE OF BOX

BOX

Setting-out equipment

The equipment necessary for the setting out of rods and boards consists of tools for drawing square and parallel lines, compasses, radius rods, triangular frames for drawing segmental curves, and trammel frames for drawing elliptical curves.

The rods upon which the heights and widths of the joinery work are drawn may be made of smooth-surfaced and whitened 6 mm pine boards, or white paper which is similar to lining paper and is obtainable in rolls.

The method of setting out joinery work on a rod with the aid of a *square and line gauge* is shown on page 258 (top). Two forms of setting out or line gauges are also shown. One has a steel rule and wooden fence and the other is made of hardwood (mahogany).

NOTE Both these gauges can be made by the joiner.

The *compasses* shown at the foot of page 258 are used for spacing out members. The wing compass is set to the size of the member, and the beam compass to the size of the spaces.

The setting out of a segmental arch using a *radius rod* is shown on page 259 (top). An enlarged detail of the radius rod is also given. Saw cuts on the rod indicate the size and position of the arch, the laggings, and the door frame head.

Details of a *triangular frame* for drawing segmental curves of small rise are given at the foot of page 259. Notice that the segmental curve is drawn by the triangular frame being rotated on the two nails marked A and B. Radius rods and triangular frames are made from straight-grained softwood, and must be marked out and made accurately.

The setting out of an elliptical arch by the *short trammel method* is illustrated on page 260. The isometric and elevation views show the trammel frame in position, and the method of using the trammel beam to mark out the curve. An enlarged detail of the grooved frame and trammel beam is given at the foot of the page.

The *long trammel method* is the most accurate way of marking out an elliptical curve. In this method the axis lengths are placed end to end, with the pencil which marks the curve in the middle of the beam. The isometric and elevation views given on page 261 show the frame in position, and the method of plotting the curve. An enlarged view of the trammel beam shows the pencil and the two adjustable pins.

The geometry of setting out an arch

The setting out of an elliptical arch from five centres is shown on page 262. In order to reduce the number of voussoir (arch brick) patterns to three, the curve must be set out from five centres. This is done in two stages.

The first drawing on page 262 shows the method of obtaining the four points on the elliptical curve. Notice that each half of the major axis is divided into three equal parts, and that so also are the upper halves of the minor axes at either side. Lines are drawn from the centre O to pass through the points on the major axis, and from the points on the minor axes to meet at the crown. The intersections of these lines give the four points marked A, B, C, and D, which will lie on the curve.

The second drawing shows the method of obtaining the centres from which the segments of the arch can be marked out. First arcs are drawn with E as the centre. Then arcs of the same radius are drawn with B and C as centres. Straight lines are drawn through the intersections to give X. Lines XB and XC are then drawn, to form the central segment of the arch (shown dotted in the drawing).

AB is then bisected in the same way. A straight line is drawn through the intersections, and meets BX at the second centre, V. AV and BV are then joined to give the second segment of the arch.

Equally, on the other side, the centre Y lies at the intersection of the bisecting line and XC. YC and YD are joined to give the third segment.

The centres W and Z lie at the points where AV and DY respectively meet the spring line.

To find the segmental curves, W, V, X, Y, and Z are used as centres for arcs passing through F and A, A and B, B and C, C and D, and D and F respectively.

The three voussoir templets are also shown.

The method of setting out the head of the door frame which is fitted to the elliptical brick arch is given at the foot of page 262. Notice that the joint lines are normal to the curve,

The setting out of a *four-centre arch* with joints in the springing and at the crown is shown on page 263. An outline of the plank from which the circular head is cut is given. The curved head may be built up in two or more sections, as shown in the enlarged details.

Details of the setting out of a *parabolic arch* and door frame head are given on page 263 (middle) with an enlarged detail of the head, which is built up in three sections. A workshop method of marking out a parabolic curve is illustrated at the foot of page 263. Notice that the cord is fixed to the square, which slides along the straight edge, and that the marker is kept tight to the edge of the square.

Roofing with the steel square

A knowledge of the geometry of roofing is essential if the use of the steel square is to be fully understood. The system of lengths and bevels is based on the right-angled triangle. It is very important that the craftsman should be able to visualise the position of the square on the roof in order to understand the method of finding the bevels.

Details of a roof, L-shaped in plan, are given on page 264. It has a span of 4 m and a rise of 1·5 m. The roof contains common rafters, jack rafters, hips, valleys, and purlins, the lengths and bevels of which can be obtained by the use of the steel square. A plan view and a specification of the member sizes are given in the middle of page 264. The constructional details given at the foot of the page show a section through the eaves and ridge, and particulars of the span and rise.

The steel square has two arms forming a right angle, one of the arms is longer and broader than the other, and is called the body, the short arm is called the tongue.

Details of the square are given on page 265 (top). An adjustable fence is shown, which is fastened to the two arms of the square with clips. Steel squares will have metric dimensions of millimetres, centimetres (10 mm), and decimetres (100 mm). 100 millimetres on the scale represents one metre of rafter, the actual size of the rafter can be obtained by stepping up the size obtained on the square ten times.

The run of the rafter, which is usually half the span, is 2 metres. 200 mm should therefore be measured along the body of the square. The rise is 1·5 metres, so that 150 mm should be measured along the tongue, this gives a rafter length on the square of 250 mm.

The marking out of the common rafter is illustrated on page 265. A section view of the rafter with the first, second, and tenth positions of the square marked on it is shown. Note that half the thickness of the ridge must be deducted from the length of the rafter.

It is usual to begin marking out at the wall plate end of the rafter, starting from the face of the wall plate as is shown on page 265 (middle).

Before the hip rafter can be marked out, its run length must be found. The run of the hip rafter on the roof plan shown on page 265 is the diagonal of a square whose sides equal the run of the common rafter, in this case 2 m. The square will be set to measure 200 mm on the body and the tongue giving a diagonal length of 280 mm. Ten times this measurement gives a hip length of 2·8 m (see page 265—middle).

The hip is marked out as illustrated in the next drawing; the square is set to a run of 280 mm and a rise of 150 mm, which gives a diagonal length of 320 mm.

The deduction for the thickness of the material at the top end of the hip rafter is explained by the diagram at the foot of page 265. A plan view shows the intersection of the two hips with the ridge. The deduction, which is half the thickness of the hip, is measured at right angles to the square.

The hip rafter is marked out in the same way as the common rafters. That is, the square is stepped up ten times beginning from the bottom end of the hip, and the necessary deductions for the thickness of the mateiral.

The *jack rafter* may be considered as a short common rafter with identical bottom and plumb bevels, but with an edge bevel which fits to the side of the hips. This bevel is obtained by placing the square on the roof as shown on page 266 (top). Notice that the size on the tongue represents the length of the common rafter, and the size on the body the run of the common rafter. To find the true length of the longest jack rafter, it is necessary to find the difference between its length and that of the common rafter. This difference is called the 'diminish' and the method of finding it is illustrated in the middle of the page. The jack rafters are shown spaced at 400 and 600 mm centres. In the first position the square is set to the edge bevel at 250 × 200 mm, and is then moved down to read 400 and 600 mm at the long corner of the shorter rafter. The difference in length between the long points of the two jack rafters represents the amount of diminish, and this is measured on the tongue of the square. A practical method of setting out and obtaining the diminish is shown at the foot of page 266.

The method of obtaining the amount of deduction for the thickness of the hip rafter is also shown on page 266. The horizontal deduction is the diagonal of a square (marked A on the drawing) whose sides measure half the thickness of the hip rafter.

The lengths of *purlins* can be found by direct measurement on the job, but the true bevels at the ends of the purlins should be found either by geometrical means or by the use of the steel square.

The geometrical method is illustrated on page 267. First, a sectional view of the purlin and a plan view of the hip are drawn. Then a development of the side and edge of the purlin is made and projected to the plan to give the two bevels.

The isometric view shows how the bevels are applied.

The method of finding the edge bevel with a steel square is shown on page 267 (middle). The purlins are at right angles to the jack rafter, so that the figures for the two bevels are the same, except that the bevels are reversed.

The drawings show the plan of the roof with the square in position, and the application of the square to the edge of the purlin. The side bevel of the purlin is rather difficult to visualise because of the position of the square in the roof. The body of the square lies on the side of the purlin as shown on page 267 (foot).

It will be observed that the triangles ABC and ABD are similar: that is, they are exactly the same shape, though different in size. (AB is proportionate to BD, and so on.) These proportions may be written down as:

$$\frac{\text{rise of common rafter}}{\text{length of common rafter}} = \frac{\text{run of common rafter}}{\text{line AD}}$$

This may be expressed as

$$\frac{\text{rise}}{\text{length}} = \frac{\text{run}}{\text{X}}$$

$$\therefore \frac{1\cdot5}{2\cdot5} = \frac{2}{\text{X}} = 1\cdot5\text{X} = 5$$

$$\therefore \text{X} = 3\cdot33$$

Notice that the rise 150 mm is measured on the body of the square, and the length of the common rafter (250 mm) on the tongue.

Geometry of domes

Domes may be used as roofs or ceilings. Domed ceilings are usually very massive, and are erected in such buildings as theatres, public halls, and ecclesiastical buildings. Small domes often form a roof covering for ventilating turrets, bell turrets, or towers.

Domes may be classified according to their geometrical shape. In the elevation view they may be pyramidal, semicircular, conical, or ogee in shape, and in the plan view square, octagonal, or circular. The geometry of domed roofs involves the finding of the lengths, bevels, and shapes of the structural members (rafters and ribs), and the development of the roof surfaces.

A typical *pyramid roof* is shown on page 268, in plan, section, and isometric view. The true lengths and bevels of the common and hip rafter are given in the middle of the page. The method of finding the dihedral bevel (the angle between the two roof slopes) or the hip backing is also shown. The development of the roof surface is shown at the foot of page 268, together with the length and edge bevel of the jack rafters.

The small *semicircular dome* illustrated on page 269 is *square* in plan. The dome is formed with 25 mm thick ribs framed into a

plate at the bottom end, and into a mast at the top end. This
structure is covered with two thicknesses of 9 mm plywood. Plan,
elevation, and an isometric view of the dome are shown at the top
of page 269. Right-angle views of each rib must be drawn in order
to find their true shape, and to do this a plan and section view of
the dome is necessary. The true shape of the common and hip
ribs can be drawn as shown in the middle of page 269. Also shown
is the development of the curved surface. Notice the stretch-out
from the plate to the crown of the dome.

A small *semicircular dome* which is *octagonal* in plan is shown on
page 270. The dome is formed in the same way as the square
dome. A plan, elevation, and isometric view of the dome is given
at the top of the page. The true shape of the rib is shown projected from the section view. Notice that a stretch-out of the curved
roof surface is made from the plan.

The *conical roof*, illustrated on page 271, is a comparatively
simple roof to set out. A plan, elevation, and isometric view of the
roof is shown, together with a plan and section view giving the
true length and bevels of the rafters. The development of the
curved surface is shown projected from the section view. The
surface would probably be covered with plywood 6 to 9 mm thick,
laid in two or three thicknesses.

The small *hemispherical* dome illustrated on page 272 can be
easily set out but is rather difficult to construct. A plan, elevation,
and isometric view of the dome is given. The ribs, identical in
shape, radiate from the mast and are covered with a plywood skin
which is built up in two thicknesses, cut to shape and securely
fixed by gluing and nailing. Because all the ribs are the same shape
their true shape can be taken from the section of the dome, as
shown. Two methods of boarding the domes are given on page 272
(foot). The first example shows the patterns required for horizontal boarding, and the second that for vertical boarding.

A small *ogee dome* is illustrated on page 273. The hip ribs are
cut on to the wall plate, and framed into the mast at the top end.
The common ribs are considered as jack rafters, and cut on to the
side of the hip rafters. The true shape of the common and hip ribs
is given at the foot of page 273. Notice the method of finding the
centres for marking out the ogee curve. The points A, B, and C on
the curve are bisected and the centres (O and O) found in the

same way as for the elliptical arch (page 262). The segmental
curves are then drawn from O and O. Notice also the method of
projecting the shape of the hip ribs from the common ribs. The
true shape of the curved surface is shown projected from the
plan view.

Intersection of mouldings

Curved or shaped mouldings or mouldings of varying widths can
be made to intersect if the sectional details correspond. A typical
example of intersecting mouldings is given on page 274. The part
elevation of a pair of entrance doors with a circular centre panel
and upper and lower panels finished with a bolection moulding is
shown at the top of the page. The architrave which forms the
finish to the opening has 87 mm wide jambs and a 150 mm wide
head.

The intersection between the curved and straight bolection
mouldings requires a curved mitre. The method of projecting the
curved mitre intersection is given at the foot of page 274. First the
section views are drawn and an elevation view of the intersection
between the curved and straight moulding projected from them.
Notice that the intersection will be curved, not straight.

Because the architraves have varying widths the intersection
between them will not be a true mitre. The method of obtaining
the mitre intersection between the vertical and horizontal architraves is also shown at the foot of page 274. Notice that the given
section is drawn first and the required section projected from it.

Bull's-eye louvre frame

The vertical section and elevation views of a louvre frame are
given on page 275 (top). The louvre boards, usually pitched at
45°, are shown housed into the frame. The shape of the ends of
each board form part of an ellipse having a minor axis equal to the
inside size of the frame plus the depth of two housings. The length
of the major axis of the ellipse is found by a line being drawn at
45° through the cylindrical shape. The setting out of the elliptical
curve on which the true shape of the four louvre boards are
shown is also given.

NOTE   In order to show clearly the size of each louvre board, only half of each is drawn.

Splayed linings

The geometrical solid upon which a *circular splayed lining* is built is the cone. A plan, elevation, and section view of a circular lining are shown on page 275 (foot). The true shape of the lining is also given. Notice that only one half of the lining is shown and that another, identical, shape is required to complete it.

A plan and elevation of a *circular splayed and panelled lining* is given on page 276 (top). Projected from the plan is the stretch-out of the circular head, showing the shape and size of each panel, the muntins, and the templet for the built-up stiles. The face templets necessary for cutting out the solid splayed circular stiles on a bandsaw are shown at the foot of the page.

NOTE   Only one templet is necessary when the splayed shapes are cut out on a bandsaw, but it is advisable to check the back edge of the shape with the other templet to ensure accuracy.

Geometry of rotary cutter blocks

Only when the moulding cutter passes through the centre of the spindle of the cutting head is the cutter shape (profile) identical with the moulding which it forms. Any alteration in the angle at which the cutter approaches the timber will alter the shape of the moulding.

The method of setting out and obtaining the various cutter shapes to form an *ovolo moulding* is given on page 277. It is necessary first to draw a plan of the cutting head showing the size of the block, the projection of the cutters, and the maximum cutting circle. The moulded section is then drawn, and from positions on this the true shape of the cutter is projected.

The first example on page 277 shows the projection of the cutter shape when using a *french head*. Notice that by passing the cutter through the centre of the spindle the approach or cutting angle may be considered as being nil, and no development of the cutter shape is necessary.

The second example on page 277 shows the projection of the cutter shape when a *slotted collar head* is used. The projection, which includes the depth of the moulding, is divided into equal parts. These positions are projected on to the cutter face. Notice that the divisions on the cutter face have now become unequal and slightly larger than those on the moulding. These divisions are called a projection scale, and on this scale the profile of the cutter is plotted as shown.

The third example shows the projection of the cutter shape when a *square block* is used. Notice that the alteration in the cutting angle from 20° to 27° has resulted in a slight alteration in the cutter profile.

NOTE   All cutting edges must be the leading edges. The sum of the cutting angle, the grinding angle, and the clearance angle should equal 90°.

Side clearance is necessary to prevent rubbing between the side of the cutter and the timber (see page 277—top). A 5° clearance is considered sufficient, if the grinding operation is carefully done, to ensure that the leading edge is cutting. Sufficient clearance also between the cutter and the cutting circle is essential for satisfactory working.

The majority of *tenoning heads* have the cutters set at an angle to give a shear cutting action with the actual cutting edge slightly curved. In order to project the true shape of the cutter it is necessary to have two views of the cutting head, as shown on page 278 (top). The end view shows the cutting circle and the side view gives the true width of the cutter. The true shape of the cutter is obtained from a right-angle view by projection from the side and end views of the cutting head.

A method of obtaining the true shape of the cutters on *scribing heads* is given on page 278 (foot). Notice that the true shape of the cutter is projected from the cutter face.

Practice lessons

1 Working from the information given:

    (a)   Set out, to a 1:5 scale, an elliptical headed door frame. Width overall frame 1 m. Rise 400 mm.

    (b)   Show clearly the joint lines on the elliptical head.

2 *(a)*   Determine, by the steel-square method, the true lengths of the common rafters of a roof 6 m span, 2 m rise.

    (b)   Determine the true length of a hip rafter on a roof of the same size.

3 *(a)*   Draw, to a 1:20 scale, a single line plan and elevation of a pyramid roof square in plan. Base size 2 m. Vertical height 3 m.

    (b)   Show on the drawing the true lengths and bevels of the common and hip rafters.

4 *(a)*   Draw, to a 1:4 scale, the intersecting mouldings illustrated on page 274.

    (b)   Draw, to a 1:20 scale, the bull's-eye window and the development of the splayed lining illustrated on page 275.

5 *(a)*   Draw, full size, the methods of setting out and obtaining the various cutter shapes illustrated on page 277.

    (b)   Show clearly, on each diagram, the cutting angle, grinding angle, and clearance angles.

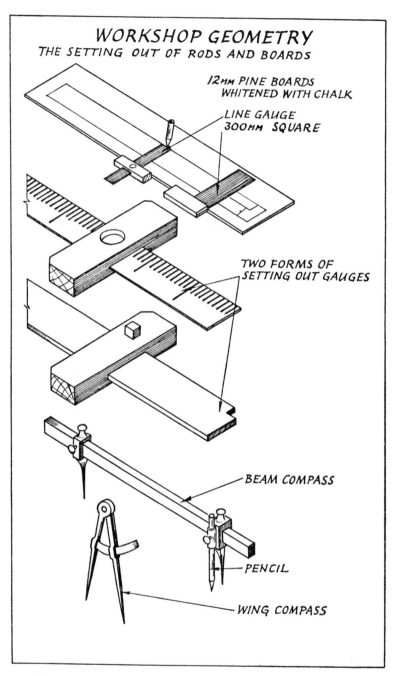

WORKSHOP GEOMETRY
THE SETTING OUT OF RODS AND BOARDS

12mm PINE BOARDS
WHITENED WITH CHALK

LINE GAUGE
300mm SQUARE

TWO FORMS OF
SETTING OUT GAUGES

BEAM COMPASS

PENCIL

WING COMPASS

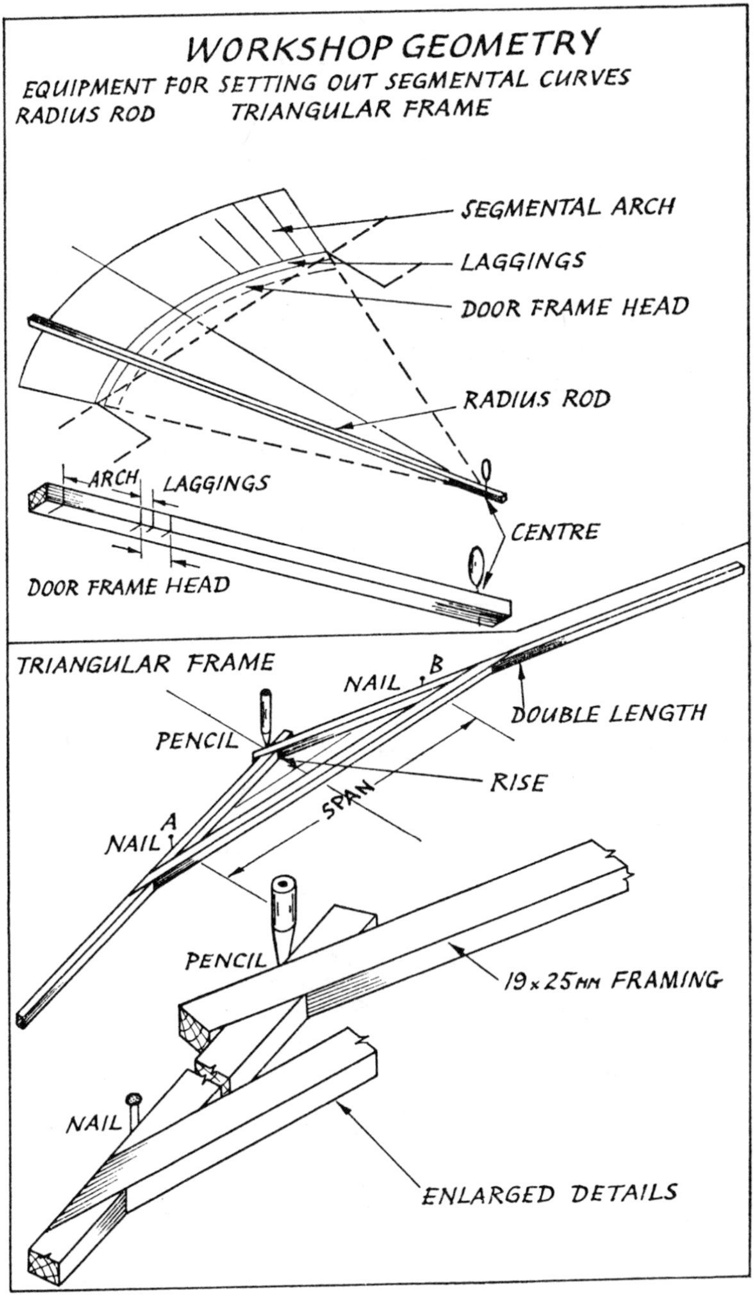

WORKSHOP GEOMETRY
EQUIPMENT FOR SETTING OUT SEGMENTAL CURVES
RADIUS ROD   TRIANGULAR FRAME

SEGMENTAL ARCH

LAGGINGS

DOOR FRAME HEAD

RADIUS ROD

ARCH   LAGGINGS

CENTRE

DOOR FRAME HEAD

TRIANGULAR FRAME

NAIL B

PENCIL

DOUBLE LENGTH

RISE

SPAN

NAIL A

PENCIL

19 x 25 MM FRAMING

NAIL

ENLARGED DETAILS

WORKSHOP GEOMETRY
EQUIPMENT FOR SETTING OUT ELLIPTICAL CURVES
SHORT TRAMMEL FRAME

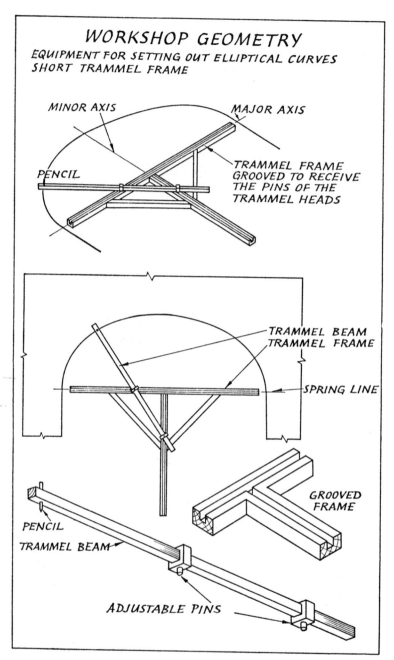

MINOR AXIS

MAJOR AXIS

PENCIL

TRAMMEL FRAME GROOVED TO RECEIVE THE PINS OF THE TRAMMEL HEADS

TRAMMEL BEAM
TRAMMEL FRAME

SPRING LINE

GROOVED FRAME

PENCIL
TRAMMEL BEAM

ADJUSTABLE PINS

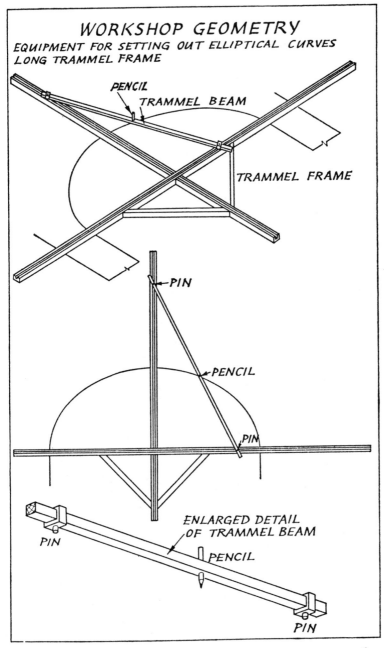

WORKSHOP GEOMETRY
EQUIPMENT FOR SETTING OUT ELLIPTICAL CURVES
LONG TRAMMEL FRAME

PENCIL

TRAMMEL BEAM

TRAMMEL FRAME

PIN

PENCIL

PIN

ENLARGED DETAIL
OF TRAMMEL BEAM

PIN

PENCIL

PIN

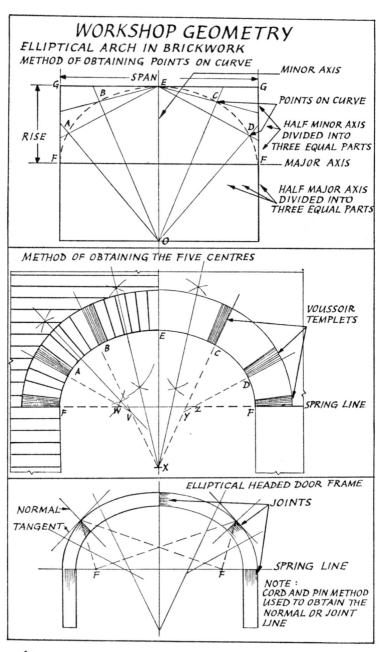

WORKSHOP GEOMETRY

ELLIPTICAL ARCH IN BRICKWORK

METHOD OF OBTAINING POINTS ON CURVE

SPAN

MINOR AXIS

POINTS ON CURVE

HALF MINOR AXIS
DIVIDED INTO
THREE EQUAL PARTS

RISE

MAJOR AXIS

HALF MAJOR AXIS
DIVIDED INTO
THREE EQUAL PARTS

METHOD OF OBTAINING THE FIVE CENTRES

VOUSSOIR
TEMPLETS

SPRING LINE

ELLIPTICAL HEADED DOOR FRAME

JOINTS

NORMAL

TANGENT

SPRING LINE

NOTE :
CORD AND PIN METHOD
USED TO OBTAIN THE
NORMAL OR JOINT
LINE

WORKSHOP GEOMETRY

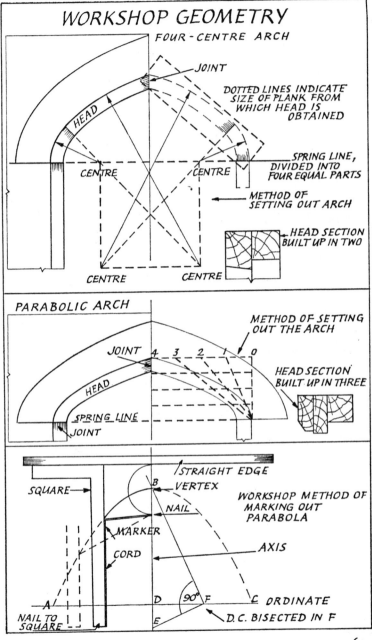

FOUR-CENTRE ARCH

JOINT

DOTTED LINES INDICATE
SIZE OF PLANK FROM
WHICH HEAD IS
OBTAINED

HEAD

SPRING LINE,
DIVIDED INTO
FOUR EQUAL PARTS

CENTRE

CENTRE

METHOD OF
SETTING OUT ARCH

HEAD SECTION
BUILT UP IN TWO

CENTRE

CENTRE

PARABOLIC ARCH

METHOD OF SETTING
OUT THE ARCH

JOINT   4 3 2 1 0

HEAD

HEAD SECTION
BUILT UP IN THREE

SPRING LINE

JOINT

STRAIGHT EDGE

SQUARE

B VERTEX

NAIL

WORKSHOP METHOD OF
MARKING OUT
PARABOLA

MARKER

CORD

AXIS

A

D   90° F   L ORDINATE

NAIL TO
SQUARE

E

D.C. BISECTED IN F

263

WORKSHOP GEOMETRY

ROOFING WITH THE STEEL SQUARE

PROPOSED ROOF

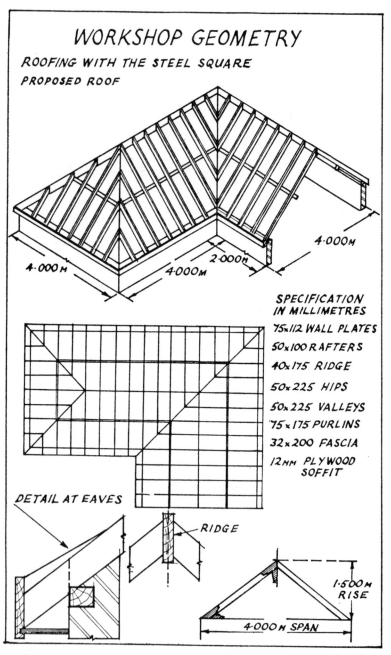

4·000 M

2·000 M

4·000 M

4·000 M

4·000 M

SPECIFICATION
IN MILLIMETRES

75 × 112 WALL PLATES

50 × 100 RAFTERS

40 × 175 RIDGE

50 × 225 HIPS

50 × 225 VALLEYS

75 × 175 PURLINS

32 × 200 FASCIA

12 MM PLYWOOD
SOFFIT

DETAIL AT EAVES

RIDGE

1·500 M
RISE

4·000 M SPAN

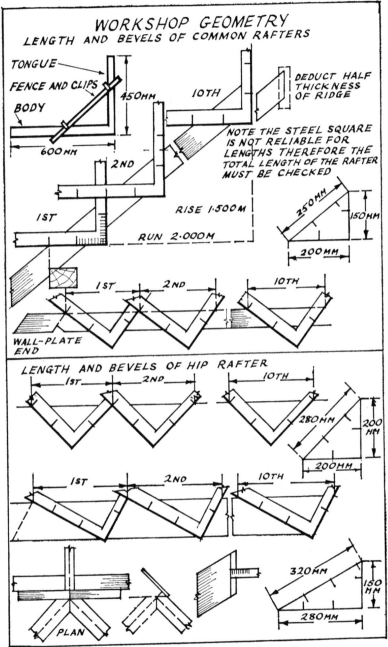

WORKSHOP GEOMETRY
LENGTH AND BEVELS OF COMMON RAFTERS

TONGUE

FENCE AND CLIPS

BODY

450MM

600 MM

10TH

DEDUCT HALF THICKNESS OF RIDGE

NOTE THE STEEL SQUARE IS NOT RELIABLE FOR LENGTHS THEREFORE THE TOTAL LENGTH OF THE RAFTER MUST BE CHECKED

2ND

1ST

RISE 1·500M

RUN 2·000M

250MM

150MM

200MM

1ST

2ND

10TH

WALL-PLATE END

LENGTH AND BEVELS OF HIP RAFTER

1ST

2ND

10TH

280MM

200 MM

200MM

1ST

2ND

10TH

PLAN

320MM

150 MM

280MM

265

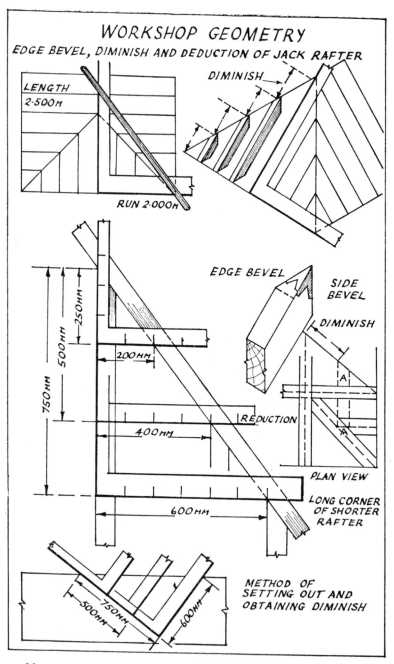

WORKSHOP GEOMETRY

EDGE BEVEL, DIMINISH AND DEDUCTION OF JACK RAFTER

LENGTH 2·500M

RUN 2·000M

DIMINISH

EDGE BEVEL

SIDE BEVEL

DIMINISH

250MM

500MM

750MM

200MM

REDUCTION

400MM

600MM

A

A

PLAN VIEW

LONG CORNER OF SHORTER RAFTER

500MM

750MM

600MM

METHOD OF SETTING OUT AND OBTAINING DIMINISH

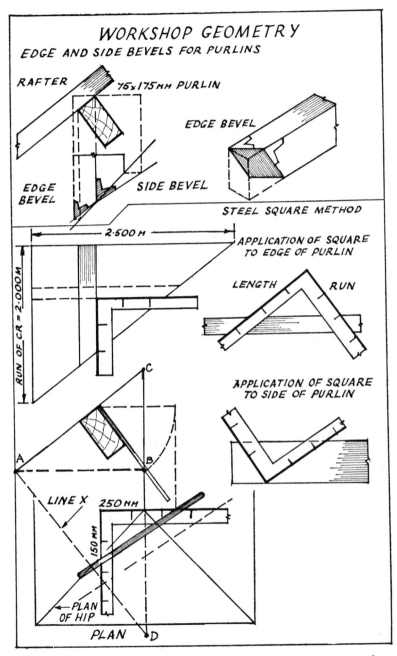

WORKSHOP GEOMETRY

EDGE AND SIDE BEVELS FOR PURLINS

RAFTER

75 x 175 MM PURLIN

EDGE BEVEL

EDGE BEVEL

SIDE BEVEL

STEEL SQUARE METHOD

2·500 M

RUN OF CR = 2·000 M

APPLICATION OF SQUARE
TO EDGE OF PURLIN

LENGTH

RUN

APPLICATION OF SQUARE
TO SIDE OF PURLIN

C

A

B

LINE X

250 MM

150 MM

PLAN OF HIP

PLAN

D

WORKSHOP GEOMETRY

SMALL DOMES
PYRAMID ROOF SQUARE IN PLAN

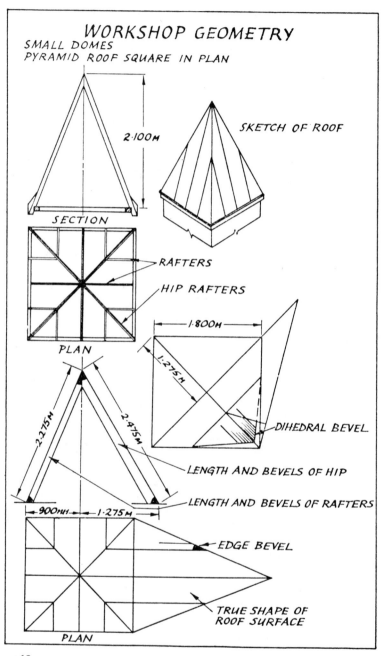

2·100M

SECTION

SKETCH OF ROOF

RAFTERS

HIP RAFTERS

PLAN

1·800M

1·275M

DIHEDRAL BEVEL

LENGTH AND BEVELS OF HIP

2·275M

2·475M

LENGTH AND BEVELS OF RAFTERS

900MM   1·275M

EDGE BEVEL

TRUE SHAPE OF
ROOF SURFACE

PLAN

WORKSHOP GEOMETRY

SMALL DOMES
SEMICIRCULAR DOME, SQUARE IN PLAN

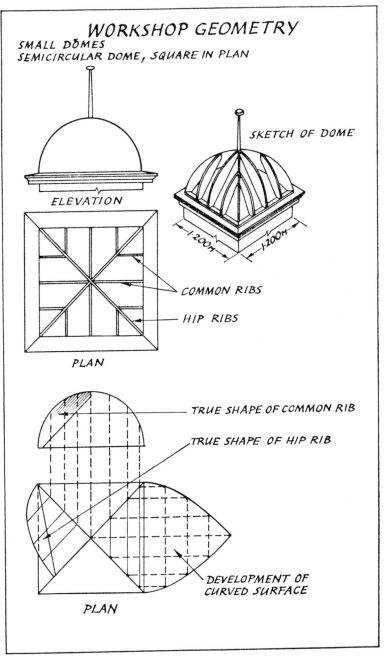

ELEVATION

SKETCH OF DOME

COMMON RIBS

HIP RIBS

PLAN

TRUE SHAPE OF COMMON RIB

TRUE SHAPE OF HIP RIB

DEVELOPMENT OF
CURVED SURFACE

PLAN

WORKSHOP GEOMETRY

SMALL DOMES
SEMICIRCULAR DOME, OCTAGONAL IN PLAN

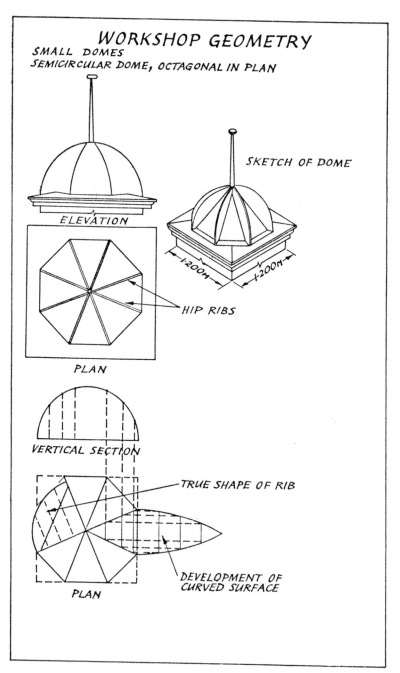

SKETCH OF DOME

ELEVATION

1·200M   1·200M

HIP RIBS

PLAN

VERTICAL SECTION

TRUE SHAPE OF RIB

DEVELOPMENT OF
CURVED SURFACE

PLAN

WORKSHOP GEOMETRY

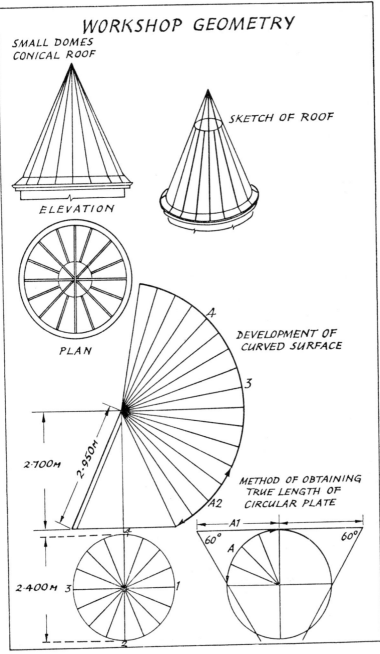

SMALL DOMES
CONICAL ROOF

ELEVATION

SKETCH OF ROOF

PLAN

DEVELOPMENT OF
CURVED SURFACE

A

3

2·700M

2·950M

METHOD OF OBTAINING
TRUE LENGTH OF
CIRCULAR PLATE

A2

A1

60°

A

60°

2·400M

3

1

2

WORKSHOP GEOMETRY

SMALL DOMES
HEMISPHERICAL DOME

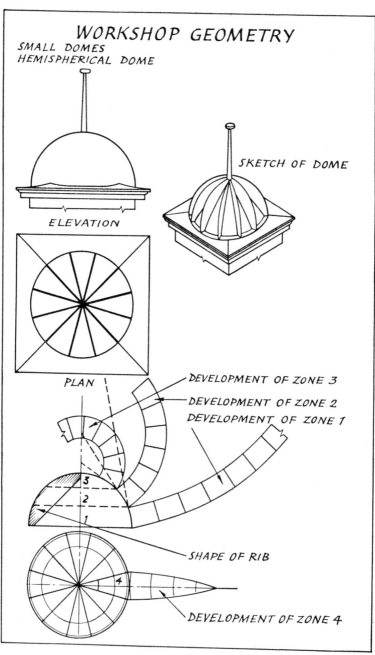

ELEVATION

SKETCH OF DOME

PLAN

DEVELOPMENT OF ZONE 3

DEVELOPMENT OF ZONE 2

DEVELOPMENT OF ZONE 1

SHAPE OF RIB

DEVELOPMENT OF ZONE 4

WORKSHOP GEOMETRY

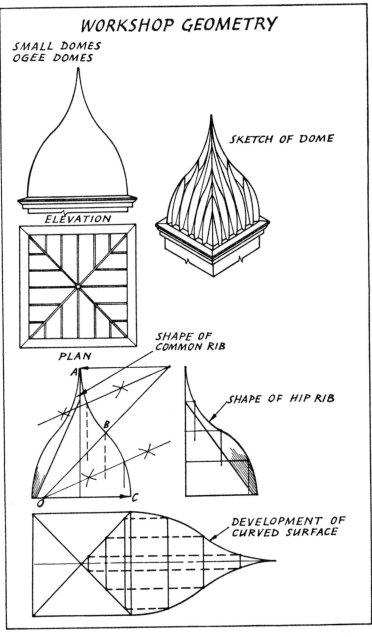

SMALL DOMES
OGEE DOMES

SKETCH OF DOME

ELEVATION

PLAN

SHAPE OF
COMMON RIB

SHAPE OF HIP RIB

DEVELOPMENT OF
CURVED SURFACE

WORKSHOP GEOMETRY

INTERSECTION OF MOULDINGS

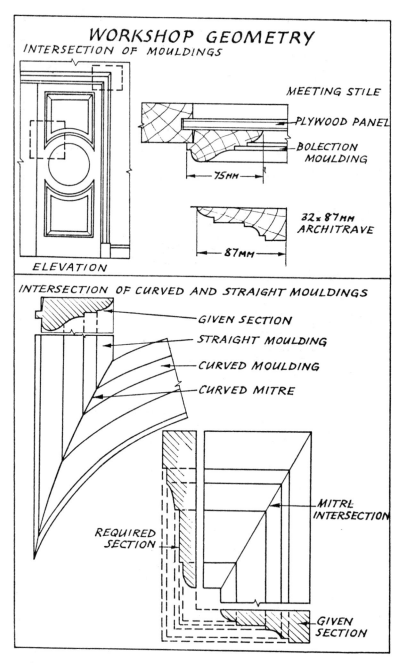

MEETING STILE

PLYWOOD PANEL

BOLECTION MOULDING

75MM

32 × 87MM ARCHITRAVE

87MM

ELEVATION

INTERSECTION OF CURVED AND STRAIGHT MOULDINGS

GIVEN SECTION

STRAIGHT MOULDING

CURVED MOULDING

CURVED MITRE

MITRE INTERSECTION

REQUIRED SECTION

GIVEN SECTION

274

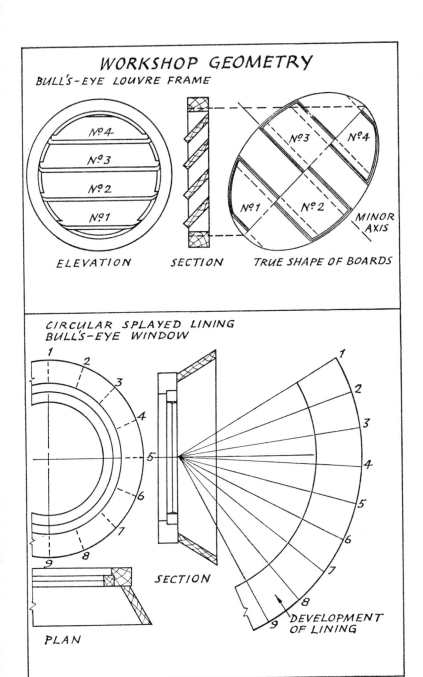

WORKSHOP GEOMETRY
BULL'S-EYE LOUVRE FRAME

N°4
N°3
N°2
N°1

ELEVATION

SECTION

N°3
N°4
N°1
N°2
MINOR AXIS

TRUE SHAPE OF BOARDS

CIRCULAR SPLAYED LINING
BULL'S-EYE WINDOW

1
2
3
4
5
6
7
8
9

SECTION

PLAN

1
2
3
4
5
6
7
8
9

DEVELOPMENT OF LINING

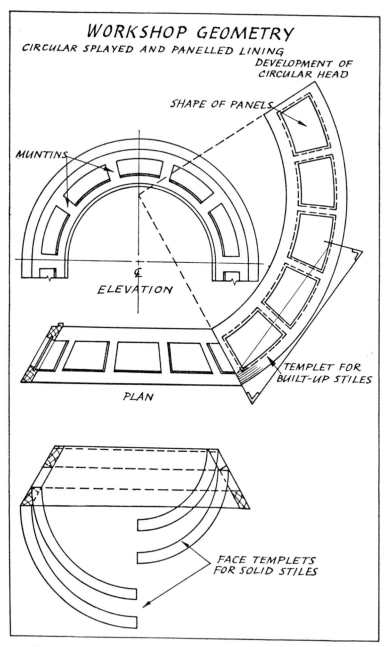

WORKSHOP GEOMETRY

CIRCULAR SPLAYED AND PANELLED LINING

DEVELOPMENT OF
CIRCULAR HEAD

SHAPE OF PANELS

MUNTINS

ELEVATION

TEMPLET FOR
BUILT-UP STILES

PLAN

FACE TEMPLETS
FOR SOLID STILES

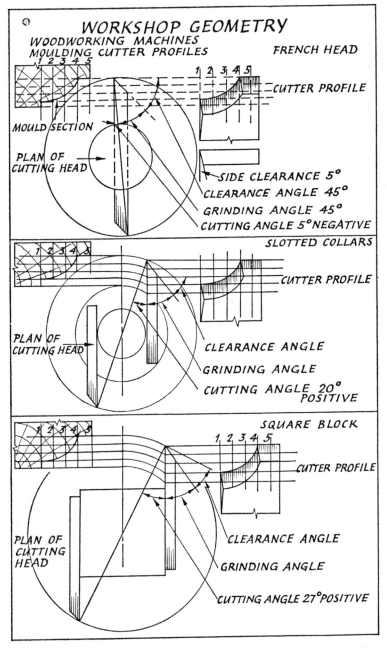

WORKSHOP GEOMETRY
WOODWORKING MACHINES
MOULDING CUTTER PROFILES

FRENCH HEAD

1 2 3 4 5

1 2 3 4 5

CUTTER PROFILE

MOULD SECTION

PLAN OF
CUTTING HEAD

SIDE CLEARANCE 5°

CLEARANCE ANGLE 45°

GRINDING ANGLE 45°

CUTTING ANGLE 5° NEGATIVE

SLOTTED COLLARS

1 2 3 4 5

CUTTER PROFILE

PLAN OF
CUTTING HEAD

CLEARANCE ANGLE

GRINDING ANGLE

CUTTING ANGLE 20°
POSITIVE

SQUARE BLOCK

1 2 3 4 5

1 2 3 4 5

CUTTER PROFILE

PLAN OF
CUTTING
HEAD

CLEARANCE ANGLE

GRINDING ANGLE

CUTTING ANGLE 27° POSITIVE

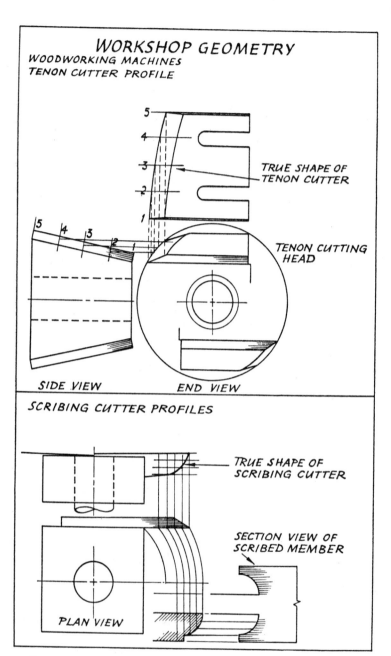

WORKSHOP GEOMETRY
WOODWORKING MACHINES
TENON CUTTER PROFILE

5
4
3
2
1

TRUE SHAPE OF
TENON CUTTER

5 4 3 2 1

TENON CUTTING
HEAD

SIDE VIEW   END VIEW

SCRIBING CUTTER PROFILES

TRUE SHAPE OF
SCRIBING CUTTER

SECTION VIEW OF
SCRIBED MEMBER

PLAN VIEW